The Narration of the Invisible

A Political Theory of Semantic Fields

Jorge Majfud

HUMANUS

NEW YORK, SAN FRANCISCO, MEXICO CITY

The Narration of the Invisible. A Political Theory of Semantic Fields
First Edition: University of Georgia. Thesis, May 2005.
Second Edition: Editorial Académica Española, 2018.
Fourth Edition, Rebelde Editores, April 2021.
© Jorge Majfud 2021.
© Humanus 2021, 2025
https://humanus.info / info@humanus.info
ISBN: 978-1-956760-27-9

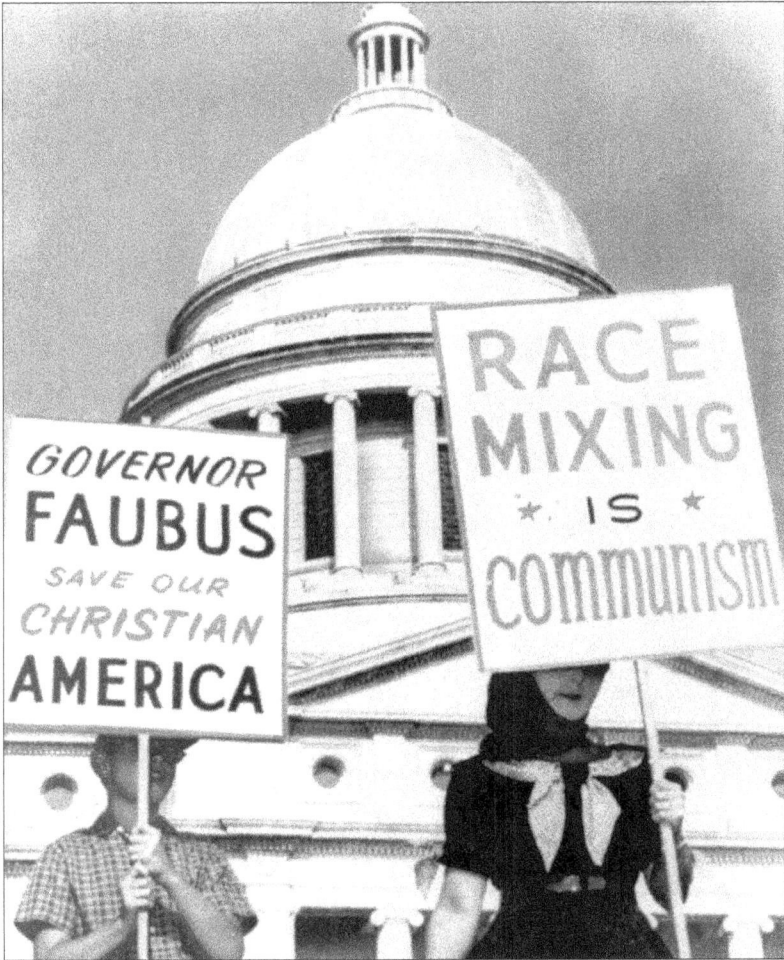

A mother and her son at a protest in Arkansas (1959) against racial integration: *"Governor Faubus, save our Christian America"*; *"Racial integration is communism"*. (Everett Collection Historical / Alamy Stock Photo)

This study on the struggle for semantic fields in social narrative was originally published as a thesis by the University of Georgia in 2005. Since then, political and social events, along with new technologies like social media, have continued to confirm the political and historical relevance of the semantic struggle (even over the ever-present weight of production and consumption systems) explored in this book. In this new edition, no significant changes have been introduced to the general study. With its strengths and weaknesses, the author has decided to present this new edition of A Political Theory of Semantic Fields *as it was presented in 2005, without revisions and with the intention of maintaining the immediate historical context.*

Table of Contents

Introduction

First Note

THIS STUDY ANALYZES two important ideological traditions that expressed and defined, to a large extent, the profile of a continent, a history, a culture—an identity—: the Latin American one. To a great extent, the analysis proceeds by contrasting two paradigmatic texts: *The Open Veins of Latin America* (1971) by Eduardo Galeano and The Twisted Roots of Latin America (2001) by Alberto Montaner. First, the main lines of a semantic dynamic are outlined, along with the process and dialectical struggle for the definition, conquest, and management of meanings—of symbols, ideolexemes, texts, and their eventual contexts—as well as the construction of a historical narrative from different reading models.

1.2—The Odyssey of Truth or the Search for the Intelligible

MADAN SARUP, analyzing the main ideas of Jacques Derrida, wrote that "deconstruction" could be understood as the critical operation by which binary oppositions can be partially unmasked (40). Binary oppositions would not, then, be a "natural form" of thought but quite the opposite: a metaphysical and, above all, ideological construction.

> Binary opposition represents a way of seeing, typical of ideologies. Ideologies often draw rigid boundaries between what is acceptable and what is not, between self and non-self, truth and falsity, sense and non-sense, reason and madness, central and marginal, surface and depth. Derrida suggests that we should try to break down the oppositions to which we are accustomed, and which ensure the survival of metaphysics in our thinking. [...] Using deconstructive methods, we can begin to unravel these oppositions embedded within each other (41).

But which tradition has prevailed—after the Middle Ages rejected novelty, the questioning of paradigms and authorities—if not the modern tradition of revolution, the permanent will to rupture and philosophical parricide? What has the best tradition of Western thought been, in the last five hundred years, if not a permanent exercise of deconstruction? The difference lies, probably, in that each previous critique proclaimed itself as a new universal center of moral and epistemological legitimation. The so-called "deconstructionism," on the other hand, renounced (as a declaration) this claim by falling into a permanent postponement of meaning, while simultaneously constructing, without escaping the circle it intended to destroy, a new center, this time paradoxical: an anarchic center.

As could not be otherwise, this innovation was soon questioned. Zavarzadeh himself criticized the annulment of oppositions as part of a new postmodernist instrumentalization of an old dominant ideology with new needs. The negation of opposites like strong-weak or oppressor-oppressed in thinkers such as Michael Foucault would be nothing more than the expression of the new capitalist order where transnational corporations dominate, thus eliminating the contradictions that arise from the social division of labor (34).

In this essay, we will take these preliminary warnings into account. However, we will propose a contrasting exercise—especially starting from the third chapter—that allows us to appreciate differences and similarities—ideological and methodological—of two widely known essays in the Hispanic world: *Las venas abiertas de América Latina* (Eduardo Galeano, 1971) and *Las raíces torcidas* de América Latina (Carlos Alberto Montaner, 2001). The importance of both can be attributed, on the one hand, to the influence they have had on their readers and, on the other, to the "representative" value that they have been conferred.

The poststructuralist deconstructive process would consist, to a large extent, in pointing out that in a pair of opposites, one of the terms is privileged, not by manifest logic, but by the force of a dominant metaphor (Sarup, 57). Our essay will recurrently use several pairs of opposites denounced by Derrida, especially pairs like development-underdevelopment, materialism-culturalism, etc. At other times, we will also use pairs like culture-nature, subject-object, and center-periphery. These pairs are essential to understand the theoretical perspectives of thinkers like Paulo Freire or Mas'ud Zavarzadeh, sometimes with the awareness of their false opposition, as in the case of the educator-educated pair for the former. Even if we can understand that what we call "natural," as opposed to "cultural," is the product of an intellectual

13

construction and, therefore, a product of "culture"—so that culture would precede "nature"—we can still suspend this dialectical objection in favor of using this pair as an analytical tool. In this way, we can analyze the ideological mechanism according to Roland Barthes' observation, in which where there is only equivalence—of meanings, of values—a reader caught in the ideological game sees a process of causes and effects. In this way, the sign has a "natural" meaning, unquestionable, when in reality, it is an unquestioned meaning. Instead of seeing a semiotic system, the reader reads into a system that relates "facts."

We will strive to make a conscious use of these pairs as intellectual constructions, though no less real nor less useful than any other—including deconstruction. After all, even if it be by ideological or theological construction, the rich and the poor, the oppressed and the oppressors exist. And although they do not oppose each other as animal categories, we can observe some economic differences, a struggle, or a social conflict.

1.3—The Two Texts in Dispute

THE TWO TITLES WE WILL ANALYZE in this essay are significant. *The Twisted Roots* directly alludes to *Open Veins* in its grammatical structure, while in their metaphorical usage, both forcefully express the theoretical and ideological principles upon which each text is written.

In the first, we notice a bleeding, the result of either an external aggression or a suicide, perhaps, but in any case, it reveals an agony caused by a hostile context. The bleeding alludes to lost riches and explains the current anemia. The explanation lies mainly in the oppressive actions of the "other," which, in turn, responds to a materialistic system that structures other orders, symbols, meanings, and institutions.

In the second case, in the case of the response, the title alludes not only to the first but also to a congenital malformation. The problem, then, lies in the "mind"—in the culture, in the education, in the philosophy—of the deformed being. And above all, in its original past. The reality is a direct consequence of a "mental state," not as an illusion but as a realization. This mental state, in turn, is an unconscious inheritance from its own history.

If in the first the oppression comes from the outside—from society, from the individual—in the second it comes from within. However, the *liberation* for both originates in the consciousness of the individual and society. What differentiates them are the subsequent steps for the full realization of the universally desired liberation.

In both texts, we will recognize each author's own readings and "models of reading" that will condition the historical narrative each constructs based on the same facts or facts selected according to their own conception of social and historical dynamics, according to a specific *logos* that must unify, in a single conception, the chaotic diversity of what is apparent—also, according to the ancient Greeks.

Although *Open Veins* and *The Twisted Roots* passionately oppose each other—or precisely because of this—they form a unity. They are united by the mystery of a vast, contradictory continent; they are united by the consciousness of failure, the search for lost time, and political and ideological passion.

The first, from 1971, synthesizes the thought of its time and transforms into a kind of bible—although a "bible for the Latin American idiot," as Montaner would say (Mendoza, 53)—. The second is no less a product of its time than the first: it synthesizes the new (neo)liberal thought of the nineties. In this, as important as the defense of certain economic and social ideas is the attack on thinkers traditionally called "leftist." In the first, we can find much of the theses of the second, although, in the struggle for meaning, these will also serve to deny the adversary.

Both, Galeano and Montaner, were exiled from their countries—Uruguay and Cuba—for their thoughts, and it is no surprise that these exiles, in turn, consolidated the profiles of their thinking, the radicalization of their ideas.

Be that as it may, both will structure a thought that will derive its intelligibility and strength from a supposed historical continuity and a supposed dialectical coherence. Both will strive to define the meaning of symbols, of facts; they will struggle for the meaning of "justice" that each carries.

In this struggle, we will recognize common elements that are, in our view, intrinsic to the "nature" of signs and their meanings, of ideas and thoughts. This fundamentally theoretical issue will be addressed in the second chapter.

1.4—Bipolar Space

IN MATHEMATICAL THINKING we can come to know the result of an equation without knowing one of its components. To these, we assign an x, a y, or a z and proceed as if we knew the complete process to later deduce the value of each term, limiting ourselves to laws we assume must govern the relationship between the parts and the whole. That is, we must presume knowledge about the unknown with the aim of understanding it.

In philosophical thought, and especially in theological thought, the approach is not very different. The difference lies in that its variables are not countable but infinite, and thus it is possible to arrive at the same result through various paths, not without a certain logic or rationality. Generally— we conjecture—intuition prefigures the answer to a mystery, physical or metaphysical, and this final outcome turns out to be the beginning of a *thesis* under the camouflaged name of a *hypothesis*. In this way, the search for truth often begins at the end. That is, with the thesis or pseudo-hypothesis—with a plausible substitute for truth. As in classical theology, one starts with revealed, unquestionable truth to traverse a long circular path of verifications and interrogations that allow us to return to the starting point, and so on. It is the prefiguration and subsequent construction of the metaphysical space.

This, of course, should not be taken as a Neoplatonic idea. We do not attribute to this "metaphysical space" an ontological category, independent of the intellect, but rather it is understood here as a phenomenology of human knowledge, of the representation of the world. We can assume that a tree is not the same as the representations we might have of it, just as the creations we develop under the name of "fiction," which we later call the "product of the spirit" or of "culture," are not the same. We thus assume the existence of both spaces, the physical and the metaphysical, which we will develop in this very essay.

The methodological alternative of the ancient Greek philosophers, in the search for truth, was not to recognize any truth before embarking on the path toward it. In this will, they differed from the biblical prophets beyond the Aegean (who, on the contrary, assumed the preexistence of revealed truth over any thought). However, not even for these daring Greeks was the path to truth, to knowledge, undertaken blindly and without potential trials. The searches begin with certain intuitions, warnings about clues that lead in a certain direction and not in another. In a more radical possibility—such as the theological and ideological traditions—the objective, the truth, must be located before starting to walk toward it.

We can observe, even in the most abstract paragraphs of the texts we will analyze in this essay, that the expression of thought and the dialogue—almost always a debate—that each writer maintains with others and with themselves, consists of a *narration of a virtual reality.* This, in my view, is the visualization of the *logos* that makes the world intelligible to the subject reflecting on it. It is what we will call the "metaphysical space," that is, that invisible space of ideas, intuitions, and emotions that will be narrated using a language born in the "physical space" and with its same continuity or will for coherence and non-contradiction.

From this premise, we will see that all human language is composed, in one way or another, of metaphors, which are, in turn, the primary means that make sign transfers possible. We will recognize that signs born from the need to represent the physical space have been resignified—under the mechanism of metaphor—to represent events and phenomena observable in the metaphysical space.

1.5—The Two Reading Models

ANOTHER PARTICULARITY WE WILL ATTEMPT to demonstrate in this essay are the theoretical models of interpretation on which the two readings of history and the meanings derived from it are based.

In the case of Eduardo Galeano we can observe a conception rooted in dialectical materialism, according to which economic infrastructures, production, and distribution of wealth determine social and international relations, as well as religious and cultural expressions. That is, in Galeano's writing there is a Marxist conception of history, as a deliberate method of analysis or as a result of his own readings of texts belonging to this philosophical line. Which, of course, is no novelty. But we must recognize this when we try to approach a different reading model and ideological conception, such as that of Alberto Montaner.

In the case of the latter, the tendency is the opposite: a supposed "mentality" is responsible for socioeconomic outcomes. Furthermore, we will see how this author devotes a large part of his book to describing formal teaching models in Medieval Europe and their introduction into the new continent as responsible for the material backwardness of its peoples. We will see how he refers to a kind of "inheritance of pernicious ideas" as responsible for a productive incapacity. Sometimes in a very direct and decontextualized manner regarding international relations. That is, the superstructure, for Montaner, is responsible for the infrastructure, for the economic and productive organization of society, for its development or ultimate underdevelopment.

We thus find opposing directions of reading: one which, to identify it, we will call *ascending*—the materialist or reductionist—and another *descending*—or "culturalist"

Even though both essayists are recognized by the public as intellectuals of the left one and of the right the other, we do not see a necessary connection between the first observation and this common recognition. A materialist interpretation of history can be used by a right-wing political position while a "culturalist" reading can be upheld by leftist groups, such as some adherents of Liberation Theology or educators like Paulo Freire, for whom the first step to changing social, economic, and production structures was not in an armed revolution that dismantled said structure but in a *conscientização*, that is, in a change from within the individual, almost with religious reminiscences.1 On the other hand, the same liberalist idea of the "free market" —of which Montaner is a proponent is a materialist reading, that is, an ascending one: the freedom of the market, of the processes of wealth production, determines a different configuration of culture and intellectual production.

---

1 From the beginning of his preaching, and especially after the 1964 military coup in Brazil, Paulo Freire was proscribed, persecuted, and finally exiled not only for being "ignorant" but, above all, for being a Marxist. In his most widespread book, Pedagogy of the Oppressed, references to Marx are not uncommon

1.6—The parts and the whole in two conceptions of history

ANOTHER CHARACTERISTIC WE CAN OBSERVE of these *reading models* lies in their own conception of the social and historical dynamic. The proponents of *Open Veins* assume from the outset, much like the first Greek philosophers, that the universe is governed by laws hidden from the eye and that, as a whole, they respond to a single articulating law: the *logos*. Each part that makes up the whole relates to the other parts according to a specific *system*. In our case, in the context of the modern and postmodern era, it is the capitalist system of production. The dynamic laws that govern domestic, power, and production relations are the same laws that structure international relations. The dominant ideology and its will to perpetuate itself in power permeates everything, like a fractal, reproducing itself at a point and in the whole, inward and outward.

The relationship of oppression and exploitation that developed countries maintain over peripheral countries is the same that, within these marginal areas, the stronger countries impose on the weaker ones and, above all, the upper classes on the lower classes, consumers on producers, etc. In the first and last instance, we can recognize that these laws are the laws that Charles Darwin saw in the wild nature of the 19th century, according to which the strongest will subdue the weakest to preserve not only the species but the vital balance of the biosphere. According to this interpretation, the function of the weak is to surrender their flesh to feed the strongest. The human alternative to this Law of the Jungle —the struggle for life for the survival of the fittest— consists of suppressing these primitive laws by imposing "social jus-tice", that is, the recognition of rights that protect the weak-est and, in this way, all of humanity. In this conception, it is understood that a necessary balance for the survival of the species cannot be established when the excessive power of the strongest is capable of annihilating not only the weakest but, through this path, the rest of humanity. We can also con-sider that any moral principle consists of the abrogation of Darwin's laws in human societies. Unless the very emergence of morality was a necessary and inevitable phenomenon of these same evolutionary laws, in which case we could say that a broader interpretation of Darwin's theory can include what initially appeared to be a contradiction: the survival of the weakest through morality. In this process of defining funda-mental terms such as "social justice," it will be necessary to redefine the semantic fields of terms like freedom and jus-tice. We will attempt to do so in the second chapter.

On the other hand, the proponents of *Las raíces torcidas* do not see a mega-structure but rather centers with relative independence. Sometimes with total independence. These centers can be, first and foremost, the individual, society, na-tional or cultural regions like Latin America. Since their des-tiny is the expression of this natural freedom of the individual and society, it cannot be the consequence of a world order but rather of their own attitude toward change or permanence. The development of certain countries or in-dividuals depends more on themselves than on their context. Similar to the psychoanalytic view of individuals, this is heav-ily conditioned by their own past. Their strengths and the chains that bind them are mental. Therefore, we have called this model of reading "culturalist," but it could also be seen, using a physics metaphor, as a centrifugal reading—from the inside out—in contrast to the centripetal reading of *Las venas abiertas*—from the outside in.

It is no coincidence, then, that the title of Galeano's book analyzed here resorts to the metaphor of bleeding, while Montaner's does so with the metaphor of a malformation. Both factors would, according to each, be responsible for underdevelopment, for the failure of Latin America. Nor is it a coincidence that, in another book, Montaner resorts to the word "idiot" for his title: beyond the disparagement, we understand that the recurrence to the mental factor—and to its structural negation—is foundational in his own "model of reading."

1.7—The Models of Reading

WHY IS IT IMPORTANT TO RECOGNIZE both models of reading?

In the dialectical struggle, the reader usually takes sides with one, assuming that two opposing theses cannot simultaneously be correct. But if we judge each thesis *within its own model of reading* it is very likely that we will recognize an internal logic that we immediately confuse with the truth. On the other hand, if we judge a thesis from an opposing model of reading, we will likely judge it negatively.

To judge each thesis more broadly, we must step outside the circle that limits each model of reading. But to step out of that circle, it is first necessary to recognize it. Once both models are recognized, we can see that we do not necessarily have to judge one as true and the other as false, but we will be in a better position to make a synthesis. Two opposing theses can both be false or both be true, depending on the model of reading used to make that epistemological judgment.

The dialectical conflict arises when the models of reading remain invisible and judgments are made from within each of them.

1.8—Authors, Readers, and *Auctoritas*

Finally, I would like to clarify that when we choose to quote reflections from generally "influential" thinkers, we do not do so with the understanding that their expressions possess the value of authority, as was intended in the Middle Ages and as is still intended today on some occasions. There are no revealed words but rather revelations of words. Therefore, we will also make the effort to shorten the bibliographic list as much as possible, with the understanding of not adorning with a pseudo-erudition that results in obscuring ideas behind a thick varnish of "authorities."

The quotes explicitly refer to an author, to a name, but above all, they implicitly carry the attitude of the readers who have granted them permanence over time. Therefore, these quotes are significant not because of their personal authors but because of their readers, not because of the truth or falsity of their assertions but because of the impact they once had on a society, which is the same as saying because of the reception these large numbers of readers were willing to grant them.

The Struggle for Meaning

2.1—What is the Name of Latin America?

LATIN AMERICA is indefinable and, at the same time, a solid intuition. We cannot deny its existence, nor can we forget that it is an imaginary construct—two human conditions of any identity.

The name "Latin America," like "Ibero-America," has its own history, loaded with beliefs, superstitions, ideology and misconceptions, assumed and forgotten. The same can be said of that continent—vague, contradictory—to which the name alludes.

"National identity" was not only an obsession of the Modern era, but, even under other names, survives powerfully in our times. Perhaps the problematic center has shifted from the "national" to the "regional" or to a less artificial or arbitrary area that we could call the "cultural identity" of a people, at the risk of being redundant. The *essentialist* component that filled the interstices of this problem as part of various nationalist projects—and which occupied intellectuals like Octavio Paz for so long—has not completely disappeared or has been transmuted into a commercial relationship of signs in conflict, in a new global context.

Any question about the "identity" of a people or an individual will lead us to the problem of symbols and meanings. When we ask about the identity of Latin America, we are asking, among other things, about the meaning of the term "Latin America." Inevitably, that definition is, at the same time, a simplification that necessarily denies the infinite heterogeneity.

To begin answering these questions, we could start by searching for the etymological origin of each word and the subsequent result of their combination. For example, what does "Latin" mean?

The search for this meaning—that is, for this identity—can (or must) go beyond any etymological precision, forgetting conflicts and contradictions. For instance, for years, the typical Latin American—which is another way of saying "the stereotypical Latin American"—was represented by the indigenous person of Aztec, Maya, Inca, or Quechua origin who preserved their ancestral traditions by blending them with Catholic rituals. What these peoples had in common was the Spanish language. Yet, all of them, in the eyes of Europeans, North Americans, and even their own eyes, were monolithically defined as "Latin Americans." The inhabitants of the Río de la Plata region were called, by Anglo-Saxons, "the Europeans of the South," not without some disdain, in the understanding that they were copies, something inauthentic. Art exhibitions in major museums in Europe and the United States classified Latin American art on one hand—tropical, indigenous, primitive, innocent, virginal like the Tahitians in Gauguin's paintings—while pieces by Figari, Torres García, or Soldi were hung in a separate hall, closer to Europe than to Mexico or Peru.

If we return to the etymology of the word *Latin*, we see a strong contradiction in this identification: none of the indigenous cultures that the Spaniards encountered in the New Continent had anything "Latin" about them. On the contrary, other regions further south lacked this ethnic and cultural component. Almost entirely, their population and culture came from Italy, France, Spain, and Portugal—countries eminently "Latin," according to the oldest history of Europe.

On the other hand, if to define with some precision the meaning of "Latin America" we correct the semantic tradition of the last century, composed, like everything, of misconceptions, and refer to a simple etymological analysis of the words "America" and "Latin," then we should also include vast regions of Canada. Merely suggesting this is enough to perceive an "identity" conflict. Of course, we should also include the United States, within which live as many Spanish speakers as in Spain. Or more.

We might then be tempted to choose the term "Ibero-America" to exclude Canada from our "identity" and thus come closer to the idea we have of "Latin America". However, the exclusive reference to the Iberian Peninsula also generates exclusions that we are not willing to accept. Even if we had or invented a term that included all the European peoples who immigrated to our continent, we would still remain in a situation of inaccuracies and unfair exclusions.

In *Valiente mundo nuevo*, Carlos Fuentes tells us:

> The first thing is that we are a multiracial and multicultural continent. That is why throughout this book the term "Latin America", invented by the French in the 19th century to include themselves in the American set, is not used, but rather the more comprehensive description Indo-Afro-Ibero-America. But in any case, the Indian and African component is present, implicit (12).

To this objection by the Mexican Carlos Fuentes, Koen de Munter responds in kind. De Munter observes that indigenist discourse has become a fashion, as long as it refers to the defense of small groups, politically harmless, folkloric, as a way to forget the large masses who migrate to cities and blend into a kind of obligatory mestizaje. This mestizaje, in countries like Mexico, would only be the central metaphor of a national project, mainly since the nineties.

> One of the leading voices in the revival of mestizaje discourse was the Mexican writer, Carlos Fuentes. [...] According to Fuentes: 'Fortunately, it was not the English but the Spanish which came here [...] because in that case we would not have had what we need for the 21st century: the experience of mestizaje' (de Munter, 92)

Koen de Munter understands this type of discourse as part of a "Hispanophile" demagogy, an "ideology of mestizaje" by which the unacceptable conditions of the current Latin American reality are overlooked. According to the same author, the Hispanophilia of these intellectuals does not allow them to remember the colonial racism of the Spain that fought against Moors and Jews while making its way into the new continent. In summary, rather than mestizaje, we should speak of a "multiple violation" (93). Later, we will see that similar ideas were noted three years earlier by Carlos Alberto Montaner, in 2001, in his search for the twisted roots of Latin America.

Apparently because the proposed term was too long, Carlos Fuentes decides to use "Iberoamerica," which, in my opinion, is much more restrictive than the one "interestingly" proposed by the French, as it excludes not only the waves of French immigration in the Southern Cone and other regions of the continent in question, but also other even more numerous immigrants who are as Latin as the Iberian peoples, such as the Italians. It would suffice to recall that at the end of the 19th century, eighty percent of the population of Buenos Aires was Italian, which is why someone defined Argentinians—proceeding with another generalization—as "Italians who speak Spanish."

On the other hand, the idea of including the indigenous component ("Indo") together with the name "America" suggests that they are two distinct things2. One might think that indigenous peoples are the ones with the most right to claim the designation of "Americans." But this is not the case. The term has been colonized just as the land, physical and cultural space, was colonized. Even today when we say "American," we refer to a single nationality: the United States'. The meaning of this term is defined by an inclusion and an exclusion, that is, by a positive and a negative semantic field (see 2.6). For the meaning of this term, it is as important to define what it means as what it does not mean. And this definition of semantic boundaries does not simply derive from its etymology but from a semantic dispute in which the exclusion of what is not American has won. A Cuban or a Brazilian may exhaustively argue the reasons why they should also be called "Americans," but the redefinition of this term is not established by the intellectual will of some but by the force of a cultural and intercultural tradition. Although the first

---

2 Similarly, the fate of the modest and "politically correct" racial term "African American" to refer to a dark-skinned American who is as African as Clint Eastwood or Kim Basinger.

Creoles who lived south of the Rio Grande, from Mexico to the Río de la Plata, called themselves "Americans," later the force of U.S. geopolitics appropriated the term, forcing the rest to use an adjective to differentiate themselves.

> Now, for the world, America is nothing more than the United States. We inhabit, at best, a sub-America, a second-class America, with a nebulous identity (Galeano, 2).

The same can be said of the term "Latin America". This identity represents, for some and others, a specific space and specific cultures that are grossly simplified by the need to label. Even if we demonstrate the heterogeneity contained within this term, the cultural groups involved will remain prisoners of it.

Amarill Chanady tells us, in Latin American Identity and Constructions of Difference:

> Because of the "impossible unity of the nations as a symbolic force", any constructions of coherent view of the nation, or sustained strategy of nation building, necessarily leads to homogenization. As Renan writes, "unity is always affected by means of brutality". What that means is not only that the nonhegemonic sectors of society are "obligated to forget", and concomitantly obligated to adopt dominant cultural paradigms in several spheres, but that "forgetting" is the result of marginalization and silencing, if not annihilation (xix).

This "obligation to forget", in its effects, does not necessarily refer exclusively to a simple forgetting but rather to a denial, that is, to the consolidation of a negative semantic field C(-). Denial can lead to a form of forgetting or silence, but it does so through a conflictive path: it is a functional forgetting, self-interested, even necessary to consolidate a positive semantic field C(+) and, through both, a meaning.

A little further, citing Homi Bhabha, Chanady notes:

> Being obligated to forget became the basis of remembering the nation, peopling it anew, imagining the possibility of other contending and liberating forms of cultural identifications (xx).

In *The Open Veins of Latin America* and in The Twisted Roots of Latin America, they speak of a single and compact Latin America. Although we assume that both authors, Galeano and Montaner, are cultured men, we also suppose that they were, at the time of their respective writings, aware of this heterogeneity. Nevertheless, it is practically ignored, making Latin America a terribly compact symbolic unity. In each case, a problem specific to "Latin America" is presented without defining, throughout the text, the idea, the limits, and the nature of this identity. It is simply assumed as given, as established. This deliberate omission is functional. Rarely is it known, when attributing a significant characteristic to the "problem", whether one is talking about Argentina or Guatemala.

It is possible that this simplification unconsciously made about Latin America is due to its brief history and to some of its own myths, such as the idea of the Patria Grande. Also to a mysterious ignorance of the different indigenous peoples who inhabited this region, many of them authors of sophisticated civilizations. We cannot make this same simplification when speaking of Europe. No one would think of confusing an Italian with a German. No one—or few—would define a typical European as a "Latino" is defined in the United States or in Europe. Personally, just as an example, I never had the consciousness of being a "Hispanic" or a "Latino" until I arrived in Anglo-America. The idea of "Latin American", however, was more familiar to me from a literary perspective, originating in the sixties. But for a resident of the Southern Cone who is not trained in Bolivarian ideology, it takes a somewhat unnatural mental effort to feel identified as a Hispanic or as a Latino.

It is also possible that this simplification is due to the predominance of *the perspective of the other*: the European one. Europe has not only been historically egocentric (at times even egolatrous, like any dominant "nation") but also the younger peoples and the pre-existing peoples in America have been Eurocentric, as a result of intellectual colonization. Few in America, without a significant ideological burden , have valued and studied indigenous cultures as much as European ones. That is to say, it is possible that our simplified and simplifying definitions of "Latin America" are due to the natural confusion always projected by the gaze of the other: all Indians are the same: the Maya, the Aztecs, the Incas, and the Guarani. Only in what is now Mexico, existed —and exists— a cultural mosaic that only our ignorance confuses and groups under the word "indigenous". Frequently, these differences were resolved in war or in the sacrifice of the other. The same occurs in Africa: the fratricidal intertribal wars arise from differences that those of us who come from other continents are unable to appreciate before two or three months of attentive observation. Other cultures, like the Japanese, see Iberoamerica as imprisoned by an external image, shaped by European thinkers. Responding to this assertion, Richard Morse argues that this continent does possess its own culture, but it is more Western than that of the Nordic countries themselves (Arocena, 40). In Japan, the Western also exists, but always separate from "the Japanese" (41).

In any case, even considering Latin America as an extension of the West (as the extreme West), its names and identities have been, mainly since the mid-19th century, a function of negation. In July 1946, Jorge Luis Borges observed, in the magazine Sur, this same cultural habit restricted to Argentinians.

> [The nationalists] ignore, however, the Argentinians; in the debate they prefer to define them in terms of some external fact; of the Spanish conquerors (let's say) or of some imaginary Catholic tradition or of the "Saxon imperialism" (Borges, *Ficcionario*, 216).

2.2—Methodological Considerations

Causes and Effects

A COMMON MISUNDERSTANDING ARISES when human sciences like history, sociology or economics implicitly assume the dynamics of the physical sciences as their own. Even when economics assumes the modus operandi of traditional medicine as its own, it begins to construct this deception. Medicine seeks the causes of a disease to suppress it; once this is achieved, the desired consequence is more or less direct. However, social logic does not necessarily respond like a biological body—and here I exclude Darwinian logic, which, as I will explain later, is far broader than a simple game of the fittest organisms prevailing over the weaker ones. That is, in long-term human dynamics, we cannot alter one part without directly altering the whole; we cannot suppress a cause and obtain a direct effect, since that cause is, at the same time, a consequence of its own effects, an effect of its effects. Put differently, each cause creates its own context, which in turn influences the cause itself.

In the name of this arrowed dynamic, it is assumed that the observation of causes and effects is objective, thereby eliminating a new dimension that would destroy this temporal linearity—the subjectivity or particularity of the observer, *the theorist.* Even language itself is structured according to this linearity where tenses are ordered according to a rigid logic of precedence: past, present, and future. According to this temporal order, the cause always precedes the effect, the consequence. However, from a human perspective, we can understand that this order is simply borrowed from the physical world, since we know that a present can be explained both by its past and by its future. Thus, we can find that the cause of a present event may lie not in the past but in a motivation, that is, in its future.

This linear model of *cause and effect* denies or ignores that an effect can, in turn, be the cause of effects that may even contradict the original cause. For example, when changes in the cultural landscape of a country are projected based on a population trend, it is implicitly assumed that the cause-phenomena will continue to occur in the same scenario, as if these phenomena did not change the scenario itself, which, in turn, would influence the original effects—population growth. If, for instance, we assumed that the causes driving immigration would remain unchanged for a certain period of time and failed to recognize that this same immigration would produce its own "effect" in its context—national and international—we would be projecting a scenario indifferent to the supposed causes that generate it. On a more general level, if we assert, with Marx, that the consciousness of an individual and of a class is the result of their economic context, of the orders of production, would we not be considering that this economic order is also the product of a specific consciousness, of a specific intent, whether in good or bad faith? Moreover, if consciousness were solely the consequence of socio-economic causes, Marxism would never have been invented by Marx nor transmitted through the reading of certain books like Capital. This does not negate the undeniable discoveries of dialectical materialism by taking the opposite stance, but rather expands the positive semantic field —which we will explore further ahead— in a symbiotic understanding of culture.

In the famous Cuban film *Memories of Underdevelopment* (Alea, 1969), the protagonist reflects ten years after the Castro revolution. His central reflection revolves around the particular character of the women he interacted with at some point, who serve in the narrative as explicit metaphors for the European and Latin American character. Here, the frustration of not having materialized cultural changes —which remain almost unaltered— through a radical shift in economic infrastructure and forms of production becomes evident. This constitutes an internal critique of a radical materialist view. In other words, the cause-and-effect relationship between the base and the superstructure is not a linear one but rather dialogical or symbiotic.

However, ideologies proceed by drawing this path of causes and effects, resulting in a clearer course of action than in an awareness of the complexity of reality. By siding with a limited group of ideas, forcing the historical narrative, highlighting certain events, and suppressing others, they succeed in "rationally" explaining a vaster and more complex reality. In this essay, we will analyze two of the most significant ideological perspectives, in our view, due to their tradition and their influence on contemporary thought: the vision of dialectical materialism, represented by Eduardo Galeano in The Open Veins of Latin America, and a postmodern current represented by The Twisted Roots of Latin America by Alberto Montaner. Since both are actors in the political arena, they will spare no effort or arguments in confirming their ideological precepts, omitting or suppressing their own theoretical and methodological doubts. What one considers a cause for the other will be a pure effect. We can observe, for example, that the abolition of slavery in the 19th century, as Eduardo Galeano asserts, was driven by infrastructural reasons—economic, productive interests, etc. In response, Albert Montaner denies this hypothesis by emphasizing a new ethical sensibility as the cause for the end of the commerce and direct exploitation of human beings. While Montaner's thesis requires a strong degree of faith in the goodness of those in power, we cannot entirely dismiss it as an ethical claim without turning back. The economic infrastructures of the industrial revolution have been surpassed, but today we maintain, more than ever, the anti-slavery ethical consensus, beyond practical achievements, whether real or merely discursive. This proves that while infrastructure plays a significant role in the cultural (ethical) process, it is not its only reason and foundation. We can observe that after certain production orders have been overcome, some human achievements that we might call, with some imprecision, "natural rights" are maintained and deepened. Currently, the anti-slavery ethical value alone is a fundamental dialectical resistance to oppose other possible new economic structures that could benefit from a return to this explicit type of human exploitation— all this without failing to recognize that 19th-century slavery still exists today in many parts of the world. The new ethical consciousness is capable of extending the meaning of "slavery," from the metaphor of the ancient slave to a new, more modern exploitative relationship, such as any labor or financial relationship. It would suffice to recall, for example, the right to eight hours of daily work.

As in other instances, we can see a dialogic relationship between culture (ethics) and economics, which ideologies and radical positions tend to simplify by siding with one of them and making it the center and origin of all other causes and effects observable in human reality. In certain periods of history, economic interests and needs coincide with established ethical values, and in others they do not. When they do not coincide, conflict arises, and the side with power— political, social, military, or economic—prevails, but in no case is it a one-way, arrowed relationship where one—the economy or ethics—is the cause and the other the necessary consequence. The struggle of the unionists in the northern United States, in the 19th century, against the slave-owning Confederates of the south, can be explained (primarily) by the different production systems of each side. However, the subsequent struggle of Martin Luther King, for example, does not arise from a new production need but from a motivation that, in this case, we could understand as originating from ethical consciousness in contrast to the social reality of the time.

We can find other examples of the same kind. At the other end of the continent and during the same years as the American Civil War, Bautista Alberdi wrote: "The issue of religious freedom in America is a political and economic issue. Whoever speaks of religious freedom speaks of European immigration and population" (Alberdi, *Barbarie*, 145). That is to say, tolerance, though we may consider it an ethical value in itself, the cause of many social orders, has also been —and is— the necessary consequence of the coexistence of different human groups, often opposed in their ideas and ethical, religious, economic, and political sensibilities, in search of long-term benefits. Similarly, we can say the same about the feminist revolution. While today we may understand it as an ethical imperative, the product of a certain historical evolution that, since humanism —since the liberation of man from the fatality of religious dogma— announced the conquest of the same rights and freedoms for the other half of humanity, it is no less true that the development of new production systems will also make the integration of fifty percent of the human capital necessary and inevitable. The observation has been noted by analysts (generally Marxists) like Mas'ud Zavarzadeh:

> In its attempt to recruit women in contemporary capitalist societies, the capitalist "free" market, which is desperately

39

> in competition with the Third World labor force, has had
> to produce new subjectivities for women so that it can re-
> cruit a self-sustaining and efficient work force (204). [...]
> An expanded labor force in which "independent" women
> can play a role (66)

On the other hand, even though it may seem contradictory or paradoxical, we can also view the feminist phenomenon as a "consequence" or as a result of similar struggles to
Marxism in the 20th century. But if we were to take this observation as the sole "cause," we would be grossly oversimpli-
fying a much more complex reality.

We can see this fact purely as part of a cause-effect dynamic that has been functioning uninterrupted until today—the capitalist system's need for labor, for that new
(post-industrial) reserve army—or consider, on the other
hand and simultaneously, the purely ethical value of this ideological and social change which, whether we like it or not,
is dynamic and progressive, beyond the "causes" that motivate it. In other words, we can understand that its meaning
*is not imprisoned by its origin, just as, from an etymological per-
spective, the "contradictory" meaning of a word that has undergone a long historical journey is not. An observation that, by the
way, will not be taken into account by either Eduardo Galeano*
or Alberto Montaner. In *Crítica de la pasión pura* (1998), to
clarify this point, I used the example of a shopping center in
Montevideo (21). This shopping center is the result of repur-
posing an old prison. Tourists who are unaware of this history or who are not attentive architects will likely never
realize the dramatic change in the building's function, even
though symbolic parts of it and some of its structure were
preserved. For them, the meaning will not depend on the

building's past meanings but on its present. However, a specialist can explain that present by its past. The same can be said of other types of symbols. For example, the gesture of taking off one's hat and bowing before someone once signified absolute submission to a sovereign—and even the offering of one's head—when does it mean the same thing in our time? Now, returning to the ethics-economy dynamic, we can ask what meaning

a new "ethical value" has in itself. Why and how did it come to be? Was it formed by the dictate of history, of a productive necessity, of an ideology and community security? In other words, is it possible to reduce it to economic causes or to attribute it to a higher motivation such as the (gnostic) concept of "human progress" or "divine perfection"? Or does it simply possess inherent value, making it unnecessary to reduce it to an origin or refer it to a goal?

If we adhere to the first hypothesis, we can say that the industrial revolution in England and the United States alone led to the liberation of slaves and women, incorporating them as workers and salaried consumers. Public security systems are also affected by this same dialectic. While it is true and explicit that society must protect the weakest for moral reasons, it is equally true that there are personal interests for each member of society in this: if the weakest, the marginalized, lack health coverage or have their basic needs unmet, illness and violence will increase, two factors that turn against the strongest sectors of the same society. That is, according to this logic, a dominant system only grants a benefit to the oppressed if it results in new gains for the oppressors and the perpetuation of the system. However, on the other hand, it would make no sense for the oppressed to relinquish their gains, however insufficient, in this powerful dynamic, even if, to some extent, they serve to preserve the same system that oppresses them. Because the oppressed are not always passive actors and always have the option to change or accelerate history—by changing the structures of oppression, changing consciousness, or both.

It is not surprising, then, to understand that an infrastructural change in our era of globalization will redesign social relations between peoples and individuals under new ethical needs. Only by paying attention to new production processes can we foresee that an increasing demand for liberty through diversity will become inevitable; vertical powers, more typical of feudal systems of the Middle Ages (agrarian culture), of states, of large industries, and of large unions (industrial culture) will gradually be replaced by a greater atomization of individual and intellectual production (information age) that will pave the way for the achievement of a Disobedient Society. However, the "ethical consequences"—such as civil disobedience, individual freedom, and tolerance for diversity—will, at the same time, be causes of the same order from which they arise. That is, they will be both cause and consequence.

None of this is coincidental. It is not coincidental that ethics and economics have close and sometimes unsuspected ties. As I argued in 1998, in *Critique of Pure Passion*, morality is the *consciousness of the species*, the individual's renunciation in favor of the group, of society. In its functional roots, this renunciation is not selfless—though we assume it to be so and though the same selflessness is part of a "higher" morality—but necessary for the survival of the species and the individual. And, therefore, from this perspective, we can see culture and religions as integral and fundamental parts of the theory of Evolution from an angle opposite to the traditional one, which viewed only the triumph of the fittest. Without the need, thereby, to reduce religions to this single material-ist aspect. A symbiotic perspective, a non-exclusive dialectical dynamic between super and infrastructure, between culture and biological need, assumes that all perceived or yet-to-be-perceived factors affect the same process. What must be de-termined is *to what extent*, in a given situation, one predomi-nates over the other, as these conditional relationships need not be equitable. But every time we deny one dimension to privilege another, we are establishing the narrow codes of a reductionist ideology.

To conclude, let us remember that we also cannot claim that our position, our way of understanding the world, is not "ideological," since, like anyone else's, it is based on a privi-leged set of ideas that help us understand the rest of the world. Nonetheless, we can try to avoid a type of ideology that we find inconvenient: reductionism or thinking that does not include self-criticism, simplification, and political interest.

2.3—Signs and language

Words and numbers

A NUMBER SIGNIFIES THE UNIVERSE of infinite objects, ele-ments, concepts, and anything that can be individualized into units grouped into a specific set. The "3" signifies a unique grouping of units that are not ontologically individualized. When we signify "3," we can refer to a set of keys, days, ideas, or planets. For this reason, mathematics is often contrasted with literature, because one is the realm of abstraction while the other is the realm of the concrete, the embodied, of ideas and emotions. This, which can be upheld as a first approximation, is an intuitive idea but no less arbitrary.

Every word is also an abstraction. When we signify *tree*, we are abstracting from our own experience and collective experience. The word *tree* does not refer to anything concrete but rather to an infinitely variable set of the same unit. A *number* is a set stripped of its qualities, while a *word* is something with all the qualities of the same set stripped of its quantities. Even when I intend to directly name a unit, defined by an identity, such as when I signify the name of a person—a concrete individual—that I know, *Juan R.*, I am making an abstraction. There are infinite Juan Rs, but his friends can recognize common elements that we identify with him: his physical appearance, his character, some anecdotes we have shared with him and others he has told us, etc. But my Juan R. is surely not the same as the Juan R. of his brother or of Juan himself. In any case, *Juan R.* like *tree* are abstractions, that is, symbols that represent to the reader a certain quality of something. Juan R. aims to indicate a specific person, just as "3 apples" aims to indicate a set of concrete objects. It could be said that in this last case, the abstraction of the number "3" disappears when indicating the concrete objects it is related to, the apples. But let us observe that "apples" is not a lesser abstraction. Which apples are we referring to? Suppose that the apples are not in our hands and refer to a future promise. Then *apple* represents the infinite universe of different types of apples. It would only cease to be a qualitative abstraction if I imagine the apples with their particular shapes, shines, and colors. But this is no longer a symbol (the word-symbol) but a figurative image constructed by the imagination as a direct visualization.

We have, then, that the possible set of meanings of *3 apples* is equally infinite as the sets "3" and "apples." But their semantic fields are different. The C(-) of 3 apples is larger, being the intersection of the two negative fields of the terms that compose it. As can be seen, the language we are using in this last paragraph is borrowed from mathematical language, so we can clarify the idea using a metaphor from that discipline. We can say that the set of odd numbers is infinite, but it belongs to the set of natural numbers. There is another set, also infinite, of even numbers that does not belong to the first but does belong to the set of natural numbers.

Abstraction, in the case of a word, is not quantitative (as with numbers) but *qualitative*. The quantitative can be measured, while the qualitative depends on a subjective judgment. That is why the former traditionally belongs to the realm of science, while the latter is identified with the universe of art and philosophical speculation. Both are forms of abstraction, though different forms. Without abstraction, there is no symbol, because the symbol needs to be identified with only a part of the referred object while simultaneously being identified with a larger set of those same objects. This gives it significant flexibility while making the transfer of signs possible, without which an infinite combination of signs and terms for the infinite creation of meanings would not be possible.

Abstraction, Transfer, and Dynamics of Meanings

In other words, the term "apple" is identified with a class of elements, *but with none of them in particular*. It is an abstraction that transcends the limits of the concrete—which *must* do so to become language. We could not imagine a language composed of rigid terms that indicated only concrete and unique elements.

Instead, we have a language that is articulated by the abstraction of its elements and the concreteness of its discourse. Its sign elements —a signal, a word, a text, an attitude, a "fact"— are inherited from a culture and resignified by a concrete context and by a concrete reader. The expression of an idea, an emotion, or the perception of a physical phenomenon will make use of these tools based on abstraction to, in their combination, define a fact or a concrete experience.

We could think of the existence of certain symbols that are born alongside the object they signify. But that symbol could not exist if it were not built with meanings from the past. The word "Internet," which is almost a proper noun, was born to signify a new phenomenon, but let us see that while the phenomenon itself was a combination of already known phenomena —the book, television, etc.—, the very word Inter-net is the composition of two ancient words. Now, if the communication phenomenon of the Web were to disappear due to a catastrophe, the symbol would survive, although its meaning would continue to vary. This variation of meaning always depends on experience, that is, on the conjunction of the phenomenon —physical or metaphysical— and the reader. The reader, the final and original recipient of the sign, is both passive and active. The meaning they attribute to the sign will depend on themselves and on the context, while the context will depend on all the texts they are aware of, on them as a personal and intellectual particularity, and on other readers.

On December 15, 2004, the newspaper *Clarín* of Buenos Aires, in one of its headlines, announced: a new virus hides in Christmas cards. Twenty years ago, there would be no doubt: the information referred to a plague transmitted through cardboard Christmas postcards. Today there are no doubts either, although the meaning is different: in the new context, by "virus" we no longer refer to a biological infection; by "Christmas cards" we do not mean the classic postcards we sent and received by mail (traditional). Also, the reflexive "hides" is a metaphor applied to any type of virus —biological or computer—, but let us note that none of the words used in the headline is new as a sign. Both, "virus" and "cards" support each other to shape the meaning of the entire phrase and each of its parts —and vice versa. The words, the signs, have been resignified by a changing history, by a new context, by the structure of the phrase, of the text, by new readers.

Symbols are related to a past and a future. They are neither born nor die with the object. We use existing symbols to indicate new ideas, objects, and phenomena. These will modify both the original meaning of the inherited sign as well as the readers of the inherited sign. But when concrete objects and phenomena disappear, the sign will survive, and with it, a large part of its meaning modified by the latest experience, until a new experience takes place. Symbols are not "natural" like the things and phenomena they indicate. The word "apple" was created by a group of men and women who are no longer here. What we understand as apples, on the other hand, are natural elements. However, both the word "apple" and the set of objects it refers to can be considered of the same category —as natural—, in the semiotic understanding that they are preexistent to the experience of the reader. Both the physical space that surrounds us and the language in which we were born possess a similar nature. We can modify them only in part, but we must deal with their preexisting rules. We can modify the physical universe by building a house, a garden, and an entire city, but we will always do so by relying on its own laws, physical laws and cultural laws. We do the same with a novel or with language itself.

Abstraction and Definition

One of the central ideas we will develop in this essay is the view that every discourse is an attempt to build a *positive semantic field* while increasingly defining a *negative semantic field*. A particular idea can be named, for example, by the term *existence*. But we observe that the C(+) of this term is excessively extended; it tells us a lot and nothing at the same time. If we attempt to define the proposed term a bit more, we could say "philosophy of existence" or "existentialism." At this point, we have established a greater negation, a C(-) that encompasses everything that does not pertain to the act and history of speculation, thought, etc. But even so, the phrase will remain with a very high degree of indefinition. This indefinition would weaken the semantic value if we, the readers, did not understand that behind this expression there lies a greater definition established in discourse, in books, and in years of struggle to define those ideas that aim to be identified with the term existentialism. The first question will always be "What is existentialism?" That is, immediately, the proposed term will be demanded to provide a definition. The successive "existentialism is..." will lead to a narrative about the metaphysical space with the corresponding use of a progressive definition of semantic boundaries, defining as clearly as possible the limit between C(+) and C(-). When this definition between what it is and isn't must remain unresolved, undefined, with a broad margin of ambiguity, the discourse will be required to define "why this border is ambiguous, undefined." This once again confirms the will—of the discourse and the reader—for a semantic definition, even when a conceptual indefinition is intended.

We cannot say that a diffuse boundary of semantic fields necessarily calls into question the value, truth, or utility of the symbol, as Choudhary claims by opposing mathematical symbols to literary symbols. However, Choudhary makes an observation about the will to fix semantic boundaries as an attempt to explore a meaning "in terms of truth" (437). In words quoted from Ludwig Wittgenstein himself, "many words in this sense then don't have a strict meaning. But this is not a defect. To think it would be like saying that the light of my reading lamp is no real light at all because it has no sharp boundary (438)."

Now, the degree of abstraction is not determined solely by the expansion of the C(+) of the symbol but by the figurative diversity that this field can contain, even if it is narrow. A mathematical expression that links "a falling stone and the

Moon that does not fall"3 is an expression whose C(+) is capable of containing two seemingly opposite, contradictory, or independent figurations. That is, we must distinguish between indefinition and abstraction.

2.4—Physical Space and Metaphysical Space

Reality and Fiction

BOOK CATALOGUES, LITERARY CRITICISM and library shelves are primarily organized according to the antagonistic classification of "fiction" and "non-fiction". The practice is as useful as it is misleading. What we call *fiction* —poetry, short stories, novels— can easily claim the same right as dreams to be considered the cultural expression of a truth, of the deepest reality of a human being or a society. When we study the literature of the Middle Ages or 16th-century Spain, we observe the "idealization" of certain psychological and moral types that almost always seem improbable to us due to their excessive virtue or their unacceptable moral prejudices. However, this idea of idealization, exaggeration, or improbability—referring to moral virtues, as in *El Abencerraje*, from 1561— is above all determined by our own sensibility; that is, it is the judgment of early 21st-century readers. Now, if we pay attention, most of "popular art," such as soap operas and romance novels, are idealizations or improbabilities in the

---

3 Reference by Ernesto Sábato to Isaac Newton's law of gravitation in On Heroes and Tombs (271).

sense that we will hardly find among us a reality that matches these stereotypes. But here, what is important is not what we can call "reality" in a pretended scientific or objective sense. If there is a law that runs through the history of literature—especially fiction—it is the one that refers to the need for verisimilitude. Fictions, from the so-called mythological and fantastic to the most realistic, share a minimum degree of verisimilitude. The improbabilities of medieval literature and the no less improbable stories of modern soap operas have been and are popular because of what they have of verisimilitude. Beyond an analysis that exposes their ideological value and their "unrealism," it is important to note here that these stories are what they are because they have been recognized as "verisimilar" by a particular sensibility at a specific historical moment and in a specific place. What is "realism" if not a plausible reality? What we consider implausible today was plausible in its time, and it is from this recognition that we begin to form an idea of the men and women who read it with enthusiasm and passion. It is here, then, that "absurd," "implausible," or "arbitrary" fiction becomes an invaluable element of knowledge and, therefore, a "real object." The plausible is no longer a substitute for reality but the strongest indication of a sensitive, ethical, and spiritual reality of a people. And it is in this sense that the study of a people's sensibility—both ethical and aesthetic—through its fiction, gains a far more significant and irreplaceable value than a supposed historical study through "facts," since these "facts" are not judged through that sensibility but through ours. All of which does not mean that one is exclusive of the other but quite the contrary: it warns us of the partiality of each and the need for their complementarity in every study.

On the other hand, what is classified as *non-fiction*—history books, essays, chronicles, reflections—would hardly be able to dispense with the imagination of its author or the prejudices and myths of the society from which it emerged. If the Ptolemaic mathematicians were able to prove the "reality" of a universe with the Earth at its center, which modernity radically rejected—until recently; relatively, today—how can we not doubt the absence of fiction in each of those meticulous accounts of the Medieval Crusades4?

We can try to define a point of support to avoid a sterile relativism with no way out. Given the breadth and virtual impossibility of defining "reality" in absolute terms, we can define what we understand by "reality," integrating the understanding that the ontological category of the physical world is not sufficient to limit this concept—ultimately, a metaphysical one. We can start by saying that "reality" is any starting point from which we construct a narrative, a discourse, a representation of the world. Mas'ud Zavarzadeh, for example, at one point wrote: "Implicit in my approach, of course, is the assumption that culture (that is, the 'real') at any given historical moment, consists of an ensemble of contesting subjectivities" (5). From his perspective as a critic and theorist analyzing the cinematic phenomenon, "culture" is his starting point, the "reality" to which a film is referred as both a reflection and a shaper or reproducer of its own

---

4 See, for example, Runciman, Steven . *A History of the Crusades. The Kingdom of Acre and the Later Crusades.* Cambridge: Cambridge University Press, 1987

cultural origin. From another perspective, for example a psychological one, we can see culture as either a starting point or an endpoint. In the first case, culture is the "real"; in the second, it is the "construction" or product of another reality: the human mind. For a late 19th-century physician, for example, dreams were the product of a certain physiological condition (such as indigestion) and, therefore, the fictional reflection of biological reality. This latter case, of course, refers to a reductionist or materialist reading, for which the real is the physical, biological, economic world, and so on. The reality of a descending reading may contradict this assertion by starting from a cultural, intellectual, or psychological phenomenon: even a physical illness can be caused by a mental attitude, and the cause is no less real than the consequence.

In summary, we can say that the (pseudo-ontological) difference between reality and fiction is an ideological confirmation, the epistemological legitimation of a paradigm and a specific worldview.

Narration of the metaphysical space

Let us begin with the reflections of a famous Spanish philosopher. The quote may be lengthy but it is also necessary:

> Ideas, like money, are, in the end, nothing more than a representation of wealth and an instrument of exchange [...] Neither does the body eat money, nor does the soul nourish itself on mere appearances [...] He who warms ideas in the focus of his heart is the one who truly makes them his own; there, in that sacred hearth, he burns and consumes them, as fuel. They are a vehicle, nothing more than a vehicle of the spirit; they are atoms that

> only serve through the motion and rhythm they transmit, impenetrable atoms, like the hypothetical ones of matter that give us Heat through their motion. From the same chemical components come poison and antidote. And the poison itself—is it in the agent or in the patient? What kills one person gives life to another. Is evil in the judge or in the accused? Only tolerance can extinguish human malice in love, and tolerance only springs forth powerfully upon the collapse of ideocracy (Unamuno, 167).

Here we see how *what is seen* in the metaphysical space of speculation is narrated as if it were an objective observation made by a chronicler at a sporting event or a scientist in their laboratory. Then, to confirm it, a metaphor from the physical world is used. In this case, in the metaphor of money, the ambiguity is double. However, the philosopher forces the definition and then forces the metaphor. If we recognize the metaphor and its connection to metaphysical observation as valid, we will be recognizing the validity of their thought, of their truths. There remains the possibility of recognizing a connection of metaphysical observation with the history of money, with a part of it and not its entirety, since in the use of a metaphor, a complete identification of it with the objective of the explanation would not make sense. But which part?

We are always more inclined to call *truth* what integrates into a cognitive unit that is ours prior to discovery. "With the same chemical components, poison and antidote can be made. And the poison itself, is it in the agent or in the patient? What kills one person gives life to another," says Unamuno. Here we see that the truth of a proposition derives from its coincidence with a simple metaphor, perhaps not noticed in its surprising logic but immediately verifiable:

with the same components, poison or antidote can be made. As Socrates would say, we accept it because it was knowledge that was there, within us, and reasoning only makes it conscious. In another way, we could say that we accept it because a signic transfer occurs that establishes a harmonious integration with our previous knowledge. A new relationship has been established between the new cognitive unit and the preexisting totality. That new unit could come into conflict with the whole, with the cognitive foundations—though never absolutely—if and only if it were capable of surviving autonomously until a new complex cognitive unit is reconstructed upon it: it would be a new paradigm, a new conception of the world.

"Only tolerance can extinguish human malice in love, and tolerance only springs forth powerfully upon the collapse of ideocracy," insists the famous philosopher. Here we see the same problem again. On what basis does the author affirm that *only tolerance can extinguish malice in love*? Is it an act of faith? Where has he seen it, where has he verified it? Is he narrating an experience as one might narrate a horse race seen at a racetrack? Is he narrating what his intuition has seen from his own experience? We would lean toward accepting the latter possibility: both the author has seen it in his experience and the reader has verified it in their own, based purely on deep intuition, which is why they recognize *truth* in the previous statements. However, this "seeing in one's own experience" is terribly valued by pure subjectivity that, moreover, would be unprovable and only acquire a character of truth when recognized by other subjectivities, that is, by its *intersubjective* possibility. On one hand, it is not known under what law the metaphysical observation of ideas can be related or associated with money; on the other, we do not know what logical or epistemological law leads from tolerance to love. Yet, the philosopher presents them as a necessary cause-consequence, and nothing else is what we constantly do when narrating an idea: we *construct* it, like a painter constructs their composition, rarely resorting to reasoning, syllogism, or logic.

The dual reality: physical and metaphysical

I will start from a principle: every *truth* is a metaphysical construction.

This thought—the construction of truth—, in my understanding, works in the following way: the writer narrates a hermeneutic reality they are observing or have observed, not using their senses but their intuition. Each statement is the account of that observation. At the same time, that metaphysical reality must have a minimal order of coherence because it must share similar laws with the physical space, such as the possibility of being narrated as an observable physical and temporal fact, the need for some coherence, intelligibility, or sensible perception. This metaphysical space, where ethics and intellectual speculation exist, always exists. It is a parallel and symbiotic construction to the world we call "physical." Both the physical world and the metaphysical one together form what we can now truly call reality. Both arise simultaneously from the first split between the real and the unreal. The physical world emerges when the gods ascend to the heavens. We cannot deny the existence of the physical world or the metaphysical world; we can only question their natures, which one predominates over the other. Do we see physical reality through our prejudices and convictions? Or are our judgments, prejudices, ideas, and convictions indebted to the physical world? The questions are not mutually exclusive, they are not alternatives. According to my metaphysical observation of reality, both possibilities must be accepted in a symbiotic relationship. Just as an intellectual space conditions and influences the other, so too does the inverse hold true.

Historical Separation of the Two Spaces

From a contemporary point of view, we can say that language arises from the physical space and only through metaphors and semiotic transfers can it reach the metaphysical space and describe it. However, in a reciprocal and symbiotic way, the metaphysical space will act upon the physical space in the form of myths, ideologies, cultural paradigms, etc.

This latter point expresses a clear idea, but we must make a clarification. There is no evidence to suggest that, in ancient, prehistoric times, men and women distinguished between the physical world and the world of their beliefs, ideas, and superstitions, *quite the opposite*. Or at least the distinction between spirit and body, between magic—art—and physical law was not as clear as it is today. Nevertheless, we can recognize the ontological duality. We can easily distinguish a physical world—its idea—with its own existence, and another space where our ideas about that (presumed) preexisting space are developed. Because the physical world may be preexistent, but we can never have the slightest knowledge of it except through ourselves, through our faculty of comprehension, through our consciousness. We are condemned to live with the paradox that the radicals eliminated: our consciousness is subsequent to the physical world, but the physical world would not exist without our consciousness that grants it the preexistent attribute. The radicals, like George Berkeley, resolved this paradox by simply denying the physical world. Which proves that, although the physical world seems to be the support of consciousness—for a materialist conception of the Universe—it is entirely possible to deny its existence before denying the existence of the one who perceives it. Descartes' cogito ergo sum can be understood in the broadest sense: if I think, it's because I exist, but my existence does not prove the existence of the physical world, of what is perceived. Even in dreams, I think and perceive; what I dream and what I imagine is a reality without physical support, apparently, but it is undeniable existence.

Since the Greeks, and before, truth is what the fleshly eyes cannot see. "Truth likes to hide," said Heraclitus, and Plato understood that a man who can only see horses and not the *form*, the *essential idea* of the horse, had eyes, but not intelligence (Majfud, 69). The world functions according to a *logos* or *nous* hidden, and the mission of thought is to be able to see it behind the apparent. Psychoanalysis, Marxism, and structuralism also seem to tell us that to understand is to see what is not seen, to discover the hidden order behind appearance, the invisible law that relates a set of prime numbers by a particularity in their divisibility, etc.

But, since the same phenomenon or a series of phenomena can be explained according to different *logoi*, it turns out that the *power-to-see* of some consists in the *not-seeing* of others. Like a guide, the one who believes he sees guides the presumed blind, while describing to him what the other does not see, but can touch.

The objective element

The expression "historical fact" has its semantic center of gravity in the noun-term *fact*. This, in turn, is strongly linked to a scientific tradition that refers to an objective, observable, and verifiable phenomenon. From an epistemological perspective, an objectively observed and verified fact constitutes the first condition attributable to an assertion to be identified with (a metaphysical precept:) "the truth."

According to the Pythagorean phrase made famous by Galileo Galilei, "the Book of Nature is written in mathematical characters" (Tarnas, 263). However, we can invert this same expression—and with it the concept—in this way: we understand the physical world, the quantifiable world, by translating it into numbers. This seems to be suggested by Chaos Theory. In other disciplines, there are also axiomatic units, metaphysical foundations. In history, the verification of certain facts is vital for any attempt to establish syntheses and theoretical conclusions that claim to be true. Yet, due to the great complexity in the concatenation of historical facts, the ideas that summarize these facts in general and intelligible statements can be supported by a selection of historical facts that will never result in definitively verified conclusions. Not only because of this complexity of the facts themselves, but also due to another variable in the equation: the reader. 5

Chronicle, essay, and fiction

When we write a short story or a novel, we simply describe what we are *seeing* in our imagination. However, the process of narration is the same as when we describe something we are observing directly. Something similar happens when we draw: sometimes we follow the construction of our hand, but when we manage to anticipate what we are seeing, the result is usually better or, at least, more secure and spontaneous. Often, when I draw, I observe the result, but as soon as I can anticipate it and see the drawing fully completed before executing it, the drawing fulfills my expectations more fully. When we describe a fact and a full circumstance of something that did not happen, when we create fiction, we also proceed as if we were simply describing something we are witnessing, as if we were chroniclers of a world external to ourselves. That world, which is not the physical world, is what I call *metaphysical space*, and in the symbiosis of both lies what I understand as reality.

The same as we do when writing a novel, we do when we declare any thought, whether ethical or practical (I am doing

---

5 Christopher Braidier, analyzing Baroque painting, mentions to us the paradox of perspective discovered in the Renaissance. Considered a model of objectivity, it is the product of a point of view. The world is objective only from the point of view of a subject (Braidier, Christopher. Barroque self-Invention and Historical Truth. Burlington, Vermont: Ashgate Publishing Limited, 2004. p 91-93).

nothing else now). When we say that a car stopped because it ran out of fuel and will run again when we refill the tank, we are engaging in a dialogue with a past and a future that exists only as a representation. It's just that this fact is less evident and guides a large part of the dynamics of our thoughts. We will try to explore this idea by analyzing various texts that, initially reasonable or deductive, later reveal themselves as *assertive* and are carried out according to certain techniques that we will also seek to highlight: *transfer*.

> Truth? You say truth? Truth is something more intimate than the logical agreement of two concepts, something more profound than the equation of the intellect with the thing [...] It is the intimate union [*metaphor*] of my spirit with the Universal Spirit [*direct observation of the metaphysical space*] (Unamuno, 170).

In this paragraph by the philosopher, "something more" does not mean an expansion of the C(+) of truth but quite the opposite, as it is followed by the qualifier intimate, that is, "something more intimate than the logical agreement of two concepts," which results in a negation of meaning, a definition of the C(-) greater and a narrowing of the C(+) of the adversary.

In the following paragraph, we can see synthesized the direct narration of metaphysical space—cognitive prefiguration—and the use of metaphors as a link with the physical space:

> Logic is fencing that develops the muscles of thought, undoubtedly, but on the battlefield, it is of little use. What

good are strong muscles if you don't know how to fight?
(170).

Gradually, Unamuno becomes entangled in the metaphor and the axiomatic concept by which that which is lived is true:

> True is the doctrine of electricity in that it gives us light and transmits our thoughts over distances, among other wonders (171).

In this case, perhaps we can notice that it is not a direct narrative about the observation of metaphysical space but rather the result of a progressive construction, a consequence of the use of a concept applied to different unforeseen situations under the same "logic."

2.5—Historical Facts

A *fact* is a text

A HISTORICAL FACT IS A TEXT that has forgotten it is a text; it is not a purely objective and undeniable phenomenon, as it claims to be. Its meaning is tied to its context and to a reader. It is a text that varies according to the context and the outcome of the various struggles for its meaning. The weapons of this struggle will be re-signification, through the (re)definition of semantic fields and strategic sign transfers with their corresponding forgettings, the forgetting of its own history. Its battlefield will be the context itself. From the context will be taken the signs established in the pursuit of modifying the meanings of key signs within a thought.

When I say that a *fact* is a text, I am establishing an initial axiom. At the same time, I am establishing a grammatical identity—using the link *is*—which, in reality, signifies an inclusion: one set is included in the other, but not the reverse. While we can observe that the law of reciprocity can be fulfilled—a text is a fact—we notice that the first expression carries a meaning distinct from the second, from its semantic inversion. The axiom "a fact is a text" is, in turn, a metaphor, because only a part of one can be identified in the other. They are not synonymous nor do they become interchangeable. With this metaphor of low figuration, we are performing a transfer of meaning. That is, there is something inherent to a text that we understand to be present in a fact. This "something" is, or can be, its character as an interpretative object and subject of interpretation. In other words, like a text, a fact can be the product of symbolic construction or susceptible to perceptual alterations.

However, the same expression "a historical fact is a text" can be derived from a more general idea: a text is something that is (or can be) interpreted by relying on something beyond itself: a context and an observer who will link the two—the text and the context—in a relationship of giving-and-receiving, of extracting-and-conferring meaning.

This leads us to another question: are text and context two different ontological categories, or does their "being" depend on a semantic relationship?

Text and Context

How does the text differ from the context? Are they not the same thing but in different semantic positions? That is, in a relationship of giving-and-taking meaning in different ways?

If I were to elaborate or clarify this idea a bit, I would start by specifying that here I am understanding "text" in a broad sense. In a restricted sense, "text" refers only to a written code or message. In a more expansive sense, we can say that "text" is also any significant fact that can be taken as a unit. For example, a greeting, a street protest, an armed assault, etc.

However, all of these can, at the same time, be context—or part of a context—that contributes to the meaning of a text.

Since the scientific revolution of the early 20th century—even in the physical sciences—the "observer" has come to the forefront as an active part of the observed phenomenon. In the literary field, this "observer" who confers meaning and modifies the observed is the reader. Professor Gómez-Martínez has analyzed this under the name of the "anthropic," recognizing a post-postmodern historical moment, the final link in the author-text-reader chain (Beyond Post-Modernity, 1999). As always, Nietzsche in the 19th century had already touched on this: he wrote that "the existence of innumerable interpretations of a given text comes from the fact that reading is never the objective identification of meaning but the importation of meaning into a text which has no meaning 'in itself'" (Atkins, 28).

To make this less abstract, I will try to explain myself with more examples. The meaning of a written text is influenced, among other things, by its literary context. To put it graphically, the context of a book can be a library. But the context of any library—a literary movement, a current of thought—is, in turn, immersed in a historical, cultural, etc., context. Nevertheless, the context of a historical fact is shaped by other "facts" and by other literary texts, that is, by other texts in the broad sense of the term. However, the context of a historical event is formed by other "facts" and by other literary texts, meaning other texts in the broader sense of the term.

It seems clear, then, that the difference between text and context is not an ontological difference, but rather depends on the semantic—semiotic—relationship that one maintains with the other.

The absolute universal and the context-relative

Generally, when we speak of context, we recognize that there are many types while conceiving it as a single entity. That is, it is acknowledged that each culture, each historical moment, possesses a particular context, and that context is the one that should be used to interpret a text, a sign that "belongs" to it. At the same time, it is recognized that the context of a street protest can be the city, the country, and even the entire world. In other words, the broader the geographical area we encompass, and, if possible, the historical area, the better it will be to "correctly" interpret the text, the sign.

However, the idea of a necessary contextualization tends to deny any kind of transcendence or universality, as these are, by definition, the opposite of contextualization, of the consideration that the text and the sign do not possess a universal or permanent meaning. But let us observe that both perceptions—contextualization and universalization—are two considerations of the same thing. To contextualize would be to reduce or limit an excessively extended context, a context with universalist pretensions.

Also, the idea of a possible independence of meaning from any context, in most cases, implies validity across different possible contexts considered. That is, we could consider the extreme of a mathematical formula and say it is "indifferent" to any context. But at the same time, we can consider that its validity, abstraction, and universalization consist in its applicability to all possible contexts—that recognize it as a sign.

But let's return to an issue that, while not more complex than mathematics, involves variables impossible to abstract into x and y. Observe that when we seek to contextualize *Don Quixote*, we usually refer to the history of Spain in the 16th and 17th centuries. But to understand the Spanish situation of that era, we can go back—in time—to the centuries of Islamic rule in the peninsula and even beyond. We can also expand this context—geographically—to the tradition of French knights—and even further. We assume, then, that the more we encompass historical, geographical, and philosophical considerations, the better we will be considering the context of Don Quixote or the Battle of Lepanto. But how far? Where is the limit? If we continued to extend these contextual considerations, we would arrive at a quasi-universalization. A political or historical reading of the Battle of Lepanto would require a profound consideration of a "restricted context"; a psychoanalytic reading would likely reach back to the prehistory of humanity, to concepts like "power" or "totem," etc., which will claim some certification of being "universal."

Now, we can also separate those elements that depend more on a *narrow context* and those that aim to be stable in an *extended context* (quasi-universal). The vigil of arms of Don Quixote must be considered within a restricted context. Considering the invention of the wheel or the construction of the Great Wall of China would contribute little or nothing in this case. However, we can recognize other elements in this act, in this text: honor, courage, madness, love, etc. The current usage of the term "quixotic," like the term "sadistic"—derived from the fame of the novels of the Marquis de Sade—suggests a transcendence beyond the restricted context of the work or the author. We could even assume that quixotic or sadistic traits in humans are something "universal," like hate or love. Well, someone might argue that when Homer or Cervantes speak of hate or love, they are not talking about the same hate or love that can be understood by a man and a woman in the 21st century. But this is as improbable as its opposite. We cannot say that it is the same love or that they are different loves, just as we cannot even say that a man's love for a woman is the same as a woman's love for a man. Any attempt at definition would fall into a metaphysical area impossible to contrast with any minimal certainty. We have no other option but to understand the translated love in a text from two thousand years ago as something very similar to what we experience deep within ourselves upon hearing the same word. Simply, we are recognizing, implicitly or explicitly, that there is something in common that we share in the term love in the context of Homeric Greece or in the context of Neruda's Chile.

We can imagine that there are feelings, certain emotions that, like ideas, did not always exist in human history. The concept of *zero* is at least fifteen hundred years old; perhaps the feeling of *altruism*—beyond its infinite variations—is not innate in the human species, but it is likely that we can identify it in many behaviors of other animal species—especially in monkeys—even if we are not willing to recognize it as ancient as the feelings of love and power. But this would lead us to a psychological, philological, and semiotic analysis of the term *altruism*.

Let's look, then, at the case of a literary text. Novels like *Abaddon the Exterminator*, by Ernesto Sabato, contain complex references to events and symbols that would be emptied of meaning if the reader were unaware of the restricted context of Buenos Aires in the early seventies, such as words that only a local from the outskirts would understand, brand names with strong local connotations, or sayings and attitudes of politicians or artists of the time. Nevertheless, this novel has been read with passion all over the world, from the East to the West, both today and thirty years ago. We can recognize in this phenomenon elements that the author calls "human" that are shared by those who live at the antipodes of Argentines and speak a completely different language. Surely, the same text read by an Argentine and a Japanese is not the same. Nor is the same text read by two siblings or a married couple. But it would be an implausible improbability to assume that it is all a coincidence: an Argentine and a Japanese recognize common passions in a text that speaks of absolutely different things. These absolutely different things do not exist, therefore, and what is not different is, then, universal.

But universal—to what extent, to what moment? We do not know. But we can derive from this observation that this "restricted universal" is an "extended context." That is, what in the Modern Era we call "universal" and in postmodernity "contextual" can be seen as the unattainable extremes of the same spectrum.

This also suggests to us that signs, terms, texts—that is, everything that radiates meaning—gain strength and significance through what they affirm and deny each one. However, for analytical purposes, we can proceed in the opposite way to traditional analysis: instead of differentiating, we can observe that often—if not always—those sign elements that oppose each other are merely the same concept in a different semantic relationship.

Thus, we have observed that we can understand "text" and "context" as a semantic relationship, lacking a definition or an ontological value; in the same way, we can see that "contextual" and "universal" are two extreme variations— surely extreme, unattainable—of the same concept. Hence, we use *extended context* as a synonym for *restricted universal*.

The same can be said of concepts like "individual" and "society." I find it impossible to conceive one without the other, but tradition has divided them to create a dialectic of oppositions and thus define one and the other as if they were different essences. A man is not the same as a hundred men— an observation of physical space. But in a single human being exist both the individual and society, just as in a group of a hundred people. Out of this difference have emerged psychology and sociology, the psychological rules so distinct from the sociological ones. But this type of differentiation is more useful than unquestionable—how can we understand the meaning of trauma, as psychoanalysis does, without the cultural component imposed by a tradition, by the culture of a society?

Let us travel the same path back and forth. After this exercise, I understand that we might conjecture that from any complex concept, ideas and terms can emerge with sufficient autonomy to complement, oppose, and, through this dialectic dynamic, structure an entire text with new meanings. This would be achieved by limiting certain C(+), based on an original one, and extending new C(-), just as the city of Berlin was divided and colonized in 1949 by different nations and ideologies that opposed and disputed each other's discourse, the meanings of the city and the political world. Thus, we had one Berlin in the east and another in the west, which were radically opposed—in their ideological readings, in their dialectic and military disputes—but which, from other perspectives, remained the same city: Berlin, the ancient capital of the Germans.

It is useful to limit the semantic fields of each differently, but this is still a semantic construction solidified by the very fact of remaining unchallenged. And this will be one of the ideas we consider as we analyze the two disputing texts later.

The Universal and the Relative

As we have already noted, from the moment there is *communication* (or we assume there is), we must simultaneously recognize that those communicating share certain understandings or implicit agreements about the meanings of some signs we manage within a specific communication code. In his book Beyond Postmodernity, the essayist José

Luis Gómez-Martínez says something similar, and in doing so, he uses examples and conclusions we can analyze from another perspective. For example, Gómez-Martínez reminds us that, from an anthropic viewpoint, the ultimate meaning of certain symbols, such as expressions of laughter or fear, transcends cultures and thus can be taken as universal references. "A look of joy, sadness, or distress, or a scream of panic, are expressions that precede any cultural contextualization; they 'symbolize' human states of a root referent—of universality in human discourse—of the possibility of communication that postmodern discourse insists on denying us" (26).

According to this reading, we can accept that there are symbols or communication codes that depend on cultural context, while others we might call "universal" or "transcendent" as they arise from the human condition, independent of culture, country, or historical moment. This immanent dimension of humans can serve not just as the starting point of an interpretation but also as its endpoint. In fact, it is the foundation of a profound humanism and the basis of what we know today as Human Rights: the assumption that there exist transcendent, universal human values.

Indeed. And from an ethical perspective, we have always defended this "common ground" of understanding—the minimum condition for intercultural dialogue and ethical reflection. However, it can always be useful—for challenging established notions—to question it. Why do we consider Human Rights as "universal" values, independent of any culture? Without a doubt, this perspective is at least a consensus, and in its defense, our own principles stand. However, without the intent to deny them and purely for analytical purposes, we may well consider that what we call "universal" here is nothing more than one end of the same spectrum, on which the "relative" of culture lies on the opposite end. I mean, once again, that here we are not dealing with two different ontological categories but with the same thing with varying degrees of its common components. That is to say, even Human Rights—the universal in humanity—is a cultural, contextual formation, just as "the cultural" is, in turn, a human manifestation, and thus "universal."

To clarify this, we can consider some concrete aspects of these human phenomena.

In a broader historical context, even the most basic laws, such as those summarized in the second tablet of Moses— thou shalt not kill, thou shalt not steal, etc.—are the results of a historical evolution that we stopped calling "cultural" and began to consider "universal." Surely there is no people in the world where crime is an indifferent or recommended activity. Without delving into pathological cases where crime constitutes a source of pleasure, and even though in the rest of our societies crime remains a widespread practice still—why did I say *still?*—it continues to provoke the same conflict, the same rejection in the conscience. In the same way, we could consider the case of incest. There are no logical or biological reasons to justify the horror that incest produces in us; its rejection, rather than rational, is an inheritance from our prehistoric ancestors, the founders of our sexual ethics at its roots. Nevertheless, this supposed "universality" of the rejection of incest, we are dealing with a cultural phenomenon. Cultural, but one that is indebted not to a limited context—such as a Chinese or French context—but to a much broader context. So broad as to encompass a great number of centuries and, probably, in the present, almost all geographical and cultural regions of the planet. Although incest may depend on a particular culture—since a culture might not consider it a "sin"— it is, according to anthropologists, the most universal taboo known. Laughter, which others explain in its prehistoric origin as a demonstration of fear, as a request for surrender, has come to be seen as a "natural reaction," when at another time it was probably a symbol, once part of a communication code6 with different meanings. And the same could be said of a long list of gestures—such as greeting or insulting—that have cultural origins and are now considered "universal."

Culture and Context

From the moment we use the word "culture," we are semantically and a priori limiting it—a consequence of our own culture—to a narrow span of a few decades and to geographic and human regions that are often arbitrary, as arbitrary as the racial categorizations that appear so "obvious" to us. However, just as when we say "black," "Guaraní," or "oriental" we are imposing a necessary limitation on the semantic fields of each of these terms, we do the same when speaking of "Western culture" and, ultimately, when understanding "culture." I will not dwell here on the endless question of "What is culture?" But I am interested in analyzing for a moment the idea that "culture" is referred to in a sense

---

6 As an example, see: Claude Lèvi-Strauss. The Elementary Structure of Kinship. Boston: Beacon Press, 1969. Bronislaw Malinowski. Magic, Science and Religion, and Other Essays. Boston, Beacon Press, 1948.

I would call "narrow." That is, we call "culture" that which can be contrasted with another human group that shares certain elements but differs in others. Thus, we speak of "Chinese culture" and "American culture." In this way, the term "culture" proves useful from the moment it can identify what the Chinese and Americans have in common but, at the same time, what distinguishes them. For this same reason, we do not speak of a "human culture" when thinking about the last twenty thousand years.

The True Meaning

The collection designed by the editors of *Plaza y Janés*, of which *Las raíces torcidas* is a part, bears the title at the foot of the cover: *Así fue. La historia rescatada*. The first expression refers to *facts*, that is, *real* events that could or can be objectively verified with the intention of claiming the category of "truth." The second phrase is a common aspiration: every writing of history is a rewriting of facts and previous texts. The *rescue* signifies a salvation of the "true meaning." That is, the rewriting organizes the facts in such a way that the truth—the writer's thesis—is revealed and demonstrated.

2.6—The Semantic Fields

BEFORE ANALYZING THE SYMBOLIC and semantic dynamics of an ideology from a particular point of view proposed in this same essay—semantic fields—I will attempt to present that same viewpoint from the problematics of signs. I will use the annotation C(+) to refer to the "positive semantic field" and C(-) for the "negative semantic field."

Five theoretical premises

To begin, we can note five aspects that we recognize as present in our analysis:

1) The meaning of a sign is the semantic result of a positive field—what it means—and a negative field—what it does not mean.

2) The articulation of a set of symbols and meanings in a given linguistic system depends on the negative field of the semantic bodies.

3) There cannot be meaning in a sequence of independent elements. The meaning of a symbol owes its existence to the whole. The unit (the sign) does not stand on its own but through the negation it makes of the rest of the signs in the system.

4) The meaning of a sign is not limited by the semantic boundaries of the two semantic fields but encompasses the entire area of the linguistic system that constitutes the sign. These semantic boundaries are the unstable result of a permanent semantic struggle that occurs in any society.

5) Every symbolic unit—a symbol or an individual—lacks autonomous existence: it only exists *in relation and as part* of the whole (society) it integrates and seeks to differentiate itself from. No sign in the

system holds a privileged relationship with any other sign in the system, but relates to the entire whole in the form of negations. The privileged relationships we may find between two signs depend solely on the culture of the moment, as is the case with the relationship between the term white and the term black.

Integrated semantic analysis of some symbols

In Portuguese, the verb "tirar" means *to take, to grab*, but in Spanish it means the opposite—*to throw, to detach*. Hence, obviously, *"tirar dinheiro"* is not the same as "tirar dinero." Within the Spanish language itself, "tomar" can mean different things depending on its grammatical context: it can mean *to drink* or *to grab*.

However, these definitions appear relatively clear to speakers who master each of these languages. Now let us take the case of someone learning to speak Spanish. A relatively immediate step in their learning will be the definition of the relationship this sign—the word *tomar*—maintains with a positive field: that is, when assigning it a meaning. Simultaneously, we will begin to define a negative field. However, the "stability" of the sign will not be established until the negative field has been sufficiently defined. That is, until the reader-listener can establish what the same sign does not mean.

We can clarify this a bit further in another way. Let us suppose we write the word "Tacuarembó" in an internet search engine. If we are searching for the word in the overwhelming universe of words that "belong" to all languages available on the web, it is possible that we will find several matches, one of which will correspond to the object I have in mind when writing or mentioning "Tacuarembó," that is, my hometown. But I cannot be sure about what other matches—meanings—the same word may have. If I add an accent at the end, it will likely limit the search automatically to the universe of words belonging to Spanish. It is probable that in Guaraní "Tacuarembó" means *land of tacuaras*, though we cannot affirm this with certainty since we do not speak that language and in that region of America, almost no traces of that indigenous culture remain. It is also likely that the same word may mean many other things in other Asian or African languages. However, for me, it will be as important to attribute it a meaning as to deny it others. Even more important will be to deny it the possibility of meaning an unlimited set of things. If I continue my experiment by reducing the positive field and write "río Tacuarembó Chico," I no longer expect an almost infinite coincidence where the indigenous word plus the two Spanish words may refer to something different from the natural river that flows through my hometown. If I found that "Río Tacuarembó Chico" is the brand of pencils manufactured in Japan, I would surely attribute it to a deliberate reference by the manufacturer to my city rather than a mere coincidence. Now, why do I resist accepting—at first—another meaning for that expression other than the one previously attributed? Undoubtedly, because the positive field of the new semantic body falls within the negative field of the previous semantic body, leading me into conflict by not recognizing it as a second body: something cannot belong to both the negative and positive fields simultaneously without belonging to an alien semantic body.

When I say "cocina," I can establish an ambiguous relationship between the word as a noun or a verb, I can recognize its dual meaning as a noun (as a space in the house or as a culinary tradition), but these ambiguities, which can coexist perfectly well within the same semantic body, are quickly resolved with minimal grammatical context that moves from an undefined field to a clearer definition. When we say "paella is traditional in Spanish cocina," I am eliminating—practically entirely—the possibility of the noun/verb ambiguity of the word "cocina." In this process, I am not acting by addition—assigning a meaning—but by subtraction—eliminating other possible meanings. I proceed by confirming—expanding—a more precise region of the negative field. Thus, we can say that what we understand as the "definition" of a symbol is no more than the pressure we exert from the negative field onto the positive field until reducing it to its minimal expression. Its paradigmatic example is the mathematical symbol, while in art the positive field tends to expand into more vast, proprietary or shared regions, within a broad frontier with the negative field.

The same happens with the pronoun *I*. In English, I cannot omit it when I want to say *"I went there"*. The verb *went* can signify the action of a person who moved to some place, but if we do not specify which person we are talking about, the expression remains undefined to a dangerous limit for its signification. In Spanish, on the contrary, I can omit the pronoun *I*, because the verb includes it. I can say *"I went* there" or simply *"I went* there." The verb contains the person, a single person—*I*. This indication consolidates the negative field by eliminating other possible persons, so the meaning is highly defined in this sense (the rest of the brief expression negates the possibility of the other meaning of the verb *"fui"* as a conjugation of "ser"). On the other hand, if I say "they went there," the verb in Spanish can include the persons *ustedes* or *ellos*, so the boundary between the C(+) and C(-) fields remains with a still broad margin of ambiguity. Therefore, to define this semantic boundary I must add, for example, the pronoun *ellos*. "They went to Santiago" is a grammatically correct expression, as correct as the previous one, but with the difference that it has excluded the pronoun *ustedes*. Has it ceased to be ambiguous? If I know only one Santiago, yes. But if I consider that there is a Santiago in Chile and another in Galicia, I won't know which one I'm talking about until I add: "They went to Santiago de Chile." I have proceeded, again, by subtraction. I have negated meaning to other possibilities of the original sign.

In the previous expressions, the C(-) was disturbed by a manifest, even conscious, ambiguity of the C(+). It was necessary, then, to press from the C(-) onto the C(+) that was the objective of our intended signification.

Now, we might argue that there is only one positive field and that, when it comes into conflict with the positive field of another sign, we decide to "differentiate it." This objection is entirely valid but partial.

It is entirely possible—and in fact, it happens—that two positive fields come into conflict—or dispute an order of priorities—when the meanings get confused, just as a single sign can possess a broad positive field, so much so that it can encompass several meanings—ambiguous and even opposite—. But this way of viewing the reality of the sign would also be false from the moment it is incomplete.

Let's consider any arbitrary sign. Let's think of a word, such as "prison." Immediately, we can think of the building where living bodies are kept. In another instance—or simultaneously—we can think of its metaphorical use: "the body is the prison of the soul," "language is the prison of thought," etc. But surely, we will all think that this word "possesses" a limited number of meanings. Three, four, or at most ten. However, how can we deny it one hundred or two hundred different meanings when the Spanish language recognizes over half a million words?

If we open a dictionary at random, most likely, we will know the meaning of almost all the words. Now, when I immediately say that the word "prison" has two or three meanings, does that mean I have checked each of the five hundred thousand words in the dictionary? How did I acquire this immediate knowledge? How do I know that the word "prison" does not mean something else in my language? That denial is a fundamental part of the meaning of the symbol and, above all, of the dynamics of any language.

Finally, if we read the word "Nietzsche" in a Spanish text, we will probably say that "it means nothing." As we said at the beginning, from the moment the sign is recognized as such, it means something. In this case, it could mean a word from a foreign language, or perhaps a name, but it will always mean something, however vague it may be. Now, the idea of meaning nothing derives from the extensive and almost complete negative field that the sign has in the Spanish language. We have not checked each of the five hundred thousand words in the language, but our knowledge of non-meanings—that is, the negative field of the sign—provides us with a quick, immediate judgment. This knowledge is as immediate and of the same nature as its opposite: its possible positive field. Both together: the meaning.

When we read the word *tistruct* we can immediately respond that we do not know it or that "it means nothing" in our everyday Spanish. It is likely that we hesitate because we have heard a similar word—or the same one—somewhere before, or because we attribute some authority to a dictionary that contains words we never use. I may hesitate a lot or a little, but in any case, the time it takes to say I don't know it is not directly related to the number of words I know.

In summary, defining my knowledge of a symbol by the C(+) I attribute to it would be as arbitrary as doing so only by the C(-) I have of it. Ultimately, it would, in my view, be a poor definition, an incomplete one. Meanwhile, I will continue to attribute to the sign a certain meaning that derives from the tension between the two semantic areas.

Semantic Conflict

According to Whorf and Saussure, each word not only has a meaning but also a "value." This explanation seems to stem from the observation that two words can have the same meaning but different values. Thus, Pierre Hegy explains that the French word mouton has the same meaning as the English word sheep. However, Hegy says, they do not have the same value due to the existence of the English word mutton. Far from the deconstructionists, he tells us that while meaning is something stable and can be clearly defined in a dictionary, value depends on the context of the language used (Hegy, 329).

> Similarly, the sound-image used in various languages to refer to the concept of "power" may have the same meaning but not necessarily the same value. (330)

As Barthes formulated it in 1956, there are no innocent languages, "every man is a prisoner of his own language" (116). If we consider the historical context of France and the United States in the 17th century, we will see that in the first case, the language develops with an elite—courtly—consciousness, while the second lacks it. From there, Hegy follows, it is possible to understand the concept of "shared power" in this English—black power, student power, etc.—, while it is not possible to understand the word pouvoir in French as something shared: it is something taken entirely—blacks or students either have or do not have power.

The positive field will be artificially defined by identifying an unknown sign with a known meaning from our own language. But what will remain even more undefined is the negative field, that is, that accumulation of non-meanings that should solidify when attempting to establish a homologous semantic body in both languages. However, this semantic body is rooted in a particular culture, at a specific historical moment, and stems from a particular individual who is, at the same time, conditioned by others and by their own creative freedom.

When we translate a text literally—word by word—the result is often disastrous. We can rephrase a sentence, change words that isolated would have no correlation, in order to reproduce a similar *expression* in another language. In this act, we treat the entire phrase as a symbol that corresponds to another symbol—though not univocally. Nevertheless, this effort means comparing two semantic bodies from two different linguistic systems. For this, the dynamics of the two fields—the positive and the negative—are determinative.

Finally, let us note that Barthes' prison-like idea of language—already anticipated by F. Nietzsche nearly a century earlier—is of fundamental use in the analysis of ideologies in language. Jorge Luis Borges had summarized it with his inimitable style: "Man's languages are traditions that entail something of fate. Individual experiments are, in fact, minimal, except when the innovator resigns themselves to crafting a museum specimen [...]" (Borges, Obras 174). Nevertheless, we cannot overlook a possible objection that can be raised from an epistemological standpoint. Madam Sarup succinctly summarized this objection as follows:

> Nietzsche believes that we are unable to escape the constraints of languages and thus have no alternative but to operate within language. He is aware of the reflexive problem: if we say 'we are trapped within language and its concepts', that claim is in itself, of course part of the language. We wish to express our 'trappedness' but we are unable to do so other than in the very concepts which trap us. The original thought therefore eludes us, for if we could express it, we would not, after all, be trapped" (45).

In the same way, the *warning* that each language carries within it its own history and its own ideological structure is a form of 'awareness' that we can consider beyond the prison of the means it uses to express itself.

Our effort will be to point out the existence of certain semantic constructions and their —ideological— function in culture and, more specifically, in social narrative.

Symbolic creation from an integral perspective

Let us now place ourselves in the vulnerable position of someone who is unfamiliar with a symbolic system, with an unknown language into which they are entering.

Let us consider again the word "kitchen." If the same word is considered in a language foreign to me (let's say, Swahili), my mastery of the positive and negative fields will be drastically altered. With the use of a dictionary, I might try to define the positive field by establishing its relationship with the meaning in Spanish. In doing so, of course, I will not only be relating the corresponding positive field of its symbolic counterpart, but, simultaneously, I will be doing the same with the corresponding negative field, although in a still unsatisfactory and vulnerable way. I will be assigning a provisional C(-) derived from my own linguistic system without knowing to what extent it is an error and to what extent it is not.

Now, inversely, what does "nucu" mean in Makua? After consulting a native speaker, I will be able to say what it means "fool" in that language. But I still won't be able to easily define the negative field of non-meanings. When I say "m'bora nucu," or "n'cuña nucu," in an African context, I can think about what it means (a self-insult in the first case and an insult to the white boss in the second). But I won't be sure what the lone word "nucu" does not mean in another semantic or psychological context. When I hear the corresponding sound, neither. It is possible that the word has other meanings that don't appear in an initial translation, in a particular native translator, nuances that depend on a grammatical context I do not master. That is, my C(-) will be in suspense.

Let us now consider a key point for this analysis: neologisms. Let's go a bit further using a more current example. If we are in a classroom at a North American university and we hear the sound corresponding to "sheet," we quickly attribute a meaning to it. Then, when we want to ask for a sheet of paper, we can use it ourselves by trying to imitate it. The "purist" strategy will be to try to reproduce it as closely as possible to how we heard it previously. But even so, we cannot be sure that we are not conveying a different meaning than the one we originally intended, if we do not yet have mastery over the negative field of the English language. The difference between a sheet and excrement in English depends on a subtle change (for a Spanish speaker) in the pronunciation of "sheet" or "shet."

However, the precision of a sign does not depend solely on the "clarity" of the sign. That is, the precision of a sign does not depend only on its positive field but, above all, on its negative field. In this way, if our negative field of the sign is "solid," *we can alter the positive field as we wish without losing the original* meaning. A great variation of the sign will not alter the meaning. This is the case with words that are distorted for economy or simple verbal play. In English, we can shorten the word "because" to 'cos, for example. In slang jargon, even abbreviations and distortions can reach an extreme that becomes incomprehensible to someone who does not master the same negative field as the members of that particular community. In this way, a new dialect or symbolic language can emerge, and when it consolidates, we will attribute the phenomenon to the existence of new "visible" elements, that is, to symbolic variations. It is possible for a symbol to change without changing either field, but for this to happen, not only must the positive field remain unchanged for a time, but above all, the negative field must be consolidated to prevent the positive field from opening excessively to the point of jeopardizing the meaning. If I can say "'cos" instead of "because," it's because my C(-) is solid enough to affirm that "'cos" means nothing other than its variation "because." If that weren't the case, the abbreviation simply wouldn't be used. Only a "native speaker" or someone with great mastery of the linguistic system in use can make this variation — that is, someone whose C(-) of the sign is sufficiently consolidated to rule out a semantic conflict. In other words, knowing what the sign does not mean is just as important, if not more so, than knowing what it means.

It's also possible that we may need new symbols to express new ideas. In this case, the symbols in use are not only inefficient for expressing a new reality, but the negative field of the symbols in use covers the area of the new need without leaving it an outlet. The creation of the new symbol must simultaneously create its own semantic body, whose negative field covers the remainder of the semantic bodies. The word "Internet," for example, not only means something new in the reality to which the current language refers, but it also denies any other meaning. Many people play with variations like "internete," understanding that the negative field is strong enough to sustain the meaning in the variation. But if a word like "internete" entered everyday language meaning the act of "entering the Internet," then the negative field of the first would be altered by the positive field of the second, and there would no longer be the possibility of using both interchangeably.

In the case of "because" and "'cos," the sounds are very different, but the meaning is the same. Exactly the same. Why is this? Simply because the variation of the sign does not fall within the positive field of any other. And when can we perform this exercise of variations? Only when we know that the variation — or even the neologism — does not alter its negative field. As long as we are not deliberately seeking confusion, ambiguity, or a semantic conflict. In other words, if I don't master the English language like a native speaker, I will likely refrain from using a neologism in a new context, as it could mean the opposite of what I intend to convey. To do so, I must first have defined a sufficiently solid negative field: knowing what the variation does not mean. In Spanish, on the other hand, I can invent words with great freedom and with the confidence that my interlocutor will not understand something very different from what I intend to mean. For example, I can replace the word "money" with many others. "That costs a lot of cloth/wool/fly." In this case, the use of slang and the grammatical context has re-semanticized the words "cloth," "wool," and "fly" for that semantic context. By using one sign to replace another with a different positive field, I have generated a significant conflict. But that conflict has been resolved by a redefinition of the C(-) of the phrase—the symbolic ensemble—that has denied other meanings, directing it back to the C(+) that would have resulted from not deceptively substituting the word "money." We know that it is improbable to pay for a good with flies, and that improbability facilitates the reconstruction of a negative field that denies the meaning of "paying with flies." In this way, we move from a negation to an affirmation. It is true that the use of the word "fly" or "cloth" is accepted in some Spanish-speaking communities, but it was not always so. The play or the necessity had an origin, and the possibility that this symbolic conflict could have been resolved was not due to the "clear correspondence" of the symbol with its meaning, the symbol with its positive field, but rather to the stability of the negative field. When in my country I first heard the expression "no pasa naranja" (literally, "no orange happens"), I immediately attributed a meaning that was already consolidated. The noun "orange" had replaced the pronoun "nothing." Of this word, it barely retained the morpheme "na," radically altering the object (nothing for an orange). The phrase is the result of a verbal play, but it makes clear the possibility of altering signs while maintaining the meaning—or the control of what one intends to mean—thanks to a solid C(-).

But I can also segment the word "money" and say "that costs a lot of *dineretti*" (which would be an unusual expression) and still be understood by another native speaker. The positive field of the new word "dineretti" is not defined by itself, but in relation—though simultaneous—to its negative field. We can say that the word *dineretti* does not exist in Spanish because we are sure that it falls within the negative field of the set of semantic bodies of this linguistic system, a certainty that someone learning the language as a second language could not have. Then, its semantic body is free to move to the sign that best fulfills the conditions of both fields: reconstructing a homologous positive field and not meaning anything else at the same time. The context of the phrase will tend to reduce the possibilities by defining the weak positive field of the symbol through a more solid negative field.

Double entendre and metaphor

Using a specific context—symbolic or grammatical—we can split a symbol into two meanings. This ambiguity does not represent a lack of definition in the semantic body but quite the opposite: only a subject who masters the non-signifying field can create a double entendre, thus giving clarity to the new meaning without diminishing the clarity of the previous positive field.

If I say "this is a bomb" surely the meaning of "bomb" will depend on the context. If we are listening to news about the infidelity of a politician or an actor, we will understand the noun as a metaphor. That is, the new C(-) will deny the physical effects of a bomb—like the explosion of chemical elements—leaving intact only those parts of the original C(+) that can be applied to the context: the transcendent and expansive potential of an event, the drama of the immediate consequences, etc. At the same time, the term "bomb," in its new context, restricts its C(+) on one hand and extends it on the other, coming to mean, for example, "scandal." In this way, what we call a signic transfer occurs.

Opacity of the semantic body

It is possible for a negative field to be destroyed to the extent that a symbol loses its signification. This occurs when the positive field expands to an intolerable limit for the semantic body.

In a deconstruction process, for example, one can proceed not by denying meaning to a symbol but by questioning its own significant negativity.

The word "true," for example, can maintain a clear semantic body if, for ideological reasons, we create a pure negative field, thereby defining the boundaries of the positive field. Suppose a social group shares the premise that "something is true if it can be seen." This premise, fundamental for primitive men and for the most radical phenomenologists, has been challenged by post-animist religions and modern sciences. But under this premise, the word "truth" is defined within a clear semantic body.

However, when we question and destroy the previous premise with a more relativist one—"something can be true whether it is visible or invisible"—the negative field of the same semantic body will appear mixed with the positive field, which will diminish the "signifying power" of the word *truth*.

We can observe that in our time of reclamations and deconstructions, words like "normal" or "reality" have been stripped of their traditional C(-) through an almost unlimited expansion of their C(+). The reasons can be ideological, just as they were in an earlier stage and for which arbitrary and oppressive C(-)s had been defined, such as "normal" for a homosexual or "real" for a novel. When the C(+) of "normal" or "real" is excessively extended, it ceases to be useful for signification—it ceases to signify, it becomes insignificant.

Meanings of Liberation

When the Catholic Church assigns a meaning to the word liberation—liberation of the soul, disregard for social oppression—it is narrowing the semantic boundary of the word liberation, which liberation theologians then redefined by expanding the positive field to the social sphere. From here, the struggle for the meaning of liberation and of sin will be a struggle over the semantic boundaries of both terms.

In the case of the theologian Ratzinger, the response to liberation theologians does not consist of denying their ethical assumptions—such as justice, liberation, defense of the poor, etc.—but rather re-signifying them. That is, the process of opposing the foundations of the new theological movement—its total negation—consists of defining a positive body whose center should coincide with the center traditionally defended by the Catholic Church. Nonetheless, this struggle over the "meaning" of the principles of each with that of "liberation" will be conducted through a consolidation of the negative field by each contender. The reader-writer will exert pressure on the positive field of the sign, seeking greater clarity—legitimacy.

In this way, Ratzinger will proceed in several ways. Just as liberation theologians redefined the concept of "sin"—the origin of oppression—moving it from the medieval sphere of the individual to the modern sphere of society—poverty as "social sin"—Ratzinger will react by negating this extension of the positive field of the term.

In *Instruction on Certain Aspects of the "Theology of Liberation,"* Ratzinger, writes that "we cannot restrict [negative valuation of the word restriction] the field of sin [...] to what is called 'social sin'" (Theology, IV-14)

But this negation can no longer restore the order prior to liberation theologians: a social problem has been acknowledged, and the transfer of each of its components leaves no room for the indifferent. Thus, since this step backward is now impossible, one must proceed by negating through an *order of importance*. This equates to a *valuation* that, immediately, defines what is good and what is bad.

If we prioritize the urgent over the transcendent, we would be negating—according to a traditionalist and conservative view—the "true" order of priorities set by the Gospels. This, from a traditional point of view in any religion, is justifiable: post-Judaic religions (Christianity and Islam) find their justification only in the afterlife.

Later, Ratzinger himself adds: "the anguished sense of the urgency of the peoples should not overshadow [that] 'man shall not live by bread alone' [...]. Thus, in the face of the urgency to share bread, some are tempted to put evangelization in parentheses and leave it for tomorrow: first the bread, the Word later. He will later repeat this same concept: the liberation theologians have emphasized political liberation, which is valid if we consider the liberation of Israel from Egypt. Now, while this type of liberation is valid—because it is in the Old Testament—more valid and important is the liberation from sin. "By privileging political domination in this way, the radical novelty of the New Testament was denied [...] which is above all the liberation from sin, the source of all evils" (Theology, X, 7).

Another form of resignification consists of maintaining the symbol and attributing to it a meaning different—and sometimes opposite—to that assumed by the dialectical opponent. Thus, we will see a representative of the traditional Catholic Church defending those defended by their opponent (the emphases are ours):

> This call to attention *should in no way be interpreted as* [definition of the C(-)] a disavowal of all those who wish to respond generously and with an authentic evangelical spirit [Confirmation of the traditional C(+)] to the 'preferential option for the poor' [new sign—now irrefutable—of the opponent]. In no way should it serve as a pretext for those who entrench themselves in a neutral and indifferent attitude [new irrefutable sign of the opponent through a new definition of the C(-)] in the face of the tragic and urgent problems of misery and injustice. On the contrary, it stems from the certainty that the serious ideological deviations [alteration of the C(+) of the sign and value judgment of the same] that are pointed out inevitably lead to betraying the cause of the poor [resignification: the C(+) of the opponent is, ultimately, shifted to a new C(-) that presses on their own C(+) in search of a definition with clear boundaries]" (Ratzinger, Theology).

The process of redefinition will be repeated later. As an example, we will note one: "Several factors, among which we must count the evangelical leaven, have contributed to the awakening of the consciousness of the oppressed" (I-4).

Thus, the popular maxim of Marxism is the opium of the people" —religion as a numbing opium that prevents the awakening of consciousness— is turned against the very adversary from whom it originated: the opium now becomes leaven, not to impede the awakening of consciousness but to "awaken" —to raise awareness, to receive revelation— the oppressed, the people.

Paradoxically—or not—, Ratzinger accuses his dialectical adversaries of engaging in this semantic adulteration, imposing an absolute valuation of falsehood on them. Referring to the sources of the Old Testament in liberation theologians and the importance of the historical Jesus, he says: "It is true that the formulas of faith, particularly those of Chalcedon, are preserved literally, but they are attributed a new meaning, which amounts to a denial of the faith of the Church" (X, 9).

Under the title of *An Aspiration*, Ratzinger—sometimes with the tone of a compassionate father, a position that grants him a psychological privilege over the reader— spends an entire chapter defining a C(+). What should the strategy be?

I believe that in ethics and morality it is not possible to "create" values. At most, it is possible to "make conscious" certain perceptions—previously denied—using certain legitimizing rationalization. But this is not the case here. Here Ratzinger proceeds by confirming a traditional ethical center that is not questioned by the new heretics. "Taken in itself," he says, "the aspiration for liberation cannot fail to find a broad and fraternal echo in the heart and spirit of Christians" (III-1). Later: "the expression 'theology of liberation' is a completely valid expression (III-4)"—an expression that, in turn, hides a "but."

That is, he will first seek to position himself in an ethical place already consolidated in contemporary society—affirmed by the Ancient Scriptures—and then identify its corollaries with those fundamental axioms.

Thus, the dialectical hero will recognize the validity of the sign "liberation" as one of the main "signs of our time." At the same time, he will seek to appropriate these paradigmatic signs, shifting them toward his semantic center, toward the center of his C(+). If he succeeds, he will have triumphed in the struggle for the appropriation of the sign and its resignification, that is, the simultaneous definition of C(+) and C(-). The sign will not be opposed—given its powerful social acceptance—but its semantic fields will be drastically altered. The result will produce different effects, different forms of awareness, and actions and mobilizations that are often incompatible.

Now, how have these "aspirations" been translated? According to Ratzinger himself, "the aspiration for justice is hijacked by ideologies that obscure or distort its meaning, proposing struggles [...], preaching courses of action that involve the systematic use of violence, contrary to a respectful ethic, which are data of this aspiration" (Theology, II-3). In other words, the dialectical adversary has seized the paradigmatic signs, controlling their meaning. The mission is to reclaim the contested center. Ultimately, he advances part of this struggle by foregrounding the concept of "violence" as a negative agent attributable to the adversary, which must contradict the "data of the aspiration" to the point of losing legitimacy in the possession of the basic axioms—liberation, justice, etc.

However, Ratzinger's use of the sign violence is clearly defined and entirely differentiated, in its semantic fields, from the interpretation of the adversary. In his case, the border that encloses the C(-) around the C(+) is narrow, much narrower than in the case of his dialectical adversaries. With this clarity—not without a strong ideological component, in addition to theological—he leaves out a margin that liberation theologians and other social fighters of the 20th century had created. That is, he leaves out of the C(+) a more complex and subtle, though no less dramatic, problematization of the term violence. Like the discourse of other dominant ideologies, which took it upon themselves to narrow this semantic border, here the C(+) of the word violence is restricted to physical violence. Other types of violence—moral, economic—are not taken into account, types that could justify physical violence (all this despite the fact that Ratzinger will later comment on this latter concept of violence as a Marxist precept). A state of racial, sexual, or economic oppression, for example, would justify, from other perspectives, physical violence. Yet, by denying a broader meaning to the term "violence," a status quo is sustained that is, in itself, a form of silent and resigned violence, a form of oppression encouraged by the oppressors and tolerated by the victims.

Few conceptions are more "totalitarian" than those structuring the Catholic Church and centralized governments. However, this did not prevent Paul VI from issuing a warning about the dangers of Marxist analysis and its praxis, which had seduced liberation theologians, "failing to perceive the kind of totalitarian society to which this process leads" (Theology, VII-7). It is significant how two well-known opponents—Marxists and Catholic conservatives—reclaim the term "liberation" for themselves, while identifying their adversary with the label "totalitarians." Here too we find a struggle for the conquest of a paradigmatic symbol—matured by societies throughout history—for the control of its meaning.

Of course, the idea of "eternal truth" in most religions is a totalitarian idea. However, Ratzinger perceives that the idea of a totalitarian doctrine, such as Marxism and many others, carries a negative aura and therefore distances himself by criticizing it and attributing it to the dialectical adversary, without directly pointing out what differentiates one from the other: the belief and submission to God or the preservation of ecclesiastical privileges in society.

Another proof of the same is a consciousness that was never part of the traditional Catholic Church: "in certain regions of Latin America—says the German theologian—, the monopolization of the vast majority of wealth by an oligarchy of property owners without social conscience [...] constitutes other factors that fuel a violent sentiment of revolution" (VII-12). Like everyone, Ratzinger is a permanent synthesis of the dialectic of previous opposites. Even when he radically opposes those who think differently from him, he cannot help but incorporate and confirm some of the adversary's concepts.

At all times, the dialectical resource here is the same as the persuasive resource of a political declaration or a novel. It does not demonstrate but narrates a "truth" that must be received by the reader through a powerful act of faith in the writer and not in the logic of the argument.

2.7—The (Re)definition of Semantic Fields

Essayistic Prose

THE ACT OF WRITING IS THE ACT of launching oneself to conquer others' interpretations. If we can understand poetry as the self-satisfaction of language, as the communion of the world and the acceptance of semantic ambiguity, essayistic prose, on the contrary, is in constant struggle against its own instability. Philosophical or essayistic prose is obsessed with fixing ideas that risk indefinite expression and confusion or loss in interpretation. It is the continuous struggle of a conquest that the writer makes over the readers, a struggle to control a meaning that can never be fully controlled but can be stimulated and presented as a possibility.

Areas of Semantic Recognition

We start with an axiom: from the moment there is communication —or we assume there is— it is necessary to simultaneously assume a minimal agreement on certain meanings. A sign can have infinite meanings, but it cannot have all meanings. That is, it cannot have any meaning. This is another way of affirming that a sign can have infinite meanings, but it is a sign from the moment we recognize that it affirms and denies something and that it has been created to signify something similar in the writer and the reader.

Generally, we always attend to the positive meanings of a sign. We are not aware of the vast set of negations it possesses and, without which, any meaning would disappear, that is, it would cease to be what it is—a sign. We are not aware of the vast set of negations of a sign that, in turn, coincides with the set of meanings of a language.

That is, a sign or term can have as many readings as individuals, but from the moment the sign presumes to be a means of communication between two or more individuals, it is necessary and indispensable for it to take place through a semantic encounter, a certain minimal agreement on the meanings of the symbols.

But while *communication*, by definition, implies sharing a common base of meanings, the struggle for meaning also implies the same agreement7. Similarly, two adversaries facing each other in a game of chess could not oppose each other if they did not share and accept certain rules of the game. Then, two chess-like ideas will clash to demonstrate their superiority. If Las raíces torcidas opposes Las venas abiertas, it is because, in their struggle for the meaning of the symbols and ideas, there are certain implicit agreements or consensuses. These agreements that make the dialectical struggle possible range from the language, the meaning of some historical events, to the more complex regions of ethical and social dynamics, up to violently separating at the moment of ethical and semantic valuations.

---

[7] According to Roland Barthes, a language is a social institution, a collective contract that we must accept in its entirety to communicate (Roland Barthes, *Elements of Semiology*. London: Jonathan Cape, 1967, p 14)

Collective Reading

On a table, there are ten sets of three sheets each. Each set consists of a copy of the first page of *Don Quixote*, a page with several articles of the Mexican constitution, and a copy of a page from the Bible. Ten readers read, simultaneously, one set of copies each.

The post-structuralists tell us that it is not possible for ten different readers to have the same reading of the same text. That is, on the table, there would be thirty different texts. Which is understandable: each reader uses their own experience to signify, to *recreate* each word, each entire text. Nevertheless, it is unlikely that any reader would confuse *Don Quixote* with the Mexican constitution or with passages from the Bible, even without having ever read any of the three texts. If any reader were asked to describe what they had read in one of the texts and the nine others were asked to place on the table the text corresponding to the chosen reader's description, surely the nine copies would correspond to the same text from the perspective of a single reader.

That is to say, what the readers assume as an agreement —that there were three different types of texts on the table, not thirty— despite possible exceptions and confusions, is what makes it possible for the sign not to be a purely subjective, incommunicable, and unrepeatable experience but a *semantic agreement*, a "collective reading." While we can understand, from a Derridean perspective, that the meaning of the sign is unstable and undefinable, its value as a means of communication transcends that very "indefinition" and instability. In other words, that common assumption between two or more readers is what we can call a "collective reading." This idea has more the characteristics of a meta-physical conception than a verifiable phenomenon, but we also cannot deny it without denying any possibility of com-munication, of a shared interpretation of the sign. And it is what, in fact, is assumed implicitly when the struggle for meaning arises, when two dialectical adversaries aim to es-tablish a valid reading —political, theoretical, ethical, or the-ological— while simultaneously negating another possible reading.

The dialectical struggle does not recognize any reading as valid, while it assumes the possibility —or the fact— of a "collective reading" upon which it aims to act.

Semantic boundaries

Now, after accepting this *collective reading*, we can focus on the struggle that occurs for its conquest.

According to Jacques Derrida, the problem of limits is a problem of the difference established between distinct signs. No semantic boundary is guaranteed, no meaning can be "fixed" or predetermined (Sarup, 54). Later, we will explain that, for us, the relationship of difference that defines the value of a sign is not established with another sign —as in the case of opposing pairs— but rather, simultaneously, as a negation of the universe of the remaining signs that compose any linguistic or semantic system. This negation is, in fact, immediate and spontaneous in a reader; however, it is also the semantic construction established in a dialectical struggle over the meanings of the sign, almost always with an ideo-logical function. On the other hand, let us recall Gómez-

Martínez's analysis according to which, although meaning cannot be "fixed," as Derrida maintains, this impossibility can only be seen from an impossible impersonal, static viewpoint, since each reader, in fact, assigns a certain meaning upon reading. In this inference of meaning, the anthropic value, the dynamic of the reader's being, is decisive.

Every symbol possesses a meaning that is immediate and simultaneous with its reading. That is, meaning is never absent, even if it is not univocal, even if it does not appear clear to the reader. In the production of a sign's meaning, we can also notice boundaries that define it as such. But what, in turn, do these "boundaries" mean? I understand that these boundaries do not isolate the symbol, do not transform it into an autonomous unit "in relation" to other symbols, as a shell defines an egg, or as the skin of an animal that seemingly limits it as an individual within an ecosystem. On the contrary, the boundaries or semantic frontiers are internal to the sign itself; they do not separate it from the rest but include the rest. That is, a sign is not what lies within its "boundaries," but rather, these boundaries only delineate a semantic field that is in a meaningful relationship with the semantic field that extends beyond these very boundaries. For figurative convenience, we can represent the sign as a cell or as an atom whose nucleus contains the positive semantic field, $C(+)$ —what the sign alludes to— and on the outside a negative semantic field, $C(-)$, more vast —what the sign denies— that surrounds it. Another figurative (metaphorical) way to express this idea is given by figure 1: the "arrow" symbol is not just the white area as $C(+)$ but, simultaneously, the black area as $C(-)$. The borders, the semantic boundaries that separate both areas vary according to each reading. But these borders are not the limits of the sign but rather a component part of it.

Both semantic fields make up the dynamics of each sign, which is why the limits of a sign are not the semantic boundaries that separate these fields but rather the inherent limits of the linguistic system to which they belong, the limits that encompass the universe of symbols in play. The C(-) of a symbol is not a void occupied by the meaning of another symbol: the C(-) of a symbol includes, as negation and not as forgetfulness or absence—as negative gnosis and not as a lack of gnosis—the rest of the C(+) of the other symbols within the same linguistic system. In other words, negation is not ignorance but knowledge of a different sign.

The idea that we possess a *positive knowledge* of things derives from the physical world that we apprehend intuitively and sensibly. A glass is an object made of glass—not the cavity it contains[8]—, a piece of bread is the ground and baked wheat that nourishes us, etc. But even accepting this way of seeing the material—sensible—world, there is no reason to assume that a language moves physical pieces of the same nature. Even invisible social relationships can be seen as a linguistic system, where the individual—the C(+)—needs the challenge of society—its C(-)—to define themselves as a human being.

A sign, an idea, or a thought is recognized by its C(+), but its meaning depends on both this and its C(-). One cannot assert something without denying something else. This C(-) is created simultaneously with the C(+)—from the simple and vague to the complex and defined—but a dialectical contender must carefully define one and the other in their struggle for the final meaning of the sign, of the idea.

We cannot see the symbolic unit separated from its environment—context—but neither can we see it as a simple network of connections. Each symbol of a language contains all the possible meanings of that language. The difference lies in the distinct configuration of its semantic fields—C(+) and C(-).

Every sign is composed of at least one positive and one negative field, which forms a necessary and inevitable unity: what we will call from here on the *semantic body*. Without the dynamics of the two fields gravitating around the sign, the semantic body would not exist, that is, the meaning. A symbol is worth as much for what it means as for what it does

---

[8] In the *Discourse on Method*, Descartes played with the idea of a glass "full of void." In this case—he concluded—the distance between the walls of the glass would be equal to zero.

not mean, but meaning and not-meaning are, necessarily, two simultaneous and inseparable phenomena, which is to say that both are one and the same: the semantic body of the symbol at the moment of interpretation. This semantic body refers to the symbol and its own context, but it depends on the reader, on the reader's cultural, intellectual, and emotional context. That is, on their past and present as experience and on their future as motivation.

Reading process

From this same concept of semantic fields, we can see that the reading process consists of a progressively greater separation between both fields—the negative and the positive—, that is, it consists of defining what the sign indicates and, at the same time, what it does not indicate. Whoever deciphers the semantic logic of an ancient text is establishing spatial properties in this positive-negative field. As long as this separation is not achieved, the semantic body will remain with its vague limits and, even, without precise limits, which will lead the sign to a virtual void, that is, to the illusion of pure non-meaning. A dolphin in a hieroglyph from ancient Egypt can mean many things. At first, (to me) it means that the ancient Egyptians knew about dolphins. In the context of writing, however, as a symbol and as a metaphor, it could signify many other actions and attributes, a verb, a noun, an idea, a syllable, etc. "Not knowing what it means" does not mean that the sign indicates few things or nothing, but, on the contrary, that it indicates too many things at once. The mission of whoever aims to "decipher" the sign will consist of consolidating a C(-) while narrowing the C(+) as much as possible in the moment of "indefinition". Then, if it is not a deliberately "ambiguous" sign, the semantic boundaries will also be narrow, thus producing a clear semantic body.

If we use a graphical form to represent this idea (fig. 1), we can say that the "virtual emptiness" or the "illusion of non-meaning" is nothing more than the gray semantic body. The reading process will seek to restore the tension between the negative and positive fields of the symbol, thus obtaining a "clear" division of a black field and a white field.

Construction of reality

According to the Epicureans (300-0 B.C.), it is not necessary to possess instruction in logic or syllogism to interpret a sign. Anyone can do it immediately. Even animals can do it. A dog chasing its prey by recognizing its tracks is reading signs: the sign is valuable for what it is not, for the prey. The sign identifies a prey that is absent. Consequently, the dog acts (Nöth, 16).

However, we can observe a variation. What would happen if the dog identifies tracks or another sign—let's say, visual or olfactory—wrongly? In this case, the sign would be referring to a non-existent animal.

In the case of the dialectical struggle for meaning something similar occurs. However, the complexity of the dispute arises from the fact that, in general, the prey is never caught. If it is, it is not visible; if it is not, it is invented, constructed based on different interests. Thus, it is possible that two readings of the same sign indicate different realities, past or future. Since we can hardly contrast the meaning attributed to the sign with a recognizable prey at the end of the path, we focus on the most precise definition possible of the signs, that is, of the meaning of these signs—of their semantic fields.

In any theoretical construction, *historical* events will be taken as causes and consequences. Events as consequences, in general, are the starting point of a symbolic and discursive construction that will seek to explain them by resorting to other events-causes. In this way, the consequences are recognized not as the beginning of a symbolic construction but as the final result of a historical process. That is, one begins by recognizing prey—real or imaginary—to then reconstruct its possible tracks that explain or justify it.

2.8—The dispute of two texts

History of truth

THE STRUGGLE FOR MEANING—which easily materializes as an ideological struggle—also responds to a Western tradition, constructed by its Greek branch and its Judeo-Christian branch. From the first, we have inherited the powerful idea that truth lies beyond appearance and can only be revealed through analysis and reason; from the second, the equally powerful idea that The Book possesses a single truth and, therefore, a single interpretation. Different from these two currents, we can find the mystics—whose origins are in the

East—for whom the truth could manifest in many ways through each individual, directly but incommunicable—perhaps due to not recognizing a single interpretation of the mystical experience—which is why it wouldn't make much sense to speak of a struggle for meaning or a dispute for truth.

Evidently, in this essay, we deal with the first tradition—over the long term and not by chance, dominant.

Resistant ideologies and dominant ideologies

An ideology is a system of ideas that aims to describe and construct a reality greater than itself. Within this concept, we can identify at least two fundamental types of ideologies: dominant and resistant.

I understand that *a dominant ideology* is one that arises from a social group that has imposed this system on the rest of society for its own benefit. In this way, a system of external ideas is intended to be assumed as one's own thought and sensibility, spontaneous of a "free" subject, and as a social practice. This thought can develop consciously or be unconsciously reproduced through practice and through other narratives that are assumed as one's own by those who reproduce them. In both cases, the objective of the ideology remains unnoticed by those who are dominated, and at the same time, they become reproducers of their own domination. The dominant ideology creates the illusion of freedom in the dominated and, with it, the need for its reproduction. That is, the paradox that prevents self-awareness lies in the fact that a dominant ideology is a form of alien consciousness assumed (unconsciously) as one's own. An ideology is not a thought but its opposite, yet it manages to blend with it.

On the other hand, a *resistant ideology* is necessarily a response to the former. If the dominant ideology is transparent, the resistant one is opaque, visible. From the perspective of the dominant discourse, this visibility is seen as negative for order and freedom based on its own dominant codes of reading. If we compare machismo and feminism, we can see similarities and differences. Both are "isms," that is, separations. Both are ideologies, but the former is (or was) a dominant ideology, while the latter is (or was) a resistant ideology. That is, machismo can be confused with an attitude or a feeling, with an unformulated understanding, with a "practice," leading one to think that it is not an ideology because it lacks what we commonly attribute to an ideology: a system of structured ideas, almost always with an elaborate intellectual discourse. (From this perspective, a similar analysis can be made by replacing "machismo" with "capitalism") But this error occurs when we fail to recognize the two categories we outlined above, with their corresponding characteristics. Machismo is (or was) a practice, yes, but an ideological practice; it is a widespread and dominant thought and, therefore, transparent, "natural." As with another dominant ideology, capitalism, the central and legitimizing truth and the triumph (in conquering social consciousness) are one and the same. The other, feminism, in its role as resistant and rebellious, is necessarily visible. At first, like any change, it is presented by the dominant ideology as illegitimate, disruptive, dangerous, immoral, etc. Its greatest strength comes from a rationalized system of demands, always based on specific historical shifts in ethical sensibility that precede it, such as those promoted by the French Revolution first and by the Industrial Revolution later, which also generated other social demands later called "humanist," "anti-slavery," "liberating," or "pro-human rights." It is possible—and surely inevitable—that feminism loses its initial character as a resistant ideology and transforms into a dominant ideology. Part of this process will then be to maintain for an excessive period its legitimizing demand for a moral struggle against something that no longer exists, presenting it as still existing. At that moment, domination and resistance will switch their "original" positions to take on those of their adversary. It would not be surprising if in a few years "machismo" changes its name and structures a new resistant ideology that will then appear as opaque and visible; no longer as an assumed and legitimized practice but as an intellectual and organized resistance seeking a new legitimization first, and a new practice later.

Now, to approach the issue of the dialectical dispute between two classical ideologies in Latin America, we must address the question that may be the core of this struggle: is it possible to reproduce a resistant ideology that is not only (1) ineffective as a response to the dominant ideology but also (2) the cause of greater harm than the supposed domination?

The supporters of *Las raíces torcidas a América Latina* will answer not only that it is possible but also that no such dominant ideology exists. And if it does exist, it is an expression of success, which is why, rather than resisting it, we should join it, no longer as the dominated but as the liberated. Of course, this response is, in turn, part of a dominant ideology that "seduces" us into thinking this way.

The semantic struggle

The symbol-meaning dynamic, while not an objective fact and always dependent on an individual or reader, also relies on a social agreement, a history, an unpredictable and uncontrollable series of symbolic implications, and a culture that is, in turn, a permanent synthesis of other cultures and social agreements.

Symbols emerge and express their values according to a complex and ever-changing context. But these social agreements are the result of countless tensions between different *groups* that will compete for the control of each symbol—ideological, class-based, religious, philosophical, political, financial, sexual groups, etc.

The semantic struggle (Diagram 2) can be established on two fronts: (1) a struggle over *signs*, over the rejection of certain signs and the imposition of others; or (2) a struggle over the meaning of the same sign, based on a certain consensus.

Both aspirations can be framed in semiotic and dialectical terms, and both can reach the same level of conflict. A dominant ideology will express itself more in the semiotics of surrounding symbols, while a resistant ideology will base itself on a more open dialectical struggle. The former will have the virtue of transparency or invisibility, due to its omnipresence; the latter will appear as a strongly visual discourse, almost always as a threat of disorder or violence. The first is a form of "collective reading," while the other is read from a dominant ideology as destruction (of order), even if it is only deconstruction. All reasons why the former appear as "realistic" or pragmatic while the latter are carried out by intellectuals sometimes labeled as "left-wing," usually academics.

Ultimately, both forms of struggle—over the sign and over its meaning—will be reduced to the latter: in the end, everything is a struggle for the control of the meaning of the inherited symbol and its identification with the most basic and accepted terms in a society, such as justice, freedom, good, evil, etc.

Signs of high and low semantic conflict

In the dialectical dispute between supporters of *Open Veins* and *Twisted Roots*, the struggle is established over the control of the meaning of signs, especially signs like oppression and liberation, social justice and individual justice, awareness, economic liberation and mental liberation, progress and development, democracy and freedom.

When a group definitively triumphs in the administration of a specific symbol—for example, over the term *liberalism*—the dialectical struggle shifts to a struggle for or against the sign, rather than against or in favor of a meaning. At this moment, the struggle will consist of assigning a positive or negative valuation to the disputed symbol based on the dialectical contender.

This valuation of the disputed term or symbol depends, in turn, on a subsequent identification of the disputed symbol with other symbols that must confirm it—with a coincidence of negative and positive fields. These other involved symbols should preferably be symbols of *lower conflictivity*, that is, symbols more consolidated in their positive and negative valuations, in the consensus of their meanings.

Thus, for example, a political decision can be supported or rejected by *linking it* with positive or negative consequences. The attribution of "consequences" lends the appearance of a cause-and-effect mechanism, when this, if it exists in a social setting, is always of such a degree of complexity that it is nullified by the deliberate and simplifying transfer of implication.

The paradox or breakdown in communication will arise, in some cases, when the meaning attributed to a sign varies without the adversaries—for and against—realizing that this has happened. For example, when groups in favor of liberalism and groups against it are unaware that the meanings they manage are disparate and share few common areas. For an agreement on the meaning of a term between adversarial groups, the social context of the groups will be important. The term "liberal," for example, denotes and connotes right-wing political positions in Latin America; in the United States, it means the exact opposite: it refers to a left-wing position, in the same Latin American sense of the word.

If the groups of dialectical adversaries are able to agree on the definition of similar semantic fields for certain symbols, terms, or ideas, whether as a synthesis or negotiation of a previous semantic struggle, or as a result of the triumph of one group over the others, the difference that exists between one semantic definition and another, no matter how minimal, will be due to the implications attributed to each at any given moment. That is, the difference will be due to the effective possibility of implicating the disputed sign—positively or negatively—with other signs of lesser conflict, such as, in the present day, the terms development, progress, democratization, justice, freedom, etc.

Now, while it is true that transferential discourse will always seek to implicate the term in question with other terms of lesser conflict, at the same time we will observe that each of these implicated terms can, in turn, become the object of the same problematization through which it, in turn, becomes a sign of high conflict.

For example, the term *liberalism* can be re-signified, according to a number of convenient sign transfers, from other terms such as development, freedom, progress, and justice. That is, we will strive to define, with the greatest possible precision, a positive field of our own with a broad and clear negative field. To achieve this, we will use terms of low semantic conflict, that is, not only those that have a positive valuation—in case we seek to defend the term and not attack it—but also those that have a solid consensus in the interpretative society.

At the same time, each of the terms—such as the term *justice or progress*—, when taken as the center of our consideration, becomes a problematic term, that is, one of high complexity. (What does "justice" mean? What does "progress" mean? Is what we call "justice" not, in reality, an *injustice*? That which we call "progress," is it not, in fact, a *setback* from another point of view? Etc.) But this exercise is commonly avoided, taking for granted a term of low conflictivity that we use to support another term of high semantic conflictivity. If we identify *liberalism* with justice, liberty, and progress, we will not stop to problematize these three terms. The "low conflictivity" of the socially consolidated meanings of a term—positive or negative—can easily become "high conflictivity" in a problematizing development, in a deconstruction. Therefore, to preserve this "low conflictivity," it is not only necessary to choose consolidated terms but also to avoid subversively problematizing them. The dialectical feat will consist precisely in identifying and appropriating these three terms of low conflictivity to our disputed sign—liberalism—just as a dialectical adversary, such as a Marxist, will strive to achieve the same feat: to demonstrate—to relate in a cause-effect dynamic—the links between Marxism and justice, development, and progress.

All of this suggests that what we call "low conflictivity" is a transitory valuation and depends (1) on the historical moment, on the collective reading, and (2) on avoiding the problematization of the involved terms.

Therefore, every transferential discourse is always unstable and conflictive: it consists of a thought that must fluctuate in an intermediate zone between definition and indefinition. It must strive to define the meanings of the symbols in question with the greatest possible clarity, while it will avoid destabilizing them with subsequent problematizations of the involved terms. If it chooses to do so, none of the derived chain implications will be able to contradict the definition of the central terms. In other words, the negative field of a term positively implied with a central term can never overlap with the positive field of another term implied in the same way (positively).

This form of thought is the predominant dialectical form in political, theological, and philosophical discourse, as well as in much of the so-called social sciences. That is, in all thought that refers to the human being in its cultural expressions.

2.9—New Meanings for Old Signs

Renewal of the Sign

AT NO POINT IS THERE AN UNQUESTIONABLE MEANING of the sign, but we can assume consensuses or a predominance of a "collective reading" (see 2.7.3) more or less stable in a given period of time. That consensus also changes, albeit over longer periods. Its change depends on new contexts and new myths and paradigms, on the new outcomes of the struggle for meanings, and on new readers.

On the other hand, the sign is subject to the inevitability of the renewal of its meaning, each time it seeks to strengthen itself. In the transfer, in the sign tension produced by the redefinition of meaning lies the renewal, the rebirth of the sign. This renewal can occur through the exercise of a new highly figurative metaphor, through greater tension between the image or the "original" metaphorical meaning and the induced or transferred meaning. This tension can also occur in the redefinition of semantic fields through dialectical struggle. When Galeano expresses himself through the metaphor "...on the eve of World War II" (203), through two terms that cannot logically go together according to the logic of physical space—since it is understood that World War II did not have an "eve" but rather an initial process lasting several days—he is creating an image of high semantic value through an unexpected metaphor that provokes greater drama. In poetry is where these phenomena are most exposed. Even in the essays of a poet like Jorge Luis Borges the relentless will to decontextualize words to enhance them as metaphors persists: "There are also my habits: Buenos Aires, the cult of the elders [...] My astonishment that time, our substance, can be shared." Or like the bolder and more intellectual sister of metaphors: the paradox: "[...] the contradiction of passing time and enduring identity" (Borges, Works 173).

A conflict of (semantic) boundaries)

Historical anecdote tells of a Greek philosopher who defined man as a "bipedal and featherless animal." Diogenes, a contemporary and likely neighbor of the author of this definition, presented a plucked rooster to the crowd and said, "Behold, the man."

The source of this anecdote is unimportant. It also doesn't matter whether the events happened that way or were invented centuries later. What matters now is to rescue the internal logic of the anecdote, to which it owes its historical survival. Let's see that Diogenes' critique of the definition of man does not lie in his opposition to the positive field of the definition, but in its excessive breadth. That is, the C(+) of the definition "man is a bipedal and featherless animal" includes men and also a plucked rooster. This tells us that, according to Diogenes' irony, a valuable definition must have a C(+) broad enough to include the greatest number of aspects of the object we are defining and, at the same time, a C(-) solid and extensive enough to exclude everything we do not consider part of our object. This is what always happens in the construction of any definition of the type "An X is..."

The semantic struggle occurs mainly in a struggle over meaning. This struggle over meaning consists of the redefinition of meaning—of semantic fields—of a preexisting sign. These signs can be "historical facts," terms, symbols, ideas, etc. In the case at hand in this essay, the main signs in dispute will primarily be those of the first type.

Inversion of meaning and continuity of the dialectical narrative

This semantic dynamic is common in the struggle to administer the meaning of terms, ideas, or concepts like liberty or justice. But we can also find it in the texts we are analyzing here in less conflictive terms such as scarcity. Eduardo Galeano tells us, for example, that in 1970s Cuba "the essential cause of scarcity is the new abundance of consumers: now the country belongs to everyone. It is, therefore, a scarcity of inverse sign to that suffered by other Latin American countries" (70).

The sign of the ethical valuation of an act or attitude can also be inverted. For example, we can see how after detailing the intense slave trade carried out by the Netherlands and England, Galeano finds an explanation for the change in attitude of the latter: "At the beginning of the 19th century, Great Britain became the main driver of the anti-slavery campaign. English industry already needed international markets with greater purchasing power, which required the spread of the wage system" (128). He attributes the same to

Brazilian slave owners: "The century was already dying when the coffee planters, having become the new social elite of Brazil, sharpened their pencils and did the math: subsistence wages were cheaper than the purchase and maintenance of the few slaves. Of course, what was considered the abolition of slavery, for another type of reading, meant continuity under different forms. "Slavery was abolished in 1888, leaving behind combined forms of feudal servitude and wage labor that persist to this day" (55).

On the other hand, the extensive chapter dedicated by Montaner to the history of slavery in Spain and Iberoamerica does not demonstrate a differentiating data point compared to other cultures and histories such as slavery and subsequent racial discrimination in Anglo America. Responding to Galeano's thesis, but without naming him, Montaner writes: "Did England act for economic reasons, as the most cynical assert—since the industrial revolution had already begun—or was the main motivation of a moral nature?" The author provides a forceful answer, supported only by good faith in one's fellow man, who suddenly went from being a slaveholder to an abolitionist: "It seems that the latter [moral motivation] was what most influenced the change in English policy. [...] For decades, the clamor of abolitionists grew until they managed to win the hearts of some important politicians" (67). The goal, in any case, is to redefine the semantic boundaries of the meaning of abolition and then follow with an idea of mentality—or moral superiority—that explains the development of one society and the backwardness of the other. If the author achieves this redefinition—or, in other words, if the reader grants him the semantic limits proposed by the author, often through dialectical persuasion—the entire narrative will gain argumentative coherence, a natural logic that, however, belongs only to his own reading model. Once the identification of the moral factor as the cause of historical dynamics is achieved, not only is the thesis of the supporters of "The Open Veins" denied, but the author's own thesis is confirmed: it has been the particularity of a certain (flawed, inferior) morality of the Latin American continent that has been the main cause of its economic and cultural backwardness.

2.10—Sign Transfer

(De)limitations and Transfers

SIGN TRANSFER CAN be triggered by context—such as a child learning a language—or it can be directly defined by a dialectical contender. As an example of the first situation, I will briefly refer to an anecdotal comment made to me about the young son of a friend. At a certain point during a long car trip, the child began to ask his parents for water. The little one had been drinking fruit juice at his parents' initiative until it ran out. Then, every time he asked for "water" and the parents offered him "water," the child rejected it with increasing displeasure. To try an alternative, the parents offered him fruit juice, which he accepted with satisfaction. By "water" he meant "juice." Now, we can understand that for the child, the term *water* had a very broad C(+) that encompassed all drinks.

In this example, the process of incorporating the new word, *juice*, does not consist of adding a new C(+) but in negating meaning to the previous term—water—, creating a C(-) where a large part of the C(+) of the new term, juice, is "housed."

We will not pause now to analyze the empirical dimension of this transfer or learning. Let's only observe that these transfers, in culture, tend to be gradual and permanent until they radically change the meaning and function of a sign.

When on the internet we talk about a "page," we are referring to a textual unit somewhat similar to the traditional page of a printed book. This relative similarity is the cause of the transfer. Finally, we have two situations, depending on the perspective from which we view them: (1) the same sign or term, *page*, has been re-signified through a direct association with a new phenomenon, previously identified metaphorically with a traditional phenomenon; (2) the sign or term *page* has been re-signified by a transfer of meaning originating from a new context, a set of other terms and other phenomena that have found reception within its semantic space. This, ultimately, is not absolutely necessary, as the creation of neologisms is a gratuitous act. However, rather than the creation of neologisms —which are more the consequence of a conscious act than the spontaneity of the linguistic process— the new reality tends to always identify itself with terms already in use with the sole aim of leaning on a part of the inherited meaning to then redefine it by creating new meanings through the recycling of traditional signs. In fact, this process is necessary since one of the characteristics of language and signs is their permanent adaptation. If there were no adaptation and constant re-signification, a language would not endure over time, but there would also be no possibilities for reading, as this is the adjustment of the sign to the meaning and vice versa, according to the reader's experience.

Even when in philosophy we attempt to name phenomena for which we cannot find traditional formulations, we resort to terms already in use in the language rather than absolute neologisms. A neologism is usually a subtle variation of a term in current use. For example, when we use the term *transference*, we are making use of a part of its common meaning —that is, the meaning we attribute to it and assume is shared by a certain society. However, this term, like so many others daily, immediately becomes a metaphor, resigning its final meaning to the new context, a context that makes it the center of a problem and re-signifies it. Once re-signified —or simultaneously with its re-signification— the term will begin to operate in a different way than before.

We can see a particular sign transfer in the case of a yellow ribbon tied to a tree. The symbol emerged from a song that was popular during the years of the Vietnam War. The families of some war victims used it for a different purpose. Part of the meaning attributed to the symbol was preserved at the time of the transfer, but nowadays it has been almost entirely replaced by the one assigned to it by those who referred to the war.

It is true that we can say that each and every term in use undergoes this same process of transfer and resignification. It suffices to study the etymology of most words. However, this resignification can be central, that is, the cornerstone of an idea or hypothesis. In the case of the term *transfer*, its intended meaning derives from various transfers we have made to conveniently resignify it. Not only to expose its new meaning but also to use it as a new tool of transfer, a theoretical tool with explanatory purposes, for a new intelligibility of a specific idea.

In the literal translation from one language to another, we often make this kind of transfer. We know that the boundaries of semantic fields do not coincide —neither the C(+) nor the C(-)—, however, we make a limited use of this transfer until an "appropriate" contextualization of the new word in the new language redefines its semantic boundaries.

The pseudo-ambiguities of metaphors

Metaphors are privileged vehicles in this process of transfer. Even when new ideas arise for which there are no appropriate terms according to the *metaphysical space* of the writer who conceives them, they will first seek terms that contain part of those meanings to then redefine the whole term or symbol. A close example is the very use of the terms "sign transfer" that I am employing at this moment. Immediately after a sign transfer, we will have an expansion of the C(+) of the term in question, since the act of transferring does not necessarily represent a resignification of the borrowed sign but of the problematized sign. However, the subsequent redefinition of its C(-) is essential for any sign or term, which will seek to narrow the area of the C(+) when it becomes excessive. An excess of inflation of the C(+) would threaten the

strength of the sign, diluting it into a useless non-significa-
tion that, in reality, is a hyper-signification.

Both in a text and in a single term, the excess of *richness*
of symbolic indications becomes *poverty* of meaning; that is,
the more things a sign indicates —the capacity of its $C(+)$—
the less significant value, meaning the less tension the sign
will provoke in the (con)text. Even in a metaphorical text
whose readings can be ambiguous and even contradictory, a
solid area of negations is necessary. If this minimal negation,
this critical negation, does not exist, the text would dissolve
into an excessively broad $C(+)$. For example, it is said that the
prophecies of Nostradamus are rich and valuable due to the
great ambiguity of their metaphorical language. What happens is that this metaphorical language has a great capacity
to accommodate different future readings that are later identified with a prophecy. However, the value of each metaphor
does not lie in the fact that it can signify ten or a hundred
(in)different and unrelated events, but rather, precisely the
opposite: the metaphor of the prophecy gains its prestige
from a restriction of meaning, each time it is reduced to a
few situations and, even better, to a single and precise historical event. That is, its value does not lie in indefinition but,
precisely, in the strict definition of a meaning for a metaphor
that is "apparently" ambiguous, mysterious, etc. Here, ambiguity or "indefinition" are a necessary means for its adaptation to a concrete and restricted meaning. In other words,
highly figurative metaphors, like that of the lion, are appreciated for their $C(+)$ strictly limited by their improbable co-
incidences with the agonizing death of a king.

In other cases, when the metaphor of an essayist like José
Martí can be applied to different historical moments, to

different situations, its significant value still lies in the precision that the reader assigns to it, in the belief of a "lack of precision" in meaning. The reading takes place on a specific common element—historical, political, psychological—that is recognized in different situations, apparently unrelated. That is, the reading of the "ambiguous" metaphor is not at all ambiguous in its meaning, but rather possesses relatively solid semantic fields. It is similar to the reading of Newton's formula which, in the words of Ernesto Sábato, connects a falling stone and the Moon that does not fall as the same phenomenon.

Imprecision of the sign used

Quotation marks, for example, are usually used in two moments: (1) to refer to or repeat what someone else, who is not us, said, or (2) to relativize a term when we use it knowing that it does not completely coincide with our semantic intention. This way of signifying responds to the following transfer: *this is not something I am saying, it is something someone else is saying, with whom I do not completely agree but temporarily accept*.

That "someone else," in the second case, is the language itself which, when it does not aim to become poetry, is always unsatisfactory for the expression of an idea, that is, when it is assumed as a *means* toward something else that is not itself and not as the wordplay of the words. Due to this dissatisfaction or precariousness, we must develop ten, a hundred, or a thousand pages in our attempt to "define," with an endless series of signic transfers, what we cannot express with a single sentence or a single sign.

Dynamic of Transfer

Now, how are semantic fields defined? In the first place, let's recall that the narrative or the "visualization of the meaning" of a term or a complex idea takes place in the metaphysical space, which we have already discussed (see Chapter 2.4). Then, the narrative about that space will use elements from the physical space—ideas, signs, words—which, in their character as metaphors, will have value in a new, unknown space, where they were not originally born: the metaphysical space. As I suggested earlier, the very term of "transfer" may originate in a bank transaction or in an eclectic transmission, but it is used here in its metaphorical capacity to express an invisible nature: the adoption of a meaning by a sign or idea (note that we can say the same of every word we have just used, such as "nature," "adoption," etc.). The context of the text consolidates a C(-) of the metaphor or term by negating meanings that in a text of physics, electricity, or accounting could have. The context ensures me a specific C(-) that I use to my advantage to carry out a specific transfer of meaning to the term "transfer" and, in doing so, subtly extend its original C(+) of the word "transfer."

Thus, we use a term—the word "transfer"—, *on one hand for part of its semantic value* and with the aim of resignifying it later or immediately, adjusting its semantic fields according to our vision of the meaning of a particular idea in metaphysical space. That is, every symbol is imprecise, but thanks to that imprecision, we can use them as metaphors, and thanks to that margin of sign ambiguity, we can use any word, adapt it to ever-changing, unrepeatable contexts. Otherwise, abstraction would not exist, meaning each sign and each word would only signify a single object, a single idea, becoming useless, anachronistic, for any new variation, for any new reader.

Here, in this essay, the word "transfer" is being deliberately resignified to account for a *metaphysical space* that is seen by the author but cannot yet be expressed, even minimally satisfactorily, with terms in common use. Nevertheless, we can intuit a similar process in the rest of the words that have migrated from physical space to metaphysical space over time and through the "involuntary" work of the people. An example—one could conjecture—would be the word "lastima", migrated from physical space to metaphysical space as "lástima". In this case, not only has the meaning changed, but also, and very subtly, the sign itself through the written accent and pronunciation.

Transfer by implications

In his *Instructions on Christian Freedom and Liberation, Prefect Ratzinger* tells us:

> [Freedom] finds its true meaning in the choice of what is morally good. It manifests as a liberation from what is morally evil (16).

In these theological reflections, we will find countless times during our reading that a term is not derived from another in a deductive or inductive way, but is defined by the *transfer* of meaning from other symbols, terms, or ideas. Under what mechanism does this semantic transfer operate? We cannot say it is due to a simple arbitrary operation. Not, at least, in all cases. It is possible that a term receives the signifying transfer from another according to a minimum requirement of semantic "proximity" or according to a similar set of other terms involved simultaneously. That is, according to our Western culture, we can understand terms like freedom and democracy as semantically close, while there is no simple way to positively involve terms such as freedom and slavery, except through an auxiliary path of other implications. We cannot say, without explaining ourselves, that (1) "freedom will make us slaves" or that (2) "slavery will make us free." For a Muslim or an Orthodox Christian, the latter expression is not so difficult to accept, as it is understood that freedom or liberation is achieved by submitting to divine authority9. For a secular Westerner, on the other hand, it would only be possible to understand this implication through a complex series of symbolic transfers that another secular individual might recognize as true or reject as contradictory. All of this after an analysis, that is, after a series of personal transfers.

---

[9] To refute this idea, the collection of oxymorons in literature or the verses of Saint Teresa of Ávila would suffice. However, if we refer to our time, it is hardly accepted in the essay genre for oxymoron to be employed as a persuasive instrument.

Here, in the two previous aphorisms —"aphorism" from the perspective of a humanist— we can recognize authoritarian, fascist, or radical sectarian thought, but the symbolic transfer can hardly be made directly, without the series that leads to a resignification and revaluation of one of the two initially conflicting terms.

The dialectical process is not *deductive* but *implicative*. It is not about deriving some meanings from others but about superimposing them, in such a way that the falsehood of a symbolic association lies in the *superimposition* of a C(+) of one symbol over the C(-) of the other and vice versa. A valid symbolic association will be one in which the superimposition of semantic levels causes the C(+) of one to coincide with those of the other, understanding that each positive field will have an area of different size, in such a way that some can contain others. The C(-), on the other hand, may overlap with sectors of the C(+) of other symbols without producing a total negation. If this were to happen, we would understand the dialectical discourse as paradoxical or we would not accept it as valid; at least not until a redefinition of the boundaries of the semantic fields of one of the symbols or terms in conflict.

In the partial negation of a C(-) to an external C'(+), a new signification arises, a dialectical relationship that expresses a new idea and a new symbol. For example, the definition of "Paraguayan Guarani" becomes meaningful and precise when superimposing the terms Paraguayan and Guarani. The C(+) of Paraguayan Guarani is significantly smaller than the C(+) of each of the terms that compose it. That is, the new C(-) includes a broader set of negations, which gives meaning to the new symbol.

From this perspective, we can see that any discourse that tends toward "coherence" or avoids contradictions will create a *discursive tunnel*. Using this same metaphor, we can say that discourse which manages to connect a series of positive fields without interruptions in the innumerable chain of semantic implications will be presented as "true," a common ground—according to a geometric definition—of all positive fields considered in a concrete speculation.

2.11—Link and Transfer

Inclusion and Identification

IN THE PROCESS OF SPECULATIVE THOUGHT, each term—each idea—is linked to another by what we will call a *transferential link*. This link often forms a metaphor with the purpose of narrating a perception arising from the metaphysical space. This perception or visualization of the metaphysical space can originate in multiple ways. Generally, it arises from a synthesis of one's own culture but is constantly altered by one's own reflections and reconstructions. The expression of this visualization, typically laden with prejudices, emotional and ideological constructions, can be a sincere declaration of a figuration or, alternatively, an ideological manipulation, that is, a declaration with specific aims of manipulation and domination of others.

But first, let us briefly examine the function of this *link* from a grammatical point of view. The transferential link par excellence is the copulative verb "is." In essayists like Octavio Paz, this link is predominant. In others, such as Ernesto Sábato, more common links are "therefore," "reason for which," "because," "hence," which distances him from traditional poetic thought and brings him closer to the deductive style of the sciences, a field he cultivated before dedicating himself to literature.

When we say "the sky *is* blue," we are not making a signic transfer, as we have defined it earlier. The copulative verb "is," linking the noun and the adjective, is not a transferential link but rather part of a definition caused by an observation. Setting aside any phenomenological questions about the perception of blue, we can say that "the sky *is* blue" is an objective observation made about the physical space. But in this same expression ("*'the sky is blue' is an objective observation*"), we are constructing a definition that begins to move away from that supposed "objectivity" to express an idea, something not explicit in the physical space but rather produced in the metaphysical space: "X is an objective observation." By defining a concept with a direct ontological statement—X is Y—, we are establishing a foundation for future constructions, though this foundation, once consolidated, can easily be problematized and deconstructed by posing a radical question about itself. Instead of asking, "What is X?" we problematize the whole by shifting the question to a root of the original statement: "What is Y?"

Therefore, for ideological, transferential discourse, as important as defining a direct implication of value (X *is* Y, or X *is not* Z) is the *avoidance of problematization* of those points that must be foundational to the discourse.

Now, for our epistemological model, we will assume as "objective observation," without questioning the adjective, that sensory observation which is presumed to be made on the physical or material world. This same model of objective judgment is reproduced in transferential thinking. The observation is made on the metaphysical space, but with the intention of preserving its quality as an observation—of the type "the sky is blue"—on a complex fact that is ultimately defined in an invisible space. It is not noticed—or it is sought to not be noticed—that one is not observing a fact, but rather constructing the same fact through transfer. A cosmogonic fiction is narrated—if not constructed through the narration itself.

In philosophical, political, or theological texts, that *transferential link* is basic and recurrent. First, because it directly involves two semantic fields, two ideas, which may be close to each other or separate. The direct transfer without an intermediate discourse that seeks to analyze and rationalize the semantic result is characteristic of the ideological efforts of political discourses. We can see in many photographs of the protests against racial integration in Alabama in 1959, where the slogan "Racial integration is communism" appears repeatedly. The link "is" is equivalent to the mathematical symbol =, that is, it means "is equal to," but without prior proof. Most people accept Einstein's famous formula $E = mc^2$ by an act of faith. Only a few scientists have arrived at it through a deductive process that links matter, energy, and the speed of light after a mathematical reflection on time, a variable that does not explicitly appear in the formula. In the expression "Race mixing is communism," there is no need for a prior deductive path. The inclusion—total or partial—of "race mixing" within the set "communism" must be accepted as an act of faith independent of the origin of this "conclusion." However, we are not dealing with a "conclusion" (as Einstein's formula may be) but with the origin of a thought, of a discourse. In mathematical language, we can say that it is not the corollary of the theorem but its axiom presented as a corollary. What seems like a conclusion is—or can be—the starting point for a series of justifications and rationalizations that, as in classical theology, end up confirming the precept—or prejudice—and, in this way, provide it with a certain rational(ized) foundation in a world where the tradition of dialectical debate is as or more important than the religious tradition.

The same can be said of the Marxist expression "religion *is* the opium of the people." In this case, the implication is made through a highly figurative metaphor. *Religion* here is the term of *high conflict*, associated with another term that is negative and of *low semantic conflict*: *opium*.

Of course, a transferential thought, which constitutes most common usage, does not necessarily have to be so direct and arbitrary, nor does it necessarily have to be identified with ideological use. When it starts from a complex process of implications and arrives, finally, at a synthesis of the type X is Y, then we can say it is not arbitrary, but rather appears with a (misleading) appearance of deductive thinking.

The "being" of definitions

Transferential thinking can be provoked—demanded—in the paradigmatic question of traditional philosophy: "What is *x*?" For example, "What is *love*?" This interrogation demands *definitions* that, seemingly of the nature of simple observation—like "the sky is blue"—will lead us to a minimal transfer. The smaller this series of implications, the more abstract and narrow the definition: "Love *is* a form of happiness" or "Love *is* the need for the other," etc. With a set of direct implications, we will expand or reduce the C(+) of the term love. But in any case, we see how the inquiry "What is...?" will induce us, at least initially, into transferential thinking.

2.12—Language and Metaphor

The Metaphorical Function of Language

IN 1984, JORGE LUIS BORGES, with his polished style, summarized an old conviction: "all abstract words are, in fact, metaphors, even the word metaphor, which in Greek means translation" (Borges, Atlas, 70).

We can say that language is composed of metaphors. The very discipline of etymology consists in the study of *low-figuration metaphors* ("abstract words"), that is, in the analysis of the recycling of signs and their meanings through the common history of different human groups. It is likely that signs change meanings—in a collective reading—after being used extensively as metaphors. This could be the case with words like "desvelado" or "despabilado"—both allude to a candle or its component, the wick.

But some metaphors appear evident due to their close connection with a fact or a decontextualized image, which is deliberately linked with a disconnected figuration, thus provoking a greater symbolic tension to produce a transfer of meaning in the search for the "common factor" shared by both independent figurations.

The term "fuel" is strongly linked to the physical world. But by relating it in the expression "love is the fuel of the heart," we are making a metaphorical use of the term with its consequent sign transfer. To identify love with a fuel like gasoline or coal, or with a tiny part of either of them, is to provoke a transfer of meaning through a metaphor. We make the observation in the metaphysical space but using symbolic tools from the physical space. Love may belong to the metaphysical space, but fuel belongs to the physical space. Since we cannot objectively visualize the metaphysical space, we describe it using the tools of the physical space. In English, the term foreign, meaning outsider, derives from forest, meaning woods. That is, the stranger was someone who lived in the woods in Europe, a realm of mystery and the unknown. However, the subsequent historical use of the term lost its meaning of "woods" to adopt others. Foreigner or outsider still refer to the physical space, but repeated use based on a metaphor can place it in a metaphysical space, such as its transition from noun to adjective: strange, as an adjective, can refer to the unknown or, at least, the unrecognized. For example, a person or an idea. Now, strange, as a verb, can refer to something that was once very close (to me) but has now distanced itself: the process of something beloved becoming strange (noun) signifies a sad emotion, similar to nostalgia, but which is only understood with the verb to miss. Here we are already immersed in the realm of metaphysical space; the word has been completely "abducted" from the physical space by an old, prolonged, and extensive metaphorical use.

Now let's take an expression from Alberto Montaner: "capital, like life, seeks desperately to multiply" (115). This high-figuration metaphor (presented as a simple parallel through the comparative like) has a clear direction. One could also compare the desperate multiplication of capital with the desperate multiplication of death or another no less arbitrary metaphor. There is no deductive reason or necessary relationship that leads us to one expression and not the other. Simply, the author is narrating what he sees in his metaphysical space and hopes that we see the same. To achieve this, he uses a metaphorical resource taken from the physical space that, supposedly, all readers share. We understand that the natural tendency of life is preservation and reproduction. We can see this tendency as something dramatic if the failure of this quest implies death. Therefore, it is enough to associate life and its main characteristic with any other element—in this case, capital—to "visualize" the dynamics of the analyzed element. First, the choice of metaphor must be appropriate to the idea, to the author's metaphysical image; second, after being persuaded by the parallelism of one variable with the other, we must make an act of faith in the author's choice. If these acts of faith are repeated, then the goal of convincing us of their truth will have been achieved, under the most convenient title of "demonstration."

Also using a grammatical parallelism or its symbolic antagonism, we can notice another more interesting relationship. We can observe this same thing in the metaphors represented by both titles. In *Las venas abiertas*, there is a tragic process of bleeding; in *Las raíces torcidas*, the deformation of a being, of a culture, is pointed out.

Metaphorical thinking

> It is not divinely human to sacrifice oneself for the sake of ideas, but rather to sacrifice them to us, because the one who reasons is worth more than what is reasoned, and I, a living appearance, am superior to my ideas, appearances of appearances, shadows of shadows (Unamuno, 168).

We see that at the beginning of the paragraph there is a statement that denies a very common one: idealism, according to which it was ethically superior to die for one's ideas, whether the deceased is a revolutionary, national hero, politician, scientist, or philosopher. This observation is made on the author's metaphysical world as if it were a direct observation on the physical world. However, this fact, which threatens to appear arbitrary, must be supported by other observations on other areas of this metaphysical space. The pseudo-deductive link is the term "because": "because the one who reasons is worth more than what is reasoned." That is, the man who produces (who thinks) is worth more than his production (his thoughts). Then, to confirm the above, he transfers the meaning of the relationship between two metaphors that appear similar: man is superior to his ideas as the body is superior to its shadow, ideas are shadows of something, appearance of something, to which they owe their existence. Their existence is parasitic, it depends on something else and, therefore, possesses a lower ontological category.

Said in our language, ideas are identified with shadows because they belong to the metaphysical space, which appears as indebted to the physical space (the bodies that project the shadows). This resembles Plato's cave myth-metaphor but is in no way similar to the conception of a metaphysical world of pure forms or ideas—quite the opposite. In any case, a paradox arises: ideas are produced by humans as shadows are projected by bodies. However, bodies, humans, are conceived through those shadows, through their ideas, through a self-reflection that occurs in the metaphysical space. Therefore, we are forced to say that, if a priori we can suppose the physical space preexisting the metaphysical space, we could not conceive it in itself without the latter. The idea of preexistence, precedence, or independence of the physical space is, above all, an idea, that is, a product of the metaphysical space.

But to arrive at this statement or enunciation, it is also necessary to deny other possibilities that contradict it, which threaten to invalidate it. Or to omit them. For example, it is denied or not observed that perhaps those ideas benefit a significant number of other people, that perhaps that benefit is the very life of those other people. With this, we could refute Unamuno's "statement" by observing that, from an altruistic point of view—assuming that this term is a positively valued ideolexeme—a few ideas could be worth more than the very life of the one who sacrifices himself for them, that is, for others. Then, we could proceed with the classic strategy of the dialectical adversary. That is, we could "label" Unamuno's thought as selfish and then seek other confirmations of this association of the philosopher with the socially negative valuation term.

High-figuration metaphors

In high-figuration metaphors, the signic transfer occurs without affecting the meaning of the involved unit. That is, the terms are not immediately redefined in their semantic fields but transfer part of their meaning to the new signic unit: the metaphor. A subsequent resignification of a term through the repeated and accepted use of a metaphor can occur, but at that moment the metaphor will have lost its degree of figuration to become a low-grade metaphor, that is, an independent term, a word.

This type of metaphor—high-figuration—not only appears in the titles of Galeano's and Montaner's books but is frequent in the interior texts. As an example, we can note a few, which reveal each thinker's conception. This conception is what we call the metaphysical space.

A necessary condition of each metaphor is that they must, first and foremost, function as literary figures, then transfer their logic—their meaning—to the metaphysical space, to construct the expression of an idea that otherwise would not obtain its own figuration.

We can extract a couple of examples from *Las venas abiertas..*: "Development is a banquet with few guests [...]" (Galeano, 411). "What happens to us is like a clock that runs slow and is not repaired. Although its hands continue to move forward, the difference between the time it shows and the real time will keep increasing" (407).

2.13—The Continuity of Historical Narrative

Limitations and Utopias of Contextualization

IN THE MIDDLE AGES, the expression "breaking shoes" was synonymous with "having sexual relations." If we found this expression in a single text, we probably could not identify this correspondence. However, extensive studies of countless other texts lead us to affirm this equivalence. But what would happen if we only had a single text with this unique expression at a specific time? Most likely, the "literal" interpretation would dominate, and we would lose the sexual component. We would have a radically opposite interpretation (if we consider that making love and breaking shoes are two different acts). That is, certain studies with certain data and keys that can be inferred from specific texts lead us to think that we can "objectify" certain elements. However, we can never know what we lose along the way. Especially since a great part of the textual inevitably has been lost. I am not referring only to written texts, but to the rest of the texts that are formed and are shaped by an incalculable web of contexts and sensibilities.

Reading as a Process of Re-contextualization

As we said at the beginning, the process of reading consists of a progressively greater separation between both fields: the negative and the positive, that is, it consists of defining what the sign in question signifies and *what it does not signify*. But, at the same time, this process—of reading—is an exercise in *recontextualization*. It always tends toward an (impossible but necessary) original, imaginary contextualization. Only *decontextualization* is possible through deliberate *negation*; never through possible indifference or an impossible *emptying* of context.

Decontextualizing cannot mean *emptying* of context, as that would mean the sign loses the C(-)—the context is not just what surrounds the symbol but everything that does not signify—, losing any possibility of meaning with an unlimited C(+).

A museum is an area of decontextualization. But something similar is a novel, any book. Reading is an effort of contextualization, but it always occurs outside the context we imagine, whether spatial or temporal. Its context is always the context of the reader, but in the reading process this is transparent.

With decontextualization, we increase the tension of the semantic poles: we perform an aseptic operation on the C(-) of the symbol-object and highlight the presence and limits of the C(+). Of course, in this decontextualization, the only phenomenon is not that of "making clearer" the semantic field of the symbol—C(+).C(-). It is possible that it may be altered, exalted, or distorted by the very operation of decontextualization. That is, the definition of a "purer" C(-) not only means a narrowing or redefinition of the limits of the C(+); it can also radically alter the C(+) with a subtle manipulation of it. In any case, we see that decontextualization is responsible for the new meaning.

Resistance of the Symbol

We are thus faced with two types of signs: (1) those that are dramatically altered in their "original" meanings, that is, those meanings that derived from their original context or are strongly linked to it—in this case, the context is identified with its own C(-); or (2) those other symbols that resist alteration of their meanings more, that is, those that retain their C(+).C(-) with greater independence from its circumstantial context, like mathematical signs, certain traffic signs —for conventional signs— or signs that refer to primary emotions, such as laughter or crying. Etc.

Significant Decontextualization

The book *The Twisted Roots of Latin America* begins with some quotes. Among them, one from Simón Bolívar: "The only thing that can be done in America is emigrate (1830)". More than one might be tempted to underline this expression and refer it to our own context —associations are always inevitable—: the current phenomenon of emigration from Latin American countries. Prophetic words?

We can always find prophetic words in any historical document. We could find prophetic words in a Sumerian tablet as much as in the verses of Nostradamus or in a writing of Simón Bolívar. But for that, a decontextualization is necessary. In fact, the meaning of a symbol depends —among other things— on its context. To make a new use of that same symbol, it is necessary to "pluck it" from its context. In that decontextualization, the symbol will lose part of its meaning and will retain another part, which, in turn, will go on to create a new meaning in a new context. This is what we have called, elsewhere, signic transfer.

In Montaner's quote there is, of course, a re-contextualization. In this process, we must argue, there is a transfer of meaning and, therefore, an "alteration". What we understand with that quote is not what the person who said it — Simón Bolívar— might have thought, but rather the one who quoted it —Alberto Montaner. We could argue, moreover, that Bolívar expressed that idea in a moment of fury and frustration, which does not represent his sustained thought throughout his life —assuming that someone could maintain the same thought throughout a lifetime—. Etcetera. But here —as in any place, as always—, it is about constructing a new narrative based on old narratives, old interpretations of reality, like building a mosaic using pieces from other mosaics.

2.14—The Continuity of Historical Narrative

The Problem of Series

BOTH IN *OPEN VEINS* and in *The Twisted Roots* a historical narrative is presented as the foundation of a thesis. Both theses oppose each other; both histories can be accepted by the parties in dialectical contention, but they differ in (1) the selection of historically accepted facts and fictions, (2) the recognition of different effects for the same causes, and above all, (3) the ethical valuation of these effects.

Historical *facts* are also fictions, but fictions with pretensions of not being so, with the careful commitment that their own narrative maintains with foreign narratives, called documents, testimonies, verifications. Different, historical fictions are facts created on a void, for convenience, imagination, or the need to rescue the existential continuity from the fragmentation of memory and understanding; they are facts without support in those other fictions directly provoked by that other class of fictions we call "facts".

Any historical narrative is necessarily partial, minuscule in comparison to the infinite universe of supposed facts that occurred. Everything is based on an ontological superstition: "facts" possess an existence independent of the observer. When in physical sciences this idea was dethroned a hundred years ago; when Kant himself dealt with the same in the broader field of philosophy, even today, in the daily commerce of symbols and narratives and discussions, we proceed from the basis of this autonomy of the famous facts. We do not realize that facts are made by a narrative and not by nature. We do not realize that they are permanently remade — by each time and by each individual— and we attribute, unconsciously, an immutable character to them: what is done is done.

> The Guarani sold women and children without showing the slightest remorse. To Cortés they gave twenty Indian women [...] (Montaner, 93).

We have, then, that the difference between *historical fiction* and *historical fact* does not lie in the truth or falsity of one or the other, but in the commitment or arbitrariness that the *fact* maintains with a broader set of narratives—history, culture—that cannot be altered arbitrarily, as in fiction, but that is also not immutable and can even be vulnerable to significant radical change. What both have in common, instead, is their origin: both are symbolic constructions without autonomy in a presumed material world. Both are built on moral values, superstitions, individual and collective imagination, and, above all, both are liberated by imprecision.

In their selection, their ordering, and, most importantly, in the point of view from which these facts are observed lies the interpretative difference, the thesis, the conclusion, and, finally—and not without impossible pretensions—the truth.

Historical narrative exercises a necessary classification: certain facts are chosen according to their degree of significance—attributed by the narrator or the narrative—that is, according to their level of importance. Among the probable and possible facts, some must be dismissed while others will be highlighted as responsible for other equally significant facts for, at least, two reasons: (1) for their subsequent consequences, for their impact on a certain future, and (2) for the social scale of their impact. To say it more succinctly and graphically, it is not the same for a ruler to hunt foxes and slaughter wild boars as it is to calmly prohibit the theory of evolution or decree the abolition of slavery. The importance of each act seems obvious, since we ignore the perspective of the boars and even deny their existence.

Continuity, parallelism, and induction

Continuity will be provided by a historical *logos*. Once the logic of history is discovered, or at least the logic of the economic, productive, and social system dominant in recent centuries, the narrative will be imbued with a powerful unity and continuity. The selection of facts, then, will be immediate and will be governed by the degree of significance they possess within the structuring *logos* of the narrative.

> In this book, the aim is to offer a history of plunder and, at the same time, to explain how the mechanisms of dispossession function. The conquerors and caravels appear, alongside the technocrats in jets, Hernán Cortés and the Marines, the kingdom's overseers and the missions of the International Monetary Fund, the dividends of slave traders, and the profits of General Motors. (Galeano, 12)

The history of conquest, identified with exploitation, injustice, and violence, is continued to achieve a coherent narrative in the 20th century.

Open Veins sometimes share the historical vision that will be more characteristic of *The Twisted Roots*, thirtyyears later. It takes the form of a rebuke towards Native American cultures, for their overvaluation of the conqueror who came to bleed them dry. To this, we must add "original sins" like internal division—which Galeano describe at the end of his book, referring to the 20th century—or the lack of awareness and rebellion. Thus, for example, it describes how the conquerors Cortés and Pizarro benefited from the internal divisions of the Aztec and Inca empires and practiced intrigue and conspiracy (25).

These descriptions are made under the title "The gods returned with secret weapons," which, brought to more recent history, results in parallels like other subtitles such as: "These are the sentinels who open the doors" and "The goddess technology does not speak Spanish." To this, we must add the quote that opens Galeano's book: "We have kept a silence quite similar to stupidity... (proclamation of the insurgent Junta Tuitiva of La Paz, 1809)." A confession of evidence, Alberto Montaner might say. However, though this is not gratuitous insult but rather painful self-criticism, in the previous cases, in the cited subtitles, one can read a reproach and a desire to identify a "tradition," a self-destructive attitude.

In these pages—as in *The Twisted Roots*—the narrative of various historical facts and anecdotes is often detailed and meticulous, often unnecessary to confirm the central thesis. A narrative technique more akin to digressions in a novel, meant to relieve the tension of the central story, than to a rigorous philosophical analysis Its function, I believe, is to narrate facts that no one disputes, creating a climate of complicity that will then continue onto the narration of less paradigmatic facts, those facts and explanations specific to the author who is presenting and arguing in favor of their own thesis.

The idea of a fraternal division between the Incas and Aztecs as the origin of the Indo-American defeats must be updated as a reading under the same precept of a psychological and cultural inheritance. The blame would not lie so much with Cortés and Pizarro —in a reading made by Montaner— but with the Incas and Aztecs.

To this we must add other "shortcomings" inherent to the natives that manifested before the conquest, such as superstition —the ignorance of the colonized, the "opium" of their religion—. Not only did the Aztecs mistake the Spaniards for Quetzalcoatl, but the same Incas who sought to take advantage of Potosí's silver were met with a Quechua warning: "it is not for you; God reserves these riches for those who come from beyond" (Galeano, 31).

Selection, denial, and continuity

Montaner asks —in line with his hypothesis—: "How could so few Spaniards subjugate millions of Indians into obedience? [...] There was only one method: by using the most notable Indians, the caciques and their families, as a transmission belt" (43). (Our emphasis) This idea is highly persuasive, though from a strictly epistemological perspective it remains a conjecture, an identification of one fact with another, cause with consequence: an interpretation. Its greatest virtue lies in achieving a continuous and relatively coherent narrative. Its weakness is no greater than in any other argumentative process: unity, coherence, and narrative continuity are achieved not only by arranging the elements necessary for an intelligible and continuous narrative but — above all— by overlooking those elements that do not fit into this process. This omission may, on one hand, be inevitable since it is impossible to account for the infinite universe of possible and occurred facts, while in the worst cases it may be a deliberate omission.

In this regard, we could say that if the omission of the rest of the possible signs is absolutely inevitable, the strength of the narrative would be to account only for those "transcendent" signs and disregard the infinite universe of "unimportant" elements. Of course, this depends on two premises: (1) It is necessary to define whether a fact we omit is less significant than the one we take into account or not; (2) we must start from the assumption that there is a larger set of insignificant facts and a minuscule set of significant facts, worthy of being included in a book, in a narrative, worthy of being synthesized into a few ideas, and therefore the omission of the larger set of insignificant signs would not drastically affect the theses supported by the reduced set of significant signs. One could object, at this point, that the overwhelming set of insignificant signs possesses greater significance than the reduced set of significant elements. But in this case, it is difficult for the intellect to grasp the overwhelming set of insignificant signs. What is commonly done is a synthesis —based on conjectures— of the significance that this large set could have had. For example, the so-called "people" are sometimes reduced to a psychology and a more or less unique character, as if it were not a matter of millions of differentiated and contradictory histories and individuals but of a single person.

For José Luis Gómez-Martínez, the Eduardo Galeano of The Open Veins of Latin America is an "ideological author" because he embodies these same characteristics in his rhetoric: selection within a context, contextual significance —of a logos—:

> The ideological author starts from the unavoidable contextualization of every discourse but procedurally engages in a selective deconstructive practice to utter a "truth" that, for that very reason, seeks to project as equally significant. Such would be the thesis that "the underdevelopment of

Latin America arises from the development of others"
(Gómez, 67)

Historical continuity

The region of Minas Gerais fell into poverty after its wealth
was exhausted. But since it had a "heart of gold in a chest of
iron," later, in the 20th century, North American companies
began to exploit these iron mines.

For those seeking the *logos* —or seeing the same *logos* in
different processes— every change conceals a continuity. In
the case of the exploitation of Brazilian minerals, "the exploitation [of the] *quadrilátero ferrífero* these days is carried out
by the Hanna Mining Co. and the Bethelem Steel, effectively
associated: the deposits were handed over in 1964, after a sin-
ister history. Iron in foreign hands will leave no more than
what gold left" (Galeano, 89).

> *Latin America was born as a single space in the imagination
> and hope of Simón Bolívar, José Artigas, and José San Martín*,
> but it was already broken by the basic deformations of the
> colonial system (Galeano, 332).

Signs of nascent failure: After the progressive division of
la patria, "the liberator [Bolívar] died defeated: 'We will
never be happy, never!' he said to General Urdaneta. Be-
trayed by Buenos Aires, San Martín stripped himself of the
insignia of command, and Artigas, who called his soldiers
Americans, went to die in the solitary exile of Paraguay: the
Viceroyalty of the Río de la Plata had split into four [...]" (Galeano, 432).

Once again we see that the *logos* demands unity and, therefore, a certain historical continuity. As we noted earlier, regarding the lack of communication and disunity among Indo-American peoples —and the intertribal or regional divisions, in themselves— the peoples of Latin America continue to be stripped of their wealth and their future by the conquerors, and this disunity is expressed in contemporary lack of communication. According to Galeano, even international companies show more coherence and unity than Latin American countries. This is because the infrastructure was created to serve the extraction of raw materials, meaning it was designed and built according to the needs of the countries that were beginning to develop their industries at the time (433). The railroad lines converge at the ports; the telegraph connections between Brazil and Colombia, Peru, and Venezuela are flawed. The cities of the Atlantic had no telegraphic communication with those of the Pacific, "thus telegrams between Buenos Aires and Lima or Rio de Janeiro and Bogotá inevitably pass through New York; the same happens with telephone lines between the Caribbean and the south. Latin American countries continue to identify each with their own port, a denial of their roots and their true identity" (434). For many pages, Eduardo Galeano describes the exploitation of Chilean copper, Bolivian tin, Brazilian iron, or Venezuelan oil during the 20th century. What he aims to signify is a continuation of the same story of gold and silver exploitation from colonial times. Even in this way, the intentions of the present can be questioned by using a continuity—at least a narrative one—of the past:

> [Today] there is no shortage of politicians and tech-
> nocrats willing to demonstrate that the invasion of
> 'industrializing' foreign capital benefits the areas
> where it emerges. Unlike the old one, this new form
> of imperialism would imply a truly civilizing action,
> a blessing for the dominated countries, so that *for the
> first time* the words of the declarations of love from
> the dominant power of the moment would align with
> its real intentions. (341) (The emphasis is ours)

Long before, Galeano had told us that the dispossession
had continued with the enslavement of those indigenous
people who were dedicated to agriculture and were forced to
work in mines. And he adds:

> "The dispossession continued over time, and in 1969,
> when the agrarian reform was announced in Peru, the
> newspapers still frequently reported that the Indians from
> the broken communities of the highlands would occasion-
> ally invade, waving flags, the lands that had been stolen
> from them or their ancestors, and were repelled by gunfire
> from the army" (70).

2.15—Meaning and Evaluation

Psychological Semantics and Ideological Phrases

WE CAN UNDERSTAND THAT A PART of the psychoanalytic tradition (the one that refers to healing) depends, to a great

extent, on this dynamic: making the hidden text conscious, *reassigning meaning to the symbol*, rereading the problematic text, understanding what we consider "guilt," "shame," "threat," etc., —effects of trauma— can be evaluated differently or even oppositely, thereby overcoming the "trauma," since it—as a symbol, as a text—is always a semantic construction that can be modified in its meanings. If a *past event* —symbol, text— cannot be changed, *its meaning* can. Which, in effect, comes to be the same from an ideological and psychological perspective.

Now, how, what, and why are those meanings fixed? Undoubtedly, tradition plays a decisive role in this, but it does not arrange its pieces randomly. We can observe that there is a certain intentionality in each order after discovering the greatest possible number of meanings of a symbol, a sign, or an expression, initially obvious, innocent, unquestionable— unquestioned.

Let us briefly consider what we might call "ideological phrases," so common in any society. A familiar and repeated expression is, for example, the one that asserts, *"pleasure should not be mixed with work."* Apparently—and always resorting to the cultural context—this expression has a *sexual connotation*, which is desired to be prohibited or prevented. Another possible connotation is that "work is pain, sacrifice, etc." Like *sex* in some puritanical moments in history, *work* had a solely (re)productive function. Neither sex nor work was to be practiced for pleasure, which was associated with sin, but rather out of obligation, to fulfill religious sacrifice. Now, however, if we resist identifying "pleasure" with (the sin of) sex, but rather with work itself, we can see that, on the contrary, *"it is advisable to mix pleasure with work."* We can understand that by "pleasure," we are referring to the idea that work is (or can be) an enjoyable, vocational activity. The first expression is in service of a mode of production in which the individual is an object (secondary); an object that must resign itself to sacrifice and pain as a "normal" state of their condition as a worker, as a producer. If they were to recognize that pleasure can be a positive dimension of work, a right, and finally, a meaning for their routine activity, they could reclaim a different social order. Which is, from all perspectives, subversive. The second expression, on the other hand, consists of a resignification and, therefore, a revaluation of the previous idea of (re)production, recovering the old *object* as a *subject* of freedom and pleasure.

Identification of different semantic fields

In his *Instruction on Christian Freedom and Liberation*, Prefect Joseph Ratzinger identifies power with oppression, specifying this current power—economic and technological—as concentrated:

> The new technological power is linked to economic power and leads to its concentration. Thus, both within nations and between them, relationships of dependence have been created that, in the last twenty years, have caused a new claim for liberation. (9)

In this way, he creates an explanatory context that makes the appearance of the dialectical adversary—the liberation theologians—understandable through motivations recognizable in a context of social injustice. However, this reaction of the adversary, initially justified, must reveal itself as misguided in its development and consequences:

> [The Church] has raised its voice over the centuries to warn against deviations that risk twisting the liberating impulse into bitter disappointments. At the time, it was often misunderstood (12).

Here the strategy is twofold but with a single direction: (1) the adversary is not new—it existed centuries ago in other forms and ended in failure; (2) a parallel is established that tends to identify the adversary with a historical element already known and of negative valuation, "deviated," "twisted"—like the roots of Latin America—: the Church, also back then, was "misunderstood," just as it is now. The direction of both implications consists of attributing a negative valuation to the C(+) of the adversary.

In a non-fatalistic Christian tradition, Ratzinger makes an existentialist observation: "[man] exercising his freedom, decides about himself and forms himself. In this sense, man is the cause of himself" (II, 27. p 17). Emphasis in the original.

However, from this point no consequences are derived; instead, a new concept is introduced, proceeding in this way with the first narrowing—or individuation—of the C(+) of the previous terms: "But he is so as a creature and image of God. [...] The image of God in man constitutes the foundation of freedom and the dignity of the person" (II, 27. p 17).

This semantic identification of *freedom* and dignity with "the image of God" is not deduced or inferred from any reasoning or other evidence made explicit in the text, but from dogma or faith, that is, from revealed truth. In this case, it is a theological axiom that refers all other statements—whether axiomatic or derived—to the unquestionable Revelation. (However, it remains an interpretation of the Scriptures that claims to be literal, meaning it seeks to deny its own contribution to the meaning of the sign in question.)

The definitions of the disputed terms will be made through a narrative about metaphysical space, as if it were an objective narrative about physical space:

> [Christ] has revealed to [man] that God created him free so that he may, gratuitously, enter into friendship with Him and into communion with His Life (II, 28. p 17).

Immediately, Ratzinger will confirm the axiomatic nature of his statements, which will give the entire Chapter II of his Instructions a style characteristic of classical geometry books: "Man does not have his origin in his own individual or collective action [definition of a solid C(-), through an unproven statement], but in the gift of God who created him. This is the first confession of our faith [unprovable axiom that must be accepted], which comes to confirm the highest intuitions of human thought [axiomatic basis for all subsequent speculation]" (II, 29. p 17).

Although the theologian here suggests that the axiom "confirms" the higher intuitions, this idea appears as an inversion of order, if we consider that intuitions are usually prior to any speculation—no matter how axiomatic it may be.

As is logical for a thought grounded in the axioms of Revelation, Ratzinger distinguishes two types of "freedoms": the temporal and the permanent. The temporal, as it could not be otherwise, refers to the freedom of men and women on earth (18). But there is a hierarchical difference between the two, and therefore one must be subordinated to and serve the other: "The sin of man, that is, his break with God, is [transferential link] the root cause of the tragedies that mark the history of freedom. [...] This is the deep nature of sin: man breaks away from truth [transferential metaphor] placing his will above it. By wanting to free himself from God and become a god himself, he strays and destroys himself. He becomes alienated from himself" (V, 37. p 21). The underlining is ours.

In V, 37, Ratzinger attributes to "sinners" the observance of the serpent's promise in Genesis, who promised men the possibility of being "like gods" (Gen 3, 5). In this way, a false, deceptive idea of freedom would emerge. Later we see this same—contradictory—idea of "being like God" reappear as a virtuous aspiration. Although the first ideoléxico is in the plural—which negatively identifies it with polytheism—it is not clear if this was not a later variation to differentiate the two terms and place one on the negative side and the other on the positive side of the symbol of virtue, and more recently of freedom, since Genesis does not speak of polytheism and, on the contrary, the "serpent" refers to the imitation of the Creator.

In any case, should this differentiation not be sufficient, efforts are made to more clearly define the semantic fields to align them with the previous ethical and theological valuations: "It is true that man is called to be like God. However, he becomes similar not in the arbitrariness of his whim [extension of the C(-)], but insofar as he recognizes that truth and love are both the Principle and the end of his freedom [C(+)]" (IV, 37. p 22)

Further on, Ratzinger provides more examples of theological thinking that, with a different, supposedly rational style, we can identify in an ideological rhetoric that is still atheistic: "Idolatry is an extreme form of disorder engendered by sin. [...] By replacing the worship of the living God with the cult of the creature, it distorts the relationships between men and leads to various forms of oppression (V, 39. p 22)" (emphases ours). Observe how theological elements are identified with social behaviors and values. In the following paragraph, we are presented with a narrative about metaphysical space with aspirations of rational discourse, constructed through an apparent logical, deductive reasoning. However, we can observe a manipulation of terms and signs as if they were sets of meanings, where one sign or term is identified with a part of another, just as a mathematical set can be included or can share common elements with another:

> "[...] sin is contempt for God (*contemptus Dei*). It involves the will to escape the relationship of dependence of the servant on his Father [a parallel identified with civil obedience *and* virtue *civil*]. When man sins, he seeks to liberate himself from God. In reality, he becomes a slave; *for [pseudo-deductive link] by rejecting God, he breaks the impulse of his aspiration to the infinite and of his vocation to share in the divine life. Therefore [pseudo-deductive link], his heart becomes a victim of restlessness (V, 40. p 23)*"

In the *identification* of this metaphor (23) with the social and ecclesiastical order, a certain order of social subordination is preserved and legitimized. Liberation theologians took this same complex symbol and *re-signified* it in the following way: it is not necessary to accept earthly authority to accept the divine; in fact, the opposite is understood: by accepting divine authority, earthly, political, and ecclesiastical authority is denied—or questioned. The same interpretation can be found in the words of Christ himself.

Inversion of the meaning of liberation from atheist thinkers, among whom we can identify Marxists and liberals, is "once again" inverted in the following way: by seeking liberation through materialism, the subject falls back into the oppression they denounce.

> The *sinful man*, having made himself his own center, seeks to affirm himself and satisfy his own longing for infinity by using things: wealth, power, and pleasures, despising other men whom he unjustly strips and treats as objects or instruments. In this way, he contributes to the creation of structures of exploitation and servitude that, on the other hand, he claims to denounce (V, 52. p 24).*exploitation* and *servitude* that, on the other hand, he claims to denounce (V, 52. p 24).

Next, the theologian returns to his method—continuous narration, signic transfer through identifications and overlapping of different semantic fields of signs in dispute—: "the divine gift of eternal salvation is the exaltation of the greatest freedom that can be conceived [...] This hope does not weaken the commitment to the progress of the earthly city [C(-)], but on the contrary gives it meaning and strength [C(+)]" (V, 59-60. p 34).

A political theory of semantic fields

Case analysis as an example

(Eduardo Galeano vs. Carlos Alberto Montaner)

3.1—Historical background

A dialectical dispute before the invention of Latin America

SURELY THE PSYCHOLOGICAL TRAITS most characteristic of diverse Latin America were already consolidated in the 19th century. The conception of power as an eternal source of illegitimacy stems not only from the indigenous genocide by the Spaniards but also from the Spaniards themselves, who were never fairly compensated by the Crown for their risky enterprises of discovery, conquest, and evangelization. In the epistolary literature of the 16th century, the complaint of the victors is a constant; but the complaint—which survives to this day—does not replace criticism and even less rebellion, but quite the opposite: it is a painful form of submission, of recognition of unjust authority. Unlike the thirteen colonies of the north, Latin America was conquered by commission; when the royal reward arrived, it created more complaints than gratitude. Unlike the fate of the independent pilgrims of the Mayflower, the Spaniards encountered vast civilizations that they could not displace, which they subjugated and forcefully mestized. The illegitimate gains from plunder and genocide only brought misery to the conquerors, the collapse of the Spanish empire, and a historical trauma to the indigenous and African peoples that the religious syncretism could barely mask.

But it was during the 19th century, the century of political independences and the creation of new states, that what we might call the "struggle for identity" or the awareness of a distinct existence began to take shape.

An example of this symbolic conflict can be approached through the dialectical dispute between two Argentinians, Juan Bautista Alberdi and Faustino Domingo Sarmiento. The former was born in Tucumán in 1810 and died in Paris in 1884. His friend and rival was born in 1811, also in a poor province of what would become decades later the Republic of Argentina: San Juan. He died in 1888. The former earned a law degree and achieved literary fame much earlier than the latter. Sarmiento compensated for his lesser formal education with a long political and journalistic career that culminated in his rise to the presidency of the Republic in 1868. He was also a university professor and a recognized reformer of his country's educational system. As he once predicted, the writer Sarmiento would outlast the political Sarmiento, the president. His most widely read and debated work is Facundo, Civilization and Barbarism, whose antithesis was later used in countless debates that better describe the mentality of the intellectuals of his time than the cultural categories arbitrarily identified as civilization or barbarism.

Alberdi, in opposition to Sarmiento, did not believe in primary and secondary education as the foundation for material progress but ascribed greater importance to the empirical development of manufacturing industries and agriculture. (Alberdi, Bases, 246). This, which may well seem reactionary in our time, was not so much so if we situate ourselves in the mid-19th century in some Latin American country. Even the inventions that drove North American industrial development until the following century did not primarily come from universities but from the workshops of artisans, from Thomas Edison to Henry Ford, including the Wright brothers. This, I believe, is because university education up to that point was based on scholastic models of erudition, or at best encyclopedic speculations, which had become obsolete for centuries in Europe but remained as models of culture and intellectuality in many universities, especially in Spain and Latin America until the advanced 20th century. The strictly "depository"10 and memorization-based conception of traditional educational systems was at a disadvantage compared to the inevitably freer and more creative marginal workshops and their self-taught inventors, who, on the contrary, had no other path but to experiment with the unknown.

Despite their notable disagreements, both men were products of their time and shared some common understandings. In Sarmiento and Alberdi, liberalism emerges from an admiration for the material development of Anglo-Saxon America, attributing to Spain a system and culture unsuitable for such purposes, rather than from a philosophical origin born in France or England. Both proposed the study of the English language, identifying it with industrial progress. Neither could be expected to champion indigenous causes, summarized in Alberdi's expression, who rejected the identification of the rural with the barbaric: "in America, everything that is not European is barbaric" (Alberdi, Bases, 68).

---

10 "Depository" here in the sense given by the Brazilian educator Paulo Freire.

The deconstruction of a text

The earliest documents we have of the relationship between Sarmiento and Alberdi consist of letters kept by the latter. The first, dated January 1st, 1838, and the second on July 6th of the same year (Barreiro, 1-4). In the first letter, the young Sarmiento addresses Alberdi under the pseudonym of García Román, with a baroque formality that includes expressions of humility and admiration for the man who succeeded with his publications and readings in the salons of the great city, Buenos Aires. The second letter, prompted by Alberdi's unexpected response, revolves around trivial issues of poetic techniques and grammar.

Future political events would gradually erode this literary friendship, transforming it into ideological and personal enmity. The last letters we can find from Sarmiento addressed to Alberdi date from 1852 and 1853. These are not personal letters, like the earlier ones, but rather public and part of the dialectical arena of the time. Lengthy arguments and responses, resembling passionate essays published in the form of pamphlets, caught the attention of each man's followers. In 1964, Barreiro told us that when Sarmiento "faced the polemic, he lost all composure and was shamelessly outspoken," and he quotes Lucio Vicente López, a personal friend of Sarmiento, who said, "If Facundo had known how to write, he would not have written any differently." For his part, Ingenieros summed up the dispute with an unbeatable metaphor: "Sarmiento responded with axe blows to the finely placed thrusts of his adversary" (Barreiro, 75).

Beyond these historical anecdotes, which, as anecdotes, are not insignificant, there was between Sarmiento and Alberdi a dialectical clash that represents two different visions of the Ibero-American reality of the first century of its independent history. Old booksellers and librarians have bequeathed to us a sea of writings and documents, among which is *La barbarie histórica de Sarmiento*, written by Juan Bautista Alberdi in 1875.

If we pause for a moment on this text, we will find several characteristics of the dialectical struggle of the era summarized in its pages. Alberdi's primary strategy of refutation against the author of Facundo consists of a reading of Facundo itself, whose meanings are contrary to those assumed in a "first reading," that is, a reading in which the reader grants the author the authority of administer the possible meanings, a reading that avoids critical analysis or semantic deconstruction, which assumes that the text is the final expression of a revealed logos of another reality—of a context—and not part of that unrevealed logos itself, a captive part of its own context. In a dialogue of the political and historical context with the text Facundo, Alberdi seeks to uncover and decipher a logos inherent to the text that ultimately contradicts or undermines its own author. "While the author claims to have written about the process of the caudillos," he writes, "the book demonstrates that he has written the Manual of the Caudillos and Caudillismo" (24).

The author of *Facundo*, moreover, is a personal adversary, but the text that seeks to reveal the new logos, the new reading of the same text, must present this fact as nonexistent or, at least, irrelevant. However, at the outset Alberdi accuses Facundo of being rambling and its author of being pedantic

(Alberdi, 12). Indeed, a particular egolatry can be noticed, at least, in Sarmiento's writings, in his self-representation as a man chosen by history. Even as a selfless martyr for liberty and for the Republic. A characteristic that is common among other Ibero-American leaders of the time, which reveals a personality that must be nuanced by the formal codes of discourse of the era. In the selection made by Barreiro and even in the anthology by Berdiales, it is enough to read the introduction of each speech to notice the repeated reference to the author's own "self," a rarely used resource in Hispanic letters. These compilations are from the mid-20th century. Nevertheless, Alberdi seems to have noticed it already in the European editions of Facundo: Sarmiento, he tells us, places his own portrait in his book Facundo "instead of that of his hero" and does well, because the name of this book should have been Faustino. (Alberdi, *Barbarie*, 21). "He who does not understand [Facundo] in the opposite way of what the writer intends, does not understand Facundo at all" (25). That is, if the text aims to read the logos—psychological and cultural—of Facundo Quiroga, what it actually does, according to Alberdi, is narrate the characteristics of its author, Faustino Sarmiento. This proposal represents a lucid deconstruction of the text and an early hermeneutic reading of it. On the side, let us observe that the text in question avoids identifying itself with a traditional rhetorical genre, from where the possible readings could be made, which gives it an added literary value. "I believed I could explain the Argentine Revolution through the biography of Juan Facundo Quiroga," says Sarmiento (20). However, *Facundo* resists classification into a clear genre: it is both chronicle and fiction, essay and novel; it is a political and proselytizing work, as well as the philosophical confession of a man.

Now, if we apply the same hermeneutic exercise that Alberti proposes to his own text, we can also uncover new readings of both the author and his adversary. We can understand that Juan Bautista Alberdi read history from a materialist, or proto-materialist, perspective, while Domingo Sarmiento approached it from a culturalist, superstructural, and even metaphysical viewpoint. Of course, both interpretive frameworks were not unknown in mid-19th-century Europe, though neither seems consciously aware of these codes of interpretation they employed so freely and personally.

The Conflicts of Modernity

Before delving into these ideological differences, let us briefly contextualize the disputed text within the dominant paradigm of its time: the *logocentrism* of Modernity. We will begin with a brief conceptual introduction. I will draw from a 3,000-year-old myth—or what remains of it—the Greek myth of the Minotaur, as I find it deeply significant for this purpose.

In the legend of Theseus, the Minotaur is a product of sin, born of the union between King Minos's wife, Pasiphaë, and the white bull given by Poseidon to the king. Poseidon punished Minos for refusing to sacrifice the beautiful bull by making his wife fall in love with the beast. The offspring of this union, the Minotaur, was imprisoned in a labyrinth designed by the architect Daedalus and fed with the bodies of Athenian youths. Daedalus did not build a prison or a bunker with thick walls—which would seem more practical from our modern perspective—but rather a *system* with a *code* for its own vulnerability, which serves as a metaphor for nature, seemingly chaotic yet governed by an *logos* barely accessible to mortals. On the other hand, the Minotaur was not vegetarian, as one might presume of a bull, but instead fed on human flesh, which signifies the perpetual punishment of an original sin, the hidden trauma. We can understand this myth as a metaphor (as the expression of a reality *beyond the visible*) and, on the other hand, as a *constructive symbol* of modern and later postmodern thought. Modernity has been, precisely, the confirmation of much of the Greek conceptions, of their own metaphysics of truth, as something that exists in a deep and invisible center which is possible to access after discovering the code that the system itself conceals (Newtonian mechanics, evolutionism, Marxism, psychoanalysis, structuralism, etc.). Accessing the center is not only accessing the truth but also the solution to the problem, the problem of the system, and the problems that derive from it. Once Theseus reaches the center, he kills the Minotaur and escapes. That is, he solves the problem, decodes, deconstructs, and returns to the periphery. Escaping from the labyrinth is, ultimately, the process of liberation, which comes after the sacrifice of truth. Theseus's journey is from the visible periphery to the invisible center. This center, in turn, is the cause of the misfortunes of the Athenian youths. The center here, from a psychoanalytic point of view, is the unconscious; from an epistemological point of view, it is the place where the truth11 resides. "The real," theorized Lacan, is that which resists symbolization, that which cannot be represented. That which is beyond. From Heraclitus, from the earliest Greek philosophers, this, the truth, has always been "the invisible," that which is beyond appearances or observable consequences; the substituted by metaphor. It is "the hidden truth" that must be revealed in the process, and this is the "guiding thread" of a thought, the thread that Theseus uses to navigate, to avoid getting lost in his adventure toward the center and in his ultimate liberation.

From the first pages of *Facundo*, Sarmiento laments that Argentina did not have a Tocqueville who would "reveal" to France and Europe "this new way of being that has no well-marked and known antecedents" (13). In this way, the Argentine educator reproduces the paradigm of Modernity which, in contrast to the European Middle Ages, privileges and admires the new over the established, novelty and creation over immobility, while also reproducing the modern mentality by confirming a legitimizing center —Europe, France— and thus consolidating another of the contradictory traits of Latin America: being different yet similar, being on the margin but looking towards the center, identifying

---

11 History is full of significant paradoxes. One of the consequences of the Copernican revolution —*De revolutionibus* (1543)— was the loss of man's central position in the Cosmos; thus, the humanism that would focus more on the human being —including women— than on the heavens began to emerge. Once man was removed from the cosmological center, gradually and after a long and conflictive process, he would eventually become the epistemological center, under the *de-neutralized* position of the "observer." The same can be said of the birth of perspective in the Renaissance, as the fixation of "objective," "real" space from a "point of view."

with a center without belonging to it, constructing an identity based on the European gaze.

Based on these observations, which we can find in other writings of the time in different parts of the industrialized continent, it could be said that the social bodies of Latin American countries had a modern mentality —their upper class and intellectual class, both dominant in government and in the most popular media— without having belonged to it, to Modernity, without having achieved it in its material, economic, and social realization. Perhaps a glimpse of an opposing and "postmodern" thought can be found in Bautista Alberdi, when in 1942 he gave a lecture in Montevideo: "There is, therefore, no universal philosophy, because there is no universal solution to the questions that constitute it at its core. Each country, each era, each philosopher has had their own peculiar philosophy, which has spread more or less, which has lasted more or less, because each country, each era, and each school have provided different solutions to the problems of the human spirit" (Alberdi, Ideas).

The same qualification we made earlier of "sub industrial continent" alludes to the presence of a paradigm that was already present throughout the 19th century as a *social model of being*, of success and progress. This is perhaps one of the aspects that most differentiated Latin American society from the admired and progressive Anglo-Saxon industrial society: while in the North the structures of power —economic, political, religious, and cultural— were the expression of their social base —still prior to the French Revolution and following its failure— in the South these institutions, reforms, and new orders were promoted from the top of the social hierarchy. While the North American constitution (1787-1791) was the expression of a preexisting social order12, in the South it was copied, with admiration, by our greatest political leaders with the intention of making it prevail by creating, when not imposing, a new ideal or desirable order that had yet to be formed. Hence the importance that Sarmiento gave to popular education, not as a means of liberating one's own expression but as a form of discipline, of doctrinal imposition that responded to the "civilizing" ideology of the time.

Implicitly, Sarmiento acknowledges that South American social order is not expressed in its best democratic institutions but rather in the opposite way: the individual man over institutions and the Law, the leader over the assembly. In Facundo he tells us that the caudillos are the "mirror" of the societies they lead. For this reason, he first proposes to focus on the "details" of the life of the Argentine people in order to understand their "personification" in Facundo (21). That is, the "personification" of the Argentine people is not the constitution of the people nor the industrial culture of the North, but its own character identified with "barbarism," with Rosas and with Machiavelli, who "does evil without passion" (12). Here Sarmiento does not abandon his supra-structural reading of Argentine social reality —the "spirit" of a people as the omnipotent shaper of its own social reality—;

---

12 As a foundational "antecedent," we can consider the *Mayflower Compact* (1620), the first written constitution of America, discussed and signed on the ship that brought the one hundred and one Puritan pilgrims who, lost in a storm, resolved that they would obey no other government than the one they could give themselves. The form they chose to govern themselves and avoid the incipient internal divisions was that of a «government of the majority»

he notices the difference in "character" of his barbaric society with civilized society, the Anglo-Saxon society, although he does not come to realize the process of formation of one or the other nor from where he made this assessment, insisting on his project of imposing a model on a reality foreign to it, from top to bottom, or directly replacing the blood through selective immigration.

Sarmiento criticizes the Europeanization of the past and as an alternative proposes the Europeanization of the future, as if one were a deformation of an unchangeable reality and the other a reformation of a vulnerable reality. He sees in the biographies written about Bolívar "the European general, the marshals of the Empire, a less colossus Napoleon; [he sees] the imitation of Europe, and nothing that reveals America to him" (21). According to Sarmiento, the writers, the biographers of Bolívar and his character, Facundo, distorted their identities, dressing them in frock coats and stripping them of their ponchos. They Europeanized them. This Europeanization of the past is negative because it does not stem from truth and denies "the American." If Bolívar was great, it was because he emerged from the mud, "but the writer's European classical biases distort the hero" (21). Here, Sarmiento not only forgets his earlier invocation to a Tocqueville who would have revealed his science to South America, but he will once again downplay the importance of "the American" when he praises San Martín for his European education and his way of waging war "according to the rules of science" (22).

We know that Sarmiento was dazzled by European civilization first, and later by North American civilization; he understood the differences in development almost exclusively as a consequence of a "mentality," favorable in one case and unfavorable in the other. Hence, he dedicated special effort, as both a writer and a politician, to the education of his people. His reformist attempt represented progress, though it was still rooted in prejudices that today we would find difficult to accept as valid, and at their core, they represented an ideological direction opposite to the one intended to guide society.

To support the previous paragraphs, it will suffice to recall the great Argentine reformer's conception of education, not as a form of liberation or knowledge but as one of order, social discipline, and obedience, summarized in the following statement:

> the mere fact of always going to school, obeying a teacher, being unable during certain hours to indulge in instincts, and repeating the same acts, is enough to tame and educate a child, even if they learn little. This child, thus tamed, will never stab anyone in their life and will be less inclined to evil than others. You know from experience the effect of the corral on wild animals. Simply gathering them is enough to tame them through contact with humans. A child is nothing more than an animal to be educated and tamed. (Berdiales, 56)

Sarmiento believes that to educate is to discipline. The origin of barbarism lies in the (animal) instincts of those humans who do not possess European culture—if they are capable of it—or of those who have not been tamed—if they are naturally incapable, as was the case with the indigenous people. "The Indians do not think," wrote the educator, "because they are not prepared to do so, and the Spanish whites had lost the habit of exercising the brain as an organ. [In the United States] the Indians visibly decline," wrote the humanist, with a strange mix of Charles Darwin and fatalist theologian, perhaps a product of his travels through England and its former colonies,—"destined by Providence to disappear in the struggle for existence in the presence of superior races..." (Sarmiento, Conflicts, 334).

Taming humans for a productive order, which should be led by the most capable, the civilized elite of the great city, without losing sight of the European model, the only possible model of civilization. The future depends on this discipline, just as the best of the past was due to the influence of ideas imported from the center of civilization. An idea, in turn, that Alberdi will warn against and criticize as false, denying the common understanding that Sarmiento has of the causes of Argentine independence "as a movement of European ideas, not of interests. A movement that, according to him, was only intelligible to the cities of Argentina, not to the rural areas" (Alberdi, *Barbarie*, 12).

Here Alberdi not only contrasts interests with imported ideas as the triggers of Argentine independence but also advances his critique of the city-countryside dichotomy presented in Facundo. If for Sarmiento the city represented civilization and, by extension, Europe13 —or vice versa— for Alberdi, on the contrary, "the rural areas represent what

---

13 On pages 126 and 127 of *Facundo*, we read, explicitly, this idea of the later European failure in Sarmiento. As a sample, I transcribe the following words: "Buenos Aires confessed and believed what the learned world of Europe confessed and believed. Only after the Revolution of 1830 in France, and its incomplete results, did the social sciences take a new direction and the illusions began to fade."

South America has to offer Europe," that is, the production of raw materials (13). This, in turn, aligns with his structuralist idea of power, economy, and interests.

This fundamental opposition in Sarmiento's ideological narrative, city/countryside, civilization/barbarism, is taken as the origin of other explanations but, not being explained—reduced, according to a materialist—by other factors, results in a metaphysical conception of the same order as other more common dichotomies such as light/darkness, Good/Evil, etc. While overlooking the infrastructural factors of his social reality, he revives observations characteristic of topographic determinism and then leaps back to the metaphysical, superstructural engine. Just as he contrasts the city with the countryside, civilization with barbarism, he opposes the plains of the Pampas to the mountains. Keeping in mind the literary mountains of Greece and forgetting the Andean peaks—not to mention the Asian summits—he associates one with despotism and the other with freedom and democracy (Sarmiento, Civilization, 28). Therefore, we must understand that the "freedom" of the Pampas gaucho is not true freedom because it is a barbaric freedom, without law.

The dialectical method of Sarmiento

From this observation of opposites—civilization and barbarism—located in his context, Sarmiento will undertake an intellectual exercise that we later find in more contemporary essayists: a generalization of the discovered logos to the rest of history. When comparing the decline of the interior peoples of Argentina in the 19th century, he revives the Spanish perspective of history, of their struggle against the Moors first and against the American indigenous peoples afterward: "Only the history of the Muslim conquests over Greece presents examples of such rapid barbarization, of such swift destruction," he wrote, forgetting or ignoring that much of Greek culture—the paradigm of the classical and civilization for an 18th-century European—was preserved through the reproduction of many of its texts by the Arabs. (Without stopping to consider that the greatest scientific and cultural center was Córdoba, in Moorish Spain, during the Middle Ages when most of Europe was submerged in what the Europeans themselves—the Enlightenment thinkers—would later call the "Dark Ages"). But here the goal is to identify the cause of Evil, of spiritual and economic backwardness—barbarism—and refer to it in a philosophical narrative as a theologian would proceed with Lucifer or the Original Sin. Once again, the metaphysical origin of the antagonistic axiom is revealed to us: "[...] there is something in the Argentine solitudes that brings to mind the Asian solitudes. The spirit finds some analogy between the pampas and the plains stretching between the Tigris and the Euphrates" —the emphasis is ours (29). Much later, he repeats his analytical method: "it is singular that all the leaders of the Argentine revolution were rural commanders: López e Ibarra, Artigas and Güemes, Facundo and Rosas" (66). By induction or mimesis, he explains the emergence of personalist caudillos in the pampas and the barbarian chiefs of the Asian deserts (omitting, obviously, the biblical leaders of these deserts). Subsequently, he compares the cruel dictator Rosas to the personalist leader Muhammad (65), as if there had been no despots in many other topographies and cultures, including

European ones. But the continuation of the metaphor—and the historical prejudice inherited from Spain and Europe toward the Muslim world, the closer "Other"—reinforces the arbitrary image as a coherent whole in the mind of the implied reader. The nomadic gaucho is the Arab of the desert—both tremble with poetry—and, therefore, is the reproduction of barbarism and backwardness. Like Hostos, the author of Facundo does not believe that there can be "progress without permanent possession of the land, without the city, which develops the industrial capacity of man and allows the extension of his achievements" (35).

Another example of Sarmiento's inductive method can be briefly seen in his semiotic analysis of colors when he recognizes the color red in all barbaric symbols. The flags of the "terrorist" José Artigas, the flags of the North Africans, the Japanese, etc. "I have before me a painting of flags from all the nations of the world. Only one cultured European flag predominantly features the color red [...]" (139). Incredibly, he fails to mention that the flags of those countries he himself considers the cradle and vanguard of progress and civilization, such as France, England, and the United States, already featured red in their flags in his time. Even the tricolor flag of the barbaric Artigas displays the same colors in similar proportions to these three countries, and it is highly likely that the revolutionary was inspired by these same countries when drafting his precarious constitution of 1813.

As we saw, by eliminating those elements that contradict his "inductive collection"—those data that do not belong to the set of similar clues—he achieves sufficient coherence to provoke the induction of the idea that structures the response. Every inductive method is incomplete, but in the way it is manipulated here by Sarmiento we can say that it is also a mere rhetorical device, which we might call pseudo-inductive. The collected data does not induce an idea in the writer, but rather the writer manipulates the data to induce the idea in his readers. As in the most traditional theology, the data should not question the a priori idea but confirm it; if this does not happen, the idea is not discarded, but the data is. Something similar we will find in the 20th-century texts we will analyze later. This attitude, when it leaves the realm of the most closed theology, becomes partisan politics. This is what distinguishes philosophy from ideologies.

Deconstruction and Hermeneutics in Alberdi

We could say that in 1862 Alberdi was already practicing a form of psychoanalytic analysis when he says that Sarmiento justifies the assassination of Chacho, because he was responsible for it. Sarmiento attributes victories over his montoneros to himself, but not the assassination. By trying to justify his assassin, he justifies himself (Alberdi, *Barbarie*, 40).

> The real life of Chacho does not contain a single act of barbarism equal to the assassination that he suffered [...] Since the responsibility for this act weighs on his biographer [Sarmiento], the whole purpose of the book is to justify the perpetrator of that crime, by slandering its victim. Chacho, who was never comparable to Quiroga in his attacks on civilization, has, according to Sarmiento, deserved the punishment that Facundo *did not deserve*, who was treated with a certain indulgence [...] That Sarmiento

killed the captured Chacho is a fact he claims as an honor, to cover his fear of being considered a cowardly assassin" (40).

Then, distancing himself once more from the personal controversy, Alberdi takes the same historical observations of Sarmiento and relates them to a preexisting social context, turning what for his adversary is the cause of historical events into a consequence of other structural factors—social, political, and economic.

As an example, let's recall the demonization that Sarmiento makes of José Artigas when he identifies him with the unexplained forces of the rural soul, the barbarian soul:

> The montonera, as it appeared in the early days of the Republic under the orders of Artigas, already displayed that character of brutal ferocity and that terrorist spirit that was reserved for the immortal bandit, the estanciero of Buenos Aires, to turn into a system of legislation applied to civilized society, and to present it, in the name of ashamed America, to the contemplation of Europe (Sarmiento, Civilización, 72).

Like any barbarian, like any terrorist, the struggle of the rural militiaman could not have a positive sign for Sarmiento: "Artigas was an enemy of both patriots and royalists." His principle was evil, the destruction of civilization, barbarism. His instincts are necessarily "hostile to European civilization and to any regular organization. Adverse to monarchy as well as republic, because both came from the city and brought with them order and the consecration of authority." The barbarian is anarchic, a lover of disorder, which is the opposite of "European civilization"—saving the redundancy.

Later, Sarmiento gives us another description of what he understands by a barbarian. However, the definition does not stand on its own and therefore needs to be repeatedly identified with his a priori scheme of opposites, such as city versus countryside. After narrating how Facundo loses in a fight with an officer and then has him restrained to be killed with a spear, Sarmiento concludes: "And yet, despite all this, Facundo is not cruel, not bloodthirsty; he is merely a barbarian, who cannot control his passions [...] he is the terrorist who upon entering a city executes one man and whips another, but with economy; often with discernment [...]" (198). The "instinctive" seems to be the only inherent trait in the metaphysics of the barbarian, a trait that saves and condemns him in the eyes of the civilized—for whom the only tolerable crime is one executed in a scientific manner, regardless of the fact that this results in death on an always greater scale. But it continues to be insufficient.

In this vision, everything can be reduced not only to a cultural trait —that of rural barbarism— but also to a psychological and even biological origin: the *instincts*. Instincts that, as a reformer of his country's education systems, he sought to control, appease, and subdue, as one subdues and frustrates the instincts of animals destined for production (Berdiales, 56).

Using a sociopolitical analysis, Alberdi explains that Artigas' "montonera" was rural because the Spanish power had been established in the cities (Alberdi, Barbarie, 34). Therefore, it is not a "natural" attribute of the inhabitants of rural areas, of those who did not wear tailcoats and were more exposed to cultures more distant from the European one.

> After the rural caudillo comes the city caudillo, who perpetuates himself in power, who lives without working, off the country's treasury, who executes and persecutes his opponents [...] He is not the caudillo in leggings, but the caudillo in a tailcoat; he is always a barbarian, but a civilized barbarian (36).

Alberdi goes beyond the appearance of the tailcoat and the leggings, beyond the dichotomy proposed by Sarmiento, to see not only what the countryside and the city might have in common —caudillismo, evil, etc.— but also the same ideological process that is capable of organizing these classifications to the benefit of one side: "The rural caudillos," he wrote, "did evil without teaching it through doctrine. The educated caudillos of the cities do it and consecrate it through theories that clothe barbarism with the mantle of civilization" (37). (The emphasis is ours) This lucid observation, in turn, could align with another from his dialectical adversary, which is worth another lucid definition of ideological domination: "Terror among us is a governmental invention to stifle all conscience, all civic spirit, and finally force men to recognize as the thinking head the foot that presses on their throat" (Sarmiento, Civilization, 199). Both observations, it goes without saying, transcend their own context.

Beyond this possible critical encounter, which equally serves both theoretical positions, let's see that Alberdi not only denies the decisive force of ideas as the catalyst for the struggles for independence, based on his materialist reading, but also provides some contextual data of the time, such as the near total illiteracy of the population in the early 19th century (13).

This observation is not free from questioning, since: a) it was enough for the new humanist ideas to motivate the caudillos of the time for their followers to act accordingly; and b) this knowledge of the new ideas did not necessarily have to be transmitted in writing—nor was a discursive clarity of these ideas even necessary, as they could be summarized on the face of a coin, as indeed they were later: *liberty*, equality, fraternity. More complex ideas, such as Marxist-Leninist ideas, triggered or precipitated the Bolshevik Revolution in a Russia populated mostly by illiterate peasants.

Nevertheless, this objection does not weaken Alberdi's main hypothesis—based on a materialist reading—but, on the contrary, consolidates it. What, on the other hand, demonstrates that the previous observation, whether true or false, constitutes an unnecessary ad hoc argument in Alberdi's dialectical reasoning. A digression that, in any case, served more as a refutation of the dialectical adversary than of the theory itself.

The roots of power

Sarmiento tells us, in Facundo..., that "[...] terror is a means of government that produces greater results than patriotism and spontaneity. Russia has practiced it since the times of Ivan, and has conquered all barbarian peoples" (169).

However, Alberdi will respond that Rosas did not dominate the nation through terror, but through his resources.

"Without terror, the nation is now dominated by the successors of Rosas. It is not terror, a means of government, as Sarmiento says. It is money, wealth" (Alberdi, Barbarie, 18).

And shortly thereafter he insists, emphasizing an economic and social order reason: "[Sarmiento] believes that Rosas dominated through terror and the horse. Childishness. He dominated through wealth, in which power resides" (19). And later he confirms his materialism, a mix of Karl Marx and Adam Smith: "If Sarmiento suspected that the entire nature of political power lies in the power of finance, he would not waste his time and words on foolish and ridiculous theories [...]" (41). "Sarmiento has demonstrated that he does not understand the nature and origin of power [...] Not everyone who wants to be a terrorist is one. Only those who truly terrify have the actual power to inflict harm with impunity. Rosas terrified because he had unlimited means and resources; but he did not have power because he terrified [...]" (78).

This psychological conception of the origin of power, which according to Alberdi is mistaken and Machiavellian, is also denounced as a practice to impose a different kind of power that could lead the country to a higher degree of civilization, opposing fire with fire, barbarism with barbarism, ends with means. Further on, he gives some examples of the barbarism of his dialectical adversary, quoting Sarmiento's own Facundo: "[...] terror is a means of government that produces greater results than patriotism and spontaneity (Alberdi, Barbarism, 22) [...] And then: "[...] and to restrain the heartless, even more heartless judges are needed. The judge is naturally some infamous (bandit) from times past whom age and family have led to an orderly life" (23).

The reaction at the end of the century

It will be necessary to wait until the end of the 19th century to find a consciousness that overcomes the cultural inferiority complexes—product of the logocentric rigidity of Modernity—of intellectuals like Sarmiento and Alberdi. This consciousness advocating for the indigenous will quickly transform into a reaction among new intellectuals like José Martí (Our America, 1891), Rubén Darío (The Triumph of Caliban, 1898), and José Enrique Rodó (Ariel, 1900), who will prefigure the dialectical disputes of the 20th century, dramatically flavored by the new context of the Cold War and traditional oppressions. José Martí is a clear and lucid example of this reaction against the Europeanist—rather than European—tradition, which denied the Indian, the American, and the Black, while praising or imitating the European and the North American: "The arrogant man believes that the earth was made to serve as his pedestal, because he has a facile pen or colorful speech, and he accuses his native republic of being incapable and irremediable." And shortly thereafter, he expresses his awareness of the futility of the mimicry of Latin American intellectuals and reformers: "Incapacity does not lie in the nascent country, which prunes forms to suit itself and useful greatness, but in those who want to govern original peoples, of singular and violent composition, with laws inherited from four centuries of free practice in the United States, and from nineteen centuries of monarchy in France." A proof of this direct reaction to Sarmiento's thesis can be found in the following words: "There is no battle between civilization and barbarism, but between false erudition and nature" (Martí, América). In this work—

Our América, which appeared in *La Revista Ilustrada* de Nueva York in 1891—Martí not only alludes to Sarmiento but also denies a dichotomy to create another no less arbitrary one, if we consider that there is no "natural man" who is not framed within a culture, within an inherited or constructed way of feeling and thinking. But it signifies, from many points of view, the overcoming of a mentality—though still modern—that was by then anachronistic.

Sarmiento was one of the last representatives of the intellectuals who, for most of the 19th century, admired the economic and cultural development of the United States and attempted to imitate it without success. However, the growing international predominance of the great industrial country of the north did not produce more admirers but, on the contrary, notable detractors such as Rubén Darío, José Martí, or José Enrique Rodó, authors who would mark a strong paradigm shift.

Already in Sarmiento's *Facundo*, the warning of the waning political and military power of Europe is explicitly stated. "Rosas proved—it was said throughout America and is still said today—that Europe is too weak to conquer an American state that wishes to uphold its rights" (267). The intellectual prestige of the old continent remained unaltered, but its economic and political influence began to shift towards North America, and with it, the suspicion and later the confirmation of a new form of imperialism. The new thought sought to reclaim the ideological liberation of a margin with respect to the legitimizing dictatorship of an Anglo-Saxon center. It was the reclamation of an identity in constant construction and destruction; it signified a reclamation, while also representing a reaction. It meant turning the gaze inward, while also being a rebellious and ashamed gesture, a confirmation of one's own self—in both success and failure—at the same time as a rejection of an increasingly powerful external image. It was a philosophical and humanistic reflection, while also being a political attitude. From then on, and dramatically so during the 20th century, the dialectic of opposition and rejection towards the once-admired Anglo-Saxon model developed faster than its own dreams and aspirations. The great country of the north, the new Rome, would no longer be a center of positive legitimization but quite the opposite: opposing its economic and cultural models would become a cultural necessity. The possibility of creating a model of one's own was postponed and then forgotten in the exercise of urgent resistance. If the structure of exploitation was oppressive, the marginal attitude was not liberating. The failure was twofold. Independence was incomplete; the struggle for liberation became a tradition. Pride and dissatisfaction became chronic.

Historical Transformation of the Term "Liberal"

In the origins of Latin American countries, their intellectuals were largely in favor of liberal reforms. These, in one way or another, were partially imposed against conservative forces, represented by the Catholic clergy and the landowning classes, towards the end of the 19th and the beginning of the 20th century. As in other parts of the world, Latin American liberals conceived of history and societies as an evolutionary process, always changing and naturally progressive, from less to more, and from worse to better. A (pseudo-Darwinian) conception of humanity and a valuation of time that opposed the immobility of the church and the semi-feudal aristocracy in power.

However, this historical period also coincided with the loss of the North American reference, the social, economic, and cultural model represented by England and the United States. By the end of the 19th century (as examples, we have already cited José Martí, Rubén Darío, and José Enrique Rodó), this loss of admiration, primarily motivated by the idea of "failure," first transformed into distrust and then into a reaction. From admiration, it turned into rejection—if not hatred—for the increasingly powerful industrial nation of the north. "Anti-imperialism" in reference to North America began as a reclamatory reaction and perpetuated itself as a primarily reactionary and allergic culture, where the definition of one's own identity became subjugated to the relationship of rejection towards "the empire." This does not mean there was no unequal relationship and political and economic oppression, but rather that Latin American thought was unable to create an original and independent alternative.

Alongside this rejection and distrust of the early imperialist intentions of the Great Brother from the north, those paradigms that represented it were also rejected, such as *liberalism*. In this way, we observe how in Latin America the term "liberal," which previously connoted "progress(ivism)," to the detriment of conservative forces, came to signify the opposite. But it was not merely a simple change in the semantic boundaries of the term, but in its corresponding philosophical and ideological construction. Currently, in Latin America, the terms "(neo)liberal" or "liberalism" are opposed to "progressivism." The first two represent conservative sectors, politically referred to as "right-wing," while terms like "progressive" are reserved (and preserved) to identify groups "of the left"—as long as someone does not problematize its meaning explicitly, with the intent to reclaim a "semantically lost" territory. Nevertheless, the term "liberal" is still preserved in the language to signify a personal or moral attitude that is positively valued by the left and negatively by the conservative right. But this is not the case when the term is used to refer to a political, social, or economic definition. In the United States, on the other hand, the term "liberal" represents the opposite end of the political and moral spectrum: it stands for the left that opposes the conservative right. However, here the term "liberal" has not undergone significant shifts in its semantic fields when compared to its fate in the south, for the historical reasons previously noted. Paradoxically, today the term "liberal" is used both by the left (secular and progressive) in Latin America and by the right (religious and conservative) in the United States to discredit—if not outright insult—their dialectical opponent.

I understand that not only do the meanings of a term like "liberal" depend on its symbolic and semantic context, but the very idea (as a conceptual and practical extension of its meanings) will be dramatically altered in its effects depending on the social context in which the same model is applied. But this point requires its own space for development, where the cultural conditions in the development of a given practice can be analyzed alongside its corresponding (and not necessarily preexisting) ideology.

In the Letter from Jamaica, written in 1815, Simón Bolívar observed a primary characteristic of his continent:

disunity. "Surely," he wrote, "union is what we lack to complete the work of our regeneration." This disunity was not only expressed in the increasingly fragmented division of the future Latin American countries, a reflection of the caudillo social order, but also in the internal struggles themselves.

> Yet our division is not unusual, as it is the hallmark of civil wars typically formed between two parties: conservatives and reformers. The former are usually more numerous because the rule of custom creates the effect of obedience to established powers; the latter are always fewer in number, though more vehement and enlightened. In this way, the physical mass is balanced by the moral force, and the struggle prolongs itself with highly uncertain outcomes. Fortunately, among us, the masses have followed the intellectuals (Bolívar, Carta).

These struggles between conservatives and reformers, with the characteristics attributed by Bolívar in his Letter from Jamaica were never the exclusive property of Latin American countries. However, the second term —"reformists"— which until the late 19th century was the identity of the liberals, in the following century would be appropriated by "left-leaning" groups, that is, by the semantic adversaries of the new "liberals." Despite this semantic shift, the social structure and cultural characteristics of Latin America did not change so dramatically; on the contrary. The issues under discussion remained the same —but with a different language.

3.2—The Paradigm of Failure

The Ideological Lens

ONE OF THE CHARACTERISTICS OF A DOMINANT IDEOLOGY is to erase what has a social valuation of history, identifying it with "the natural." As John Storey says, it is the "transformation of history into nature" (85). In terms of Roland Barthes, this process leads to the production of social myths. Where the consumer of these symbols sees a process of cause and effect (the naturalizing dynamics of a phenomenon), there is only an equivalence historically established between a symbol and a specific meaning or value. What is a system of values becomes a system of facts. That is, in the words of Storey himself, things, facts, lose the memory of what they are made of —they lose their history. The symbol and the facts acquire great clarity, not through the grace of analytical or rational explanation but through the force and simplicity of a statement.

The philosophical tradition of the last century has always identified the "social myth" with the construction of a dominant ideology. However, Latin American issues have stumbled upon the opposite possibility: the social myth as the construction of subaltern culture, of an ideological tradition of "resistance." For writers like Carlos Rangel (as well as for Carlos Alberto Montaner), this mythological construction is responsible —the cause— for the failure of Latin America. In From the Noble Savage to the Noble Revolutionary, Rangel vehemently and convincingly asserts this same idea:

Undoubtedly, millenarianism and evolutionism are at odds with the rationalist spirit that made the West great [...] This explains why triumphant America, the United States, has made very moderate use of the myth of the Noble Savage and maintains a healthy resistance (greater than Europe's) to the myth of the Noble Revolutionary. It also explains why failed America, Latin America, is especially vulnerable to both myths [our emphasis] (30).

A common observation

As in *The Twisted Roots*, the central thesis of *Open Veins* originates from a supposed, never-questioned observation: failure. The image of a bad death, from *bleeding out* (open veins), as well as a bad birth, as a congenital *defect* (twisted roots), leads us to the idea of failure, of an agonizing, anemic life, with a certain physical and mental disability.

However, in the end, Montaner must pause his own metaphor by acknowledging the existentialist possibility of freedom: a responsible memory could "free itself" from its own past. Something not so different—since hope often occupies the final pages of books—is expressed by Galeano: the "consciousness" of its own bleeding can stop the hemorrhage and oppression. Both dialectical adversaries will strive to appropriate the meaning of consciousness and liberation. For both, the meanings of each of these terms will contradict the meanings attributed by their dialectical opponent. But they will start from the same observation and will make it the final consequence of two different historical narratives.

From the very first pages, Galeano questions the reasons attributable to this failure but leaves intact the recognition that his dialectical adversaries make of it:

> For those who conceive of *history as a competition*, the backwardness and misery of Latin America are nothing but the result of its failure. [...] But it so happens that those who won, won because we lost: the history of underdevelopment in Latin America is, as has been said, an integral part of the history of the development of world capitalism (Galeano, 3). [Emphasis ours]

Leaving aside for the moment the significant expression in italics, let us now focus on the common idea. We see that, for his part, Alberto Montaner does not disagree with this. The first sentence on the first page of Las raíces torcidas warns us:

> Let us say it quickly: the painful hypothesis proposed by this book is that the *manifest failure* of Latin America in the economic realm, its lack of political stability, and the poor scientific performance it exhibits, are largely consequences of our particular history (Montaner, 13). [Emphasis ours]

Here Montaner presents us with what, in his view, is the heart of his book's thesis: (1) the character of Latin American society is a consequence of its particular history; (2) the result of that history is a "manifest failure". Of course, these two central points are not characterized by their originality. In fact, they are contained in the text of his dialectical adversary, as we will see later. The struggle will, therefore, lie in the valuation and administration of the meanings of certain crucial terms and ideas for the reading of "reality".

If we briefly consider our theory of semantic fields, we will see that, not at the level of sign units but of complex ideas, in these two central statements, in addition to the explicit meanings—positive fields—, they are constructed and build themselves upon certain negations that, for the meaning of the idea, are of equal importance to their respective positive fields: the twisted roots are responsible for the failure—C(+)—, not the international context—C(-)—, not the development of "national adversaries", not external debts, not international financial pressures, not the empires that have bled the continent by extracting raw materials and preventing their primitive industrialization, etc.

Since we are not dealing with a sign of immediate reading, but with the meanings of a theory—or ideology—, these negations can not only begin to be suggested from the initial statements, but the author himself will take care of outlining these semantic boundaries through the enumeration and description of their respective negations.

On the other hand, we will later see that these very negations associated with the second point will become part of the positive field —C(+)— of Eduardo Galeano's theory, thus initiating a struggle over meaning.

Now, returning to the idea of failure, let us observe that, as if completing the circle, the book *The Twisted Roots* ends in a graphic and forceful manner, in the same vein:

> The 20th century, which has just ended, was indeed a barbaric period of horrendous massacres and sinister totalitarian dictatorships (Montaner, 192).

Throughout his book, the author emphasizes the "twisted roots" that led Latin America to a recent history of civil and military violence. He does not mention the external factors that directly contributed to this fate, which are upheld by Galeano's supporters —and by some official documents from the intelligence services of various countries (see CIA)—. But, like his adversary, he confirms the diagnosis: Latin America has failed and still has not risen.

> The content of this book inevitably leads us to a final question: despite its history, is it ever possible for Latin America to leave underdevelopment behind and reach the same economic and scientific level as Europe, the United States [...]? (Montaner, 179).

Once the *failure is acknowledged as evidence* and without problematizing its common understanding, we establish not only a starting point but, above all, an endpoint. Here, the novelty lies not in discovering a reality but in explaining it, that is, we do not seek the truth in an understanding of our object but in the dialectical path that is capable of explaining it.

The observation problem becomes simplified and further solidified when the very idea of failure is shared by both supporters and adversaries as a fact of reality. We will not delve into the problematic analysis of this concept here either. We will simply accept—provisionally—the idea that the Latin American continent is a "failed" continent.

But how deep are these twisted roots of failure?

Galeano does not go beyond the official birth date of the continent in question: 1492. Montaner, however, goes back

195

to 4th-century Europe. One of these factors is the scholastic teaching of the 12th century that was imposed on the continent through Spain (13). The other is also a peninsular legacy, inherited, in turn, from Rome and the ancient Middle East: the "descending nature of power," denounced by Averroes early in the Middle Ages. He continues in depth through the times of Constantine in the 4th century and the arbitrary actions of the Popes a few centuries later (33).

For his part, Galeano prefers not to lose a certain historical horizon and concentrates his description of the "bad birth," the origin of failure, in the colonial times of Latin America. And, more despairingly, in the recounting of the failure of the founding fathers of our nations.

We can question this well-established idea from many angles. But it would be more useful to ask ourselves from what perspective we observe the failure. This leads us to ask about its opposite: what we consider "success" and the origins of that idea. Considering the words of Simón Bolívar or José Artigas, we could speak of "the failure of unity." But if we come closer in time, although the idea of a failed union still lingers in the subconscious of Latin American thinkers, the explicit reference to failure has changed its adjective. Now, the failure is, above all, economic—it is the failure of underdevelopment.

Here, the "failure" is what has been objectified, what has been taken as an *objective observation of reality*. It could be said, then, that both Galeano and Montaner do not dispute the meaning of the term failure but quite the opposite: they share an implicit agreement on its semantic boundaries, like two conflicting countries that do not dispute the movement of their own geographical limits.

All these variations of *failure* are united by a certain idea of *success*. Not just any kind of success: it is the success conceived by the Western mindset, first European success, and then American success. Ultimately, the success of development and, in its narrowest view, economic success. Erich Fromm, in The Fear of Freedom, gives us an idea of the origin of this conception when he tells us that for Calvinism, success became the sign of divine grace and failure, the sign of condemnation (102). Later, he emphasizes a psychological perspective:

> Intense activity, in Calvin's doctrine, also had another psychological meaning. The fact of not tiring in such incessant effort and achieving success, both in moral and secular works, constituted a more or less distinct sign of being one of the chosen ones (103).

And its translation into a 20th-century mentality:

> In the further development of Calvinism, frequent warnings appear against feelings of friendship towards foreigners, cruel attitudes towards the poor, and a general atmosphere of suspicion (107).

Now, the idea of *success*, which, though it seems obvious at first, is so only as long as it is not problematized. We can find another influential thinker who disagreed with the semantic boundaries of the idea of success, and consequently, with the meanings of its opposite, failure. If we consider the perspective of the Argentine thinker Ernesto Sábato, an advocate of "problematic literature," we can find a different—and opposing—interpretation of the Western idea of success.

In his essay *Hombres y Engranajes* (*Men and Gears*), from 1951, Sábato wrote:

> It is easy, indeed, to prove the superiority of the airplane over the cart, but how to demonstrate moral or political progress? [Compte and Spenser] were reduced to assuming that people wearing top hats and traveling by train were incapable of perpetrating the things the Turks did to the Armenians[...] (Sábato, Hombres, 53).

Sábato alluded, in this paragraph, to the crimes and genocides perpetrated by the most developed countries of Europe during the World Wars. A few pages later, in his critique of the "mechanistic success" of the West, which this author often calls "technolatry," he noted:

> Before, when one was hungry, one would glance at the clock to see what time it was; now, one consults it to find out if we are hungry (55) [...] Reason—the engine of science—has unleashed a new irrational faith, as the average man, incapable of understanding the world and the imposing parade of abstract symbols, has replaced understanding with admiration and the fetishism of the new magic (58).

That is, both Galeano and Montaner operate within the same semantic boundaries that define "success" in technological and economic terms, without questioning the relativity of their negative effects from an existential perspective, as Ernesto Sábato did in the mid-20th century.

3.3—The Rescue of Consciousness

Consciousness

THE ACT OF BECOMING CONSCIOUS is not only a problem when it has not been exercised, but also when we try to define it in itself. The problem arises when we consider that what some may call "becoming conscious" for others may be just another form of "alienation" or "false consciousness."

From a social and existential point of view, and through an integral analysis of the symbol, we can say that an action is conscious when it is self-questionable. That which has not been questioned cannot be understood as conscious, but rather as an assumed impulse. There is no absolute consciousness but degrees of awareness. We can say that we assume a greater consciousness of our being-in-the-world when we are capable of perceiving the non-meanings of the symbol, those meanings that were previously assumed arbitrarily without considering the possibility of their negation, their questioning. We can say that we "become conscious" of something when we step out of the boundaries of the positive field of something and consider the negative field as a possible area for positive fields. In other words, "taking consciousness" means *stepping out of one's own circle*. This "stepping out" is always partial and insufficient, but each time we are able to encompass a larger area of previously unnoticed considerations, we are enacting a new consciousness.

As we suggested earlier, the author of *The Twisted Roots of Latin America* risks being trapped in his own metaphor. Generally, a congenital defect, whether physical or mental, has no solution. Although Montaner goes back two thousand years and thousands of kilometers to explain the failure of Latin America, he admits that the solution can be immediate—in historical terms—: within less than a generation, any society can produce an "economic miracle."

"Is it possible that Latin America will ever abandon underdevelopment?" (179), was one of Montaner's final rhetorical questions. Thirty years earlier, Galeano closed his book in the same way:

> Is Latin America a region of the world condemned to humiliation and poverty? Condemned by whom? The fault of God, the fault of nature? The oppressive climate, the inferior races? Religion, customs? Could it be that misfortune is a product of history made by men, and that it can therefore be unmade by men? (Galeano, 439).

In these rhetorical questions, both positive and negative answers are implied. Here, adversaries will quickly agree on the *yes* and the *no*. Regarding the possibility of a radical change, a historical "un-failure," both would respond affirmatively. But a *yes* that is conditional, not inevitable. The bleeding will stop, the disability will be overcome when the Latin American people *take consciousness* of their true situation. This idea of a "saving consciousness" is at the foundational origin of the world's most important religions. This consciousness is also often called "enlightenment," that is, the *awakening*, the anointing of knowledge, whether through revelation, as in the Judeo-Christian-Muslim tradition, or through discovery and understanding, as in the Eastern tradition.

The conflict arises in the recognition or attribution of the meanings of these concepts, which, in their semantic origins, possess a strong positive valuation: awakening, seeing, understanding, being aware of reality. These four terms, in their origin, refer to physical space and all place primitive man safe from the dangers of a hostile external world. However, in their historical and semantic evolution, all four are taken as metaphors to describe a metaphysical space of increasing complexity. This space can be religious or ideological, as in the case at hand.

While the meaning of seeing, that is, of opening the eyes, is scarcely disputed in its positive valuation of "protecting oneself and acting accordingly to the surrounding reality," when it becomes a metaphorical instrument of a metaphysical narrative it turns into a highly conflictual term. In dialectic disputes, the strategy of defending a highly conflictual term is to associate it, implicate it, with other terms of low conflict, that is, with those signs whose meanings are neither disputed nor questioned. Within these "stable signs," the targets will be those that possess a strong positive valuation, such as the term seeing or consciousness. This means that the semiotic transfers deduced from part of their original meaning can serve different significant purposes.

According to Mario Vargas Llosa, the drama of social and economic failure in Latin America has "a single cause: a profound inability to distinguish between truth and lies, between reality and fiction" (Manual, 15). It is implied, though not proven, that the author of these words, as well as the authors of Manual del perfecto idiota, do possess this ability to distinguish between truth and lies, between fiction and reality. In this case, the dialectic dispute dissolves into mere qualification—or disqualification—of the adversary, but it is significant in that it represents an extreme, caricatured example of the frequent attitudes observable in the dialectic struggle for the administration of meaning and, consequently, for the conquest of truth.

Thus we may find that *seeing*, that is, *becoming aware* can mean for some *stopping the bleeding* that Galeano speaks of or straightening the roots, according to Montaner. But this awareness can be one's own or it can be someone else's. When a people or an individual reproduces someone else's awareness, they are exercising their own blindness. In the face of this apparent subjectivism, we must contrast one with the other according to their "usefulness" and convenience for the individual in question. That is, someone else's awareness would be one that does not benefit them to the same extent as it benefits the other, and therefore the relationship that is established is one of oppressed and oppressor. In the words of Eduardo Galeano, this latter is a reality, whereby "the oppressed are forced to make their own a memory fabricated by the oppressor, foreign, dissected, sterile. Thus they will resign themselves to living a life that is not their own as if it were the only possible one" (439).

That is, the oppressor has colonized the memory of the oppressed, preventing them from seeing, becoming aware of their situation. And has done so in a particular way: has disfigured the metaphysical space of the oppressed to make it coincide with a physical space that, were it not for deception or blindness, would not be recognized as such.

The process was denounced a few years earlier by the educator Paulo Freire14: the oppressed have recognized what is cultural as if it were natural. What has been created by men, the oppressors throughout history, has been taken by the present of the oppressed as a natural phenomenon that is not questioned, before which only resignation and acceptance are possible, as in the face of an earthquake or the biological conditions that the body imposes on human life. Social orders have been recognized as biological orders, and if in the wild it is just for a lion to exterminate a colony of deer, it is also just that among humans there are oppressed and oppressors.

Faced with this paradigmatic idea, not explicit in social life but which we could understand as "dominant ideology," Paulo Freire responded with his theory of "conscientization," a neologism in Spanish derived from "tomar conscience" (taking consciousness) and, ultimately, from the more primitive "abrir los ojos ante la realidad" (opening one's eyes to reality).

However, we will see, with precision, how a dialectical adversary will dispute the meaning of the term consciousness and the new proposed term, that of "cocientización" — an adaptation into Spanish of the original Portuguese "concientização," translated by some in a less specific way as "consciousness-raising."

In a book written in collaboration with two other writers, Alberto Montaner alludes to these theories with repeated mockery. According to Montaner, Mendoza, and Vargas

---

14 Paulo Freire. Pedagogy of the Oppressed. (1970)

Llosa Jr., Freire and his followers believe that the poor and oppressed must be "revealed the revolution, explained the truth they ignore. Not to help them reflect or listen to what they think and want. They must be 'made conscious'" (Mendoza, 211). Ironically, the authors of Manual del perfecto idiota latinoamericano invert the semantic fields —C(+) and C(-)— proposed by Paulo Freire. If in his writings the Brazilian educator speaks of a necessary collective reflection, from the bottom up, of questioning before "teaching" revealed truths, of listening to what the oppressed sectors of society think as a means to achieve consciousness by themselves, here the opposite is declared: so-called consciousness-raising means the imposition of a "revealed truth": the truth of the revolution —Marxist—. After inverting the semantic fields to redefine the meaning of concientización, it is associated with the Marxist revolutionary project (Cuban-Soviet), that is, with class struggle, more concretely with armed struggle. Therefore, what some call "liberation" is "slavery," what they call "consciousness-raising" is "unconsciousness," what they call "white" is "black," and so on. The goal is to empty the term appropriated by the adversary and give it a meaning opposite to the one previously intended, to identify a positive term with a negative one and, in this way, persuade the reader (with or without evidence) of the perverse intentions of the other's discourse, of the negative evaluation of their thinking, of the inconvenient consequences of their twisted conception. The process involves linking a term ("concientización") with others (Marxism, revolution, violence) that have already been negatively valued. This achieves a "sign transfer," for example, from the term violence (which has low semantic conflict and high negative valuation) to the term class struggle, which has high semantic conflict. From this latter term, its meanings are transferred to the term Marxism, and finally, the meaning of violence is transferred to the redefined sign of "concientización."

Consciousness —and the very sign *consciousness*— becomes the *object of dispute*, by dialectical adversaries, and in , by powers and ideologues who play their cards in society. It is possible (1) to colonize the consciousness of men and women, but also, (2) to redefine the semantic boundaries *battlefield* of the term itself, a condition that can precede the former.

To express these same ideas and intuitions, Galeano uses a highly figurative metaphor, an almost allegorical image:

> There are those who believe that destiny rests in the laps of the gods, but the truth is that it works, like a burning challenge, upon the consciousness of men (Galeano, 436).

This is his response and his final words in the 1971 first edition of *Las venas abiertas*. F. Nietzsche's "God is dead" becomes evident here. Of course, Montaner will also not turn to divinity to explain reality or base his hopes for redemption: for the Cuban writer, too, the ends and means are contested in the consciousness of the people. Only the meanings of "becoming conscious" will differ from those of his adversary. Translated into a term of lower semiotic conflict, we might say that what his metaphysical eyes see differs from what the eyes of his adversary see, both focused on the same object. It is not a closed phenomenological problem. Both observers know that they see a different logos each and will strive to impose their own by using convenient strategies and evidence. One will see the tree; the other will see the forest. Both will claim the vision of the eagle in flight.

The two adversaries will agree that the images, representations of a country and a history do not coincide with "reality" — a positivist possibility of demonstration — but rather they often represent more the social myths or the interests of a dominant ideology than verifiable facts and values.

As we will see later, Galeano will also use the expression "industrializing consciousness" (330) of the primitive North American colonies, as a precondition for their development. Here, once again, we verify the association of consciousness as the act of being able to see the present and foresee the future. This idea of consciousness is subsequent to the facts, but the thinker who attempts to read history, unravel the logos, will attribute this metaphysical condition as the cause of an observation that is not in dispute: the economic development of the northern colonies.

3.4 — Consciousness, Between Determinism and Freedom

Freedom of the individual

NEVERTHELESS, THE IDEA OF *CONSCIOUSNESS* will always be problematic and, above all, will depend on the point of view that is adopted, the model of reading that is exercised, and the valuations that are made. The idea of *consciousness* is intimately tied to the idea of *freedom*. But when we speak of "freedom," we will always be referring to something limited by its circumstances. The circumstances can be understood as oppressive, as we can see in parts of "The Open Veins," or as opportunities to exercise that freedom. Sartre, the philosopher who understood that humans are condemned to freedom, also wrote that we are what we make of what is made of us. To a great extent, noticing this dynamic is an unequivocal way of becoming conscious of our reality.

Both the supporters of *"The Open Veins"* and those of *"The Twisted Roots"* will ultimately appeal to this last resource of freedom: consciousness as a saving condition, as an option to break the chains of (1) the economic structure or (2) an equivocal or inconvenient "mentality." But can a state of consciousness be as oppressive as it is liberating? Milton Fisk warns about the often overlooked difference between imposed consciousness and non-imposed consciousness.

> Their search for a transcendent basis for freedom makes them neglect factors such as class differences in the origins of consciousness (Fisk, 175).

David van Mill, introduces the dimension of will into the problem of freedom. Analyzing Hobbes' conception of freedom, he understands that "Hobbes also distinguishes a realm of freedom based on volition, and this is where the potential tension between freedom and determinism appears." Even the thought process —of consciousness— is caught in this tension between determinism and freedom:

> In the case of voluntary acts, our thought processes are still determined by previous events and hence we have no free will in the sense of uncaused thoughts. An act of the will, for Hobbes, simply demonstrates that we have stopped the

causal chain of thoughts which moves us to particular actions (Mill, 445).

Other theorists have seen that the very claim of considering the individual as a "naturally" free subject is merely the construction of a dominant ideology—central and, therefore, not necessarily formulated, like the Marxist one—. Specifically, Mas'ud Zavarzadeh refers to capitalism, a political, social, economic, and cultural system that depends on the idea of the individual, of the different. The same critique that emphasizes the importance of the factor of individuality— the independent, the autonomous— is part of the same dominant narrative that opposes deconstructive critique, even as the latter itself is structuring or "neo-structuralist." "In this way —says Zavarzadeh—, seeing a film as a 'unique' work of art is a way to cover the dominant ideology." And further: "Ideology critique violate the principle of uniqueness" (Zavarzadeh, 3).

The ascending reading of history and the present that conditions cultural outcomes to the political and economic orders of a society is known as materialist. Also as "reductionist," inferring from it that it seeks to explain the complexity of culture through the laws of psychology and these, in turn, through biological, economic, etc., laws. That is, the complexity of metaphysical freedom can be "reduced" to simpler laws of economics and even further, to physical laws, that is, material ones. Nevertheless, Zavarzadeh rejects this critique of "reductionism" in his theoretical analyses, warning that "the actual reason for these attacks, however, is that ideology critique displace the individual by pointing out the global structures that in fact construct his seemingly 'natural' uniqueness and freedom" (4).

True freedom —as derived from his statements— would be the awareness of the laws that structure the dominant ideology in a society through (deconstructive?) critique that allows the modification or replacement of the same (political revolution) or the "liberation" of the individual in a state of consciousness (humanist revolution).

While this critique —or *consciousness*— does not occur, paradigms of our Western societies such as "freedom" and the "individual" will remain mirages, illusions in service of something contrary to the very idea of freedom: structural determinism.

> The dominant ideology preserves the notion of the free person who can enter into transactions with other free persons in the free market but who is at the same time obedient to the law of the free market that legitimizes the dominant social order (14).

In his novel *Makbara* (1980), Juan Goytisolo sums it up in a more concise and definitively ironic way; as a public advertisement, on behalf of a large company, he tells us: "Entrusting your decision-making power into our own hands will always be the surest way to decide for yourself" (28).

In this way, what we call *moral conscience* would simply be reduced to a *functional disciplining*. What we call *consciousness*, that prerequisite for all liberation —moral, political, and religious— astonishingly transforms into an opposite, negative faculty: it imprisons, oppresses; it does not liberate. Semantic salvation is a sad and timid change of prefix: it is not *true* consciousness, it is a *pseudo*-consciousness. But in this case, we make a deductive, dialectical leap, concluding with a direct definition of what *is* and *is not*, according to our own direct narrative about our metaphysical space in chaos.

Reality (psychological) as subordinate to meaning

Consciousness and *liberation* are also closely related in the thought of educator Paulo Freire, for whom one derives from the other while both can be confused. That is, one can have a "false consciousness" and a "false liberty," products of personal and social deficiencies such as "education" and "critique." Change —liberation— will come only when the oppressed "commit to the organized struggle for their liberation, begin to believe in themselves, thus overcoming their complicity with the oppressive regime" (61). But this will not be possible if a kind of "mental structure" that comes from a "social structure" and, at the same time, reproduces it is not broken. Change will come only when the oppressed "commit to the organized struggle for their liberation, begin to believe in themselves, thus overcoming their complicity with the oppressive regime" (61).

In *Pedagogy of the Oppressed*, we can observe that Freire's main readings come from Marxist texts. But his critique, although originating from this deconstructive perspective, goes beyond.

> when the leftist man sectorizes himself, he is absolutely mistaken in his "dialectical" interpretation of reality, of history, falling into deeply fatalistic positions. [For the reactionaries of the right] the present, linked to the past, is something given and immutable; for the second [for the

leftist man], the future is something predetermined, inexorable, and fixed (25).

However, these critical assessments consider that *consciousness* and *liberation* are two perfectly definable categories according to a certain social state and, therefore, objective and not relative. One is or is not free, one has or does not have consciousness. It is a positivist conception of liberty and consciousness. "Objectification" would be, for Freire, the act of perceiving oneself in a reality, becoming aware of being in the world, not merely perceiving the world as a fatality. (93).

Another perspective we can contribute, as noted elsewhere, could be had if we understand a situation of *oppression* or *liberation* not as an objective, observable, or demonstrable fact, but even as a relationship that said fact or situation maintains with its meaning and evaluation. Could a prostitute reverse the meaning of her situation from oppressed to free in the understanding of a "personal choice"? To what extent is this choice determined by the socioeconomic structure (structuralist reading), by an inherited mentality (culturalist reading), or by a purely free choice? It is possible to understand ideas like "oppression" and "liberation" in an ethical-semantic sense, which can ultimately be reduced to a purely symbolic problem —despite the initial rejection this first proposition provokes in us.

Let's look at a paradigmatic case of oppression: the case of a prostitute. In the not-so-distant past, the prostitute was condemned as a "sinful woman," both by most religions and by most secular societies. Her oppression consisted not only in economic —material— dependence but, above all, symbolic —ethical: *how* she was viewed by society, *how* she viewed herself in society, *what* kind of meanings were recognized in her and by herself. A later historical stage sought to vindicate her as an "oppressed being," that is, a product of a "sick society." Liberation theologians might call this a "social sin." The more radical revisionists would see her as a victim of an economic, social, and ideological system. The solution —as in the case of drug addicts— is to combat the origins that generate the evil; not the one who satisfies the demand. A common expression in these groups is to claim that the prostitute is not the sinner —the one who produces evil— but rather *the symptom* of a (sick) society. That is, since the meaning of prostitution remains unchanged —in its negative valuation—, the only form of liberation is the abandonment of that state —of the sign. A healthier society, then, would be a society without brothels and without prostitutes. Or, at least, without the need for either.

Now, it is also possible to view this problem from another angle. Let us suppose a not impossible situation —in fact, we can find historical examples— where the prostitute is considered a goddess. In this case, her profession —which does not exclude pleasure, as in the previous case— does not signify a state of *oppression* but, perhaps, its dynamic counterpart: it is possible that this woman becomes an *oppressor* if she is capable of manipulating a social group. In fact, we can find examples that come close to this, in the embodiment of certain entertainment stars: the sale of their sexual image — and sometimes the sale of their body— is a reason for veneration by their admirers and by ideological groups that understand that an act of *promiscuity* (Cs_1 above) signifies a state of *female liberation* (new Cs_2).

Thus, we see that the difference between *oppressed* and *oppressor* depends on a *symbolic valuation*, since in both cases the physical relationships are the same. In the first case, the moral pain of the victim is symbolic, which does not diminish the violence or pain of their situation —obviously, here I am denying the connotation of "unreal" to the term "symbolic".

While it is true that the valuation of a symbol —ethical— and its possible meanings do not depend on the mere decision of a person or a specific group, it is equally true that the historical dynamics of groups struggling for meaning have demonstrated their instability. The shameful social —and later psychological and spiritual— situation of the homosexual has changed to the point of a radical re-signification of their identity and their ethical valuation —what was once shame is now pride. What could once have been the cause of deep anguish, of an existential crisis and, often, suicide, is now revealed as a source of a normal, dignified life.

The same could be said of the symbol *prostitute*. It is likely that such re-signification is historically very distant. However, we can understand the possibility of a *liberation* of the prostitute through a single act of re-signification. That is, the physical state referred to by the symbol *prostitute* does not need to change to achieve *liberation*.

In this sense, I understand the existence of two types of revolutionaries: those in modernity who fought mainly for a change in physical state —of the symbol— and those others, primarily contemporary, who fight for a change in meaning. Both, of course, also made and make use of the manipulation of each other's objectives, but as tools. That is, modern revolutionaries also attacked the symbols and the meanings that represented oppression for them; similarly, those who fight for the re-signification of existing symbols do not abstain from structural changes. A brief example is the struggle of homosexuals: while the re-signification of their state is a priority in their social recognition, they do not stop fighting for structural changes such as legal changes —laws that allow them to marry and thus obtain legal and economic rights, etc.

Another paradigmatic example of our times is the semantic destiny of the term man. Fifty years ago, or less, its C(+) encompassed all of humanity. Feminist movements and other ideological groups defined a new C(-) in such a way that its extension to humanity was denied and restricted to the male sex. This was the result of an ideological struggle, first and foremost, and an ethical one second.

We might be tempted to parody the idea that, therefore, any human situation can be changed and liberated through a simple resignification, through a mere change of *ethical scenario*. The response begins with the fact that no resignification is *simple*. Many fail to be sufficient to invert the original value of the symbol. Despite this, we must respond that what can be viewed with irony are not absurd claims. We know, for example, that even a situation of physical oppression can be considered positively. In our societies, we do not expect a toothache to be resignified as a heavenly blessing. However, we know that for some Amazonian tribes, a cold is not considered an illness, as we understand it, but rather as a favorable sign from the heavens. And it is experienced as such. We also know that many Christians and Muslims self-flagellate during religious celebrations. Some Christians crucify themselves alive to emulate Christ on Easter. Other Shiites self-flagellate with chains. The examples, of course, do not end with these two religions. What matters here is to note that even a situation of pain and physical oppression can be lived as a positive and desirable event. Probably we can say that in most cases—excluding sexual masochists—pain is an absolute fact. But the same pain can signify *oppression* in some cases and *liberation* in others.

Now, is it possible that we consider ourselves *liberated* and even *happy* and not be so?

Yes, as long as a new act of awareness—of the symbol, of a situation—demonstrates to us, by contrast, that what we considered *liberation* and even *happiness* were—always in comparison—*oppression* and even *sadness* in the new semantic field, in a semantic field more favorable to the individual.

Awareness and meaning

I climb some stairs. I open a door, and a tall mustached man tells me to stop. It's Juan. I shoot him twice, and Juan falls dead. I am a murderer. There is nothing I can do to bring Juan back to life. There is nothing I can do to stop being a *murderer*.

I wake up. Juan tells me to keep working. The irremediable has been remedied. Then I think of a ridiculous situation. I had told Juan that his mother had been very kind to bring us food at work, and he had replied that it wasn't his mother but his wife. The others fell silent, full of mockery.

I then thought that nothing could erase that *mortifying* moment. Probably, as in the dream, there could be "solutions." That is, if (1) I died, any idea of *shame* or

215

embarrassment would cease to have meaning. At least not the same meaning I attribute to it now, which oppresses and distresses me. It could also happen that (2) the meaning of the same incident would change radically, and instead of shame, it would provoke pride, for example. Another possibility for the cancellation of the meaning of shame would be possible if (3) everything beforehand was a fiction of my own...

To awaken is to change awareness. *To resignify is to change states.*

When we awaken, we resignify events. Generally, one of the first classifications we make is determining what is *real* and what is *unreal* in our memory. It is possible that something we recall is not clearly classified as a dream or as reality, but, in general, this type of division is immediate. When the division tends to lose clarity, we can say we are facing a serious psychological problem.

In human life, meaning depends on the state in which the symbol is produced and from the state in which it is valued. Dreaming and wakefulness are two states culturally accepted as opposites. In fact, it is important—fundamental—in psychological treatment to be able to distinguish events as occurring on one side or the other. The confusion of these two states alters the valuation and meaning of events, of the perceived symbols. This is defined as psychological illness or disturbance.

It is necessary, then, to establish a clear division—according to psychology. Another possibility for confronting trauma is to resignify the events and clearly position them in one or another scenario of consciousness.

When we resignify a symbol, we are operating, on a small scale, the same alteration of consciousness.

At an existential level, we can say that the dream is the C(-) of what we call "real"—wakefulness, the C(+). But even within wakefulness, we can find hallucinations and all that material typical of dreams. However, when we problematize the sign of reality, we can deconstruct the initial statement and recognize dreams as part of the real. Perhaps even more real than certain beliefs or illusions that develop in a state of wakefulness. This is a way of altering states of consciousness through the resignification of symbols. The crime we committed in a dream has something of the real, whereas the "good manners" of wakefulness are merely an illusory mask of my hostile feelings toward Juan. Thus, the valuation of signs will depend on the state—or position—of consciousness from which these symbols are observed.

Ideological thought

According to Nietzsche, a truth is an illusion that we have forgotten is an illusion. An illusion with a will to power. In the same sense, we understand that an ideology does not seek truth or epistemological speculation but quite the opposite; its function has an objective: to induce in a social group (or in society as a whole) a behavior through specific values. It is a form of collective thought (or discourse) that is not devoid of purpose: the productivity and consolidation of a certain social class in spheres of power that are inaccessible to the rest of "society" when it is a dominant ideology, or the organization of the dismantling of that consolidated order when it is a resistant ideology.

> Our so-called will to truth is the will to power because the so-called drive for knowledge can be traced back to a drive to appropriate and conquer. Sometimes Nietzsche places this abstract will to power as an incessant figuration, not under the control of any knowing subject, but rather in the unconscious (Sarup, 51).

However, in this reasoning, "power" is understood in a unique and general way. When in an *ideological truth* we refer to power, we must define new semantic limits to imply it in a social relationship, with productive or dominative aims of some groups over others. This leads us to the revelation of new "powers," which we define by reformulating their semantic boundaries and dividing, as in a controlled mitosis (but each time with a new "DNA" order), new partitions of meanings, which, in turn, result in a limiting implication of the noun "power" with some adjective, such as "ideological," "practical," etc. This delimitation is possible by realizing that truth as power is also recognizable in the area of "factual" sciences, such as physics or chemistry. Their "truths" have traditionally been demonstrated as "illusions" (it would suffice to cite the cases of Ptolemy or Newton); however, these illusions have had great utility, which we can understand as another form of power.

But let us return to the social sphere. For an ideology, it is fundamental to understand ideas as symbols and thought as discourse (logos, in the primitive sense of the word). The denial of alternatives through the consolidation of pairs of opposites is a powerful way of defining the sign—that is, of giving it greater clarity. The valuation of "truth" in this process derives from the forced—arbitrary but interested—confirmation of a solid negative body adjacent to a well-limited and reduced positive center. Good and evil must be clearly separated. For this type of reasoning, nothing can be good and evil at the same time; therefore, the one who manages to establish this separation will proclaim themselves as a clear-sighted visionary and will be understood by others the more radical this separation is. We can define what is good and what is evil through a certain ethical reasoning that starts from moral axioms (such as the basic commandments that seek to preserve life) and arrive at more or less complex con-clusions at a complex level of social organization, or we can proceed by skipping this difficult path and establishing di-rect identifications. This is what ideological discourse chooses to practice, what we could call a "semantic manipu-lation." Not only is there an intentionality in the attributed meaning, not derived from speculative reasoning, but often there isn't even this "simulacrum" of thought; instead, it is forcibly annulled through the hypnotic play of emotions.

In this type of mindset and strategy, there can be no room for creation. It is impossible to create semantic fields with broad, ambiguous borders and oppose them to another es-tablished field with clear-cut boundaries. Ideological thought, so close to religious dogma, demands loyalty and, therefore, renounces questioning in exchange for intellectual comfort and a longed-for security, almost always motivated by the fear that stems from the very ideological discourse and feeds it.

This process that moves from the "reading" of an idea as a symbol requires an ethical valuation—good and evil—of a semantic field that lacks it. Thus, the ideological mechanism must proceed in two ways: (1) directly attributing an ethical valuation to a historical concept or (2) establishing an identity between an already established valuation and a new symbol.

In Chapter *2.15 Meaning and Valuation*, I advanced some observations on what we can call "ideological phrases," referring only to one case of traditional phrases, constructed and confirmed by tradition. Now we will quickly look at other possible, more "spontaneous" types of phrases. For example, we can consider what the expression "María is very informal" or "María is a liberal woman" means. Both expressions, in themselves, are relative from their origin: she is informal or liberal in comparison to another person or group of people who are less informal or less liberal. Now, from an ideological point of view, we need to establish an ethical valuation: is it good or bad that María is informal? Is it good or bad that María is so liberal? We see that informality can be a virtue or a flaw, depending on the situation we are referring to or the group making the valuation. To her classmates, it is a virtue; to her teachers, it is a flaw; to her friends, both could be virtues; to her parents, both could be flaws.

But an ideology that aims to dominate truth cannot afford ambiguities. It must infer a valuation or establish a symbol within what is good and another within what is bad. Each ideology will define, in its own way, different pairs of opposites that correspond to the fundamental dichotomous pair: Good-Evil. In our times, dominant ideologies are not based, as in the Middle Ages, on religious precepts, even though these play a fundamental role in ethical discourse. But a dominant ideology is precisely so not because of what it says but because of what it establishes without saying. As J. R. Hale observes, at the end of the Middle Ages there was a shift in ethical valuation, where unproductivity began to be

defined as part of evil, replacing religious values (Hale, 105).
Today, the identification of good with productivity and evil
with unproductivity continues to hold, though it is beginning to decline. But this is a valuation that is, in certain re-
spects, discursive and largely conscious within society at
large, which can sustain it even after becoming aware of it.
However, a dominant ideology is sustained by the strength
of its transparency, its invisibility. The Good-Evil dichotomy
is currently linked to the deepest foundation of Power-Re-
sistance. When we say "power," we are not only referring to
the idea that power is the force a minority has to impose its
will over the rest of society. With "power," we refer to that
force—cultural, economic, social, institutional—that tends
toward the preservation and reproduction of established social relations, whatever they may be. Of course, one of the
consequences of this status quo is the benefit of a particular
social sector. But this does not mean that in every corner of
the dominant ideology there is a voluntary and conscious
control by that minority. A dominant ideology can be fueled
by a group that benefits from it, but it can never be controlled by it, just as it can never be defeated by any resistance
group. An immediate example is found in the overwhelming
mass of films that come from Hollywood. These, like Latin
American soap operas, while having little artistic value —
without delving into defining the latter— possess an extremely high ideological value from the moment they are
consumed by the vast majority of the population. The common factor that encompasses them as a rule is transparent
because the viewer's concentration must focus on the drama
currently being portrayed and demanding a solution. In
these films, quick consumption avoids attention to criticism

and debate, making them even more powerful as uncritical vehicles for the dominant ideology. Generally, good is represented by established institutions in society, especially state ones, such as the police, the military, the judiciary, and various government agencies. They will all fight, like Superman, against Evil, that is, against those who oppose the dominant order identified with Good. Superman fights for justice by catching the villains who hide in the shadows and whose intention is "to dominate the world." The prior domination of the world by the ideology of which Superman is a part is not seen due to its transparency, its ubiquity. The drama presented through a proposed problem (there is a villain who wants to change things) does not allow us to question anything but to focus our attention on its resolution. The conflict created with prior valuations is resolved, and evil is defeated. Superman does not fight —like Zorro— to change the world, but to preserve it as it is, because what is, is good.

In other variations of the same ethical-ideological dynamic, the hero opposes the center. But he does not oppose the dominant order but specific individuals who have "become corrupt." As Zavarzadeh says, his goal is to return it to the center. That is, here too, the good rebel is part of the dominant ideology. Almost as much as the bad rebel is, who fulfills a dual function: first, to demonstrate the "openness" of the established social order; second, to provoke a "locking" of that virtuous order as a self-defense response against evil.

Another common and caricatured element in Latin American soap operas —beyond their simplistic division of good and bad— is the "reward" of the oppressed. The maid, the good slave, will suffer the punishments of the bad. By framing the problem as a battle between good individuals and bad individuals, the ideological issue of why *things are the way they are* is automatically avoided. The natural presence of good and bad on both sides —among the rich and the poor, among the oppressors and the oppressed— helps to undermine the warning about this problem. Nevertheless, there is still an important reason why the bad are —and in fact, in large numbers— among the rich, while the poor are mostly good. This reason stems from the previous observations: a *personalization* of a fundamentally social issue takes place. In this process, the oppressed is morally rewarded. This is not just a "consolation" prize, but much more: it is fundamental to maintaining the status quo, since the "moral winner" will not want —nor should, according to this ideology— to usurp the place of the corrupt rich, the bad oppressor. If the reward is no longer in heaven, at least it will be here on earth in the form of the moral pride of the oppressed.

We can summarize what we understand by ideology. An ideology is a system of ideas aimed at social power, domination, or liberation, always for its own benefit. This system of ideas can be articulated in a literary discourse (conscious or deliberate) or it can consist of the reproduction of a social practice (unconscious). Generally, the former are resistant ideologies, while the latter are dominant ideologies.

Pair of opposites order/anarchy

A clear example of semantic manipulation, constructed by ideological discourse, is the definition of the opposites order/anarchy. This can only be considered a "tension" if it is formulated as such, from a dominant ideology. If we quickly analyze each member of the pair, we will see that such a dichotomy does not exist. First of all, because every "order" is a particular form of disorder. My order is another's disorder, if we free ourselves from the prejudices of what is "commonly accepted."

We can analyze this issue by referring to the nearly infinite examples of coups d'état that have occurred throughout history around the world. However, we will quickly examine the problem posed by the play *Squad Towards Death,* by Alfonso Sastre. I choose this example because there is an overwhelming amount of literary criticism on the meaning of "order" and "disorder" with their respective ethical evaluations of each.

Obviously, for an army (the only social framework of *Squad...*) "order" is that which assimilates human beings to machines: geometric formation, mechanical movements that mimic ancient clockwork pieces or more modern robots, are "the virtue of the true man," the institution where fathers sent their sons "to become men," etc.. Anything that expresses feeling, emotions, a predominance of nature's irregularities over the abstraction of line and number, will be seen as "disorder." Abstract order—geometric and algebraic; inhuman—requires a unity to which the parts that compose it are absolutely subjected. If we consider that these "parts" are individuals, we will know what "order" means for a militaristic ideology (though not necessarily "military") that seeks to impose itself on a society striving for the freedom of individuals and—through them, of society—: the so-called disorder. This martial conception of armies may respond to a "practical reason," but it certainly also—and perhaps, above all—responds to a traditional, historically constructed conception of a social group prepared for war.

Through this path, the term "anarchy" was systematically identified by dominant and, in a certain way, reactionary ideologies with chaos. From a mathematical point of view, "chaos" is what has no (intelligible) order; from a physical theory point of view, "chaos" is that which still possesses an order, albeit a complex one: an order highly sensitive to initial conditions. The ideology intervenes here by identifying "chaos"—that is, death, entropy—with anarchy. A society that loses its head (anarchy = decapitation) also loses its body—it dies. However, such an idea assumes, at the same time, that a society is composed of a part with the capacity to think—and thus, to be free—and a corporeal remainder (the "mass") that is incapable of both.

Ideological conclusion: anarchy is death, therefore, one must kill to preserve "order," that is, life.

The characters of *Squad to Death* are trapped in this ideological game, just as the readers or the audience are. But the characters are forgiven, as they are immersed in their circumstances. They cannot act in any other way except by reproducing what they already know. They are aware of their anguish—ethical and existential—but they are not aware of the ideological trap that chains the psychology of each one, in different ways.

To the existential anguish, then, a "psycho-social anguish" is added: ideological oppression. The tension between the social man and the existential man is the eternal self-others tension. The other, a criminal tension, created by a social structure of symbols and dominations: the fear of freedom.

In this sense—in a relationship of ideological oppression—it is infinitely more likely that the oppressed will recognize themselves as ethically and morally at fault than the oppressor will. The main reason lies first in the fact that the oppressor is not recognized as such but, on the contrary, as a benefactor of society from which he benefits. In this sense, it should not surprise us that in the case of former officials, they are always recognized and honored for their long trajectory of "service to their country and society," when we could well see that this service has been amply paid for and for which we should understand that, in reality, society and the country served the honoree in a life without needs or oppressions.

Ideology and creativity

Ideologies proceed by posing dichotomies and, simultaneously, deny the creativity of alternatives. "You have two paths, this one or the other—one good and the other bad." The creativity of the individual and of society can enter their discourse only as a masking instrument. In their practical objective, ideology will deny the plurality of paths by creating two poles: order and chaos, good and evil. The two poles are constructions that will be identified with a certain order and a certain good as they correspond to the ideological interests of a certain class or a certain division caused by the same ideology. Different options cannot be the same good or the same order; they must be mutually exclusive.

Left/Right Polarization

"Which side are you on?" This is the question that looms over any conflict, whether it is warlike, political, or dialectical. Implicitly, "side" means that there are only two options: this one or that one, one or the other, your side or the adversary's side. In any political or sports competition, the contenders must ultimately be reduced to two. This may be a mechanism established on purpose or it may be a "natural" redistribution —ideological. Followers of a sports competition usually regroup on the side of one of the two traditional clubs, thus creating the major contest known as the "classic." The same happens with political party followers. Even if there are many —like sports clubs— the movement of some and others will ultimately lead to regrouping under the banner of one of the two main contenders: in this way, one will be on one side or the other, on the right or on the left. When there are many political groups, they will form coalitions and ultimately alliances to confront the "common enemy."

The left/right dichotomy is one of the most powerful in the ideological imaginary. Beyond its anecdotal historical origin, it likely stems from the fact that humans have two hands, both of which are the most direct extensions of the brain, of the will, etc. However, the vision that these hands oppose each other is ideological, as we could see them as collaborating —like the eyes that focus on a single center— moving forward rather than divergently.

An ideology is a simplification of the world. But when it is a combative or dominant ideology, this simplification reaches its maximum extremes. This is necessary in order to identify the adversary with evil and with rigidly preestablished semantic fields. Moreover, let us not forget that the real battlefield —physical or dialectical— of ideologies is not the academic or philosophical sphere but the political one, the one that is closest to the majority of contemporary populations.

Idea of social mobility; society/individual

The idea that an individual can change their social status by ascending to a higher one is ideologically a bearer of a *paradoxical status quo*: true for some individuals, it is false for society as a whole, which remains structured in social layers. As a theoretical and spiritual principle, it assures us of social mobility and change. However, the change of "social class" is a statistical improbability even in democratic societies.

Through an individual superstition, a social body that contradicts it is sustained. The individual and society are one, separated by an artificial idea of themselves.

Ethical valuation of the semantic body

A dominant ideology is consolidated with the confusion of nature and culture. In this sense, and from a semiotic perspective, Paul de Man says that an ideology is precisely "the confusion of linguistic with natural reality, of reference with fenomenalism" (Man, 19). On the other hand, James N. Laditka expresses a common idea of our era that "[the] narrativity may well be the nature of the world, or at least that partition of our world that we can come to Know" (Laditka,

308). At first glance, both ideas seem contradictory. But they are only so if we place them on the same plane. There is no danger of collision if we place them, like on a highway, on different levels: Man refers to an ideological will or an epistemological confusion; Laditka is speaking from an ontological point of view.

The semantic body does not have ethical value by itself. However, an ideology (especially a dominant one) will seek to establish clear correspondences between both meaningful fields. Semantic bodies that remain undefined, excessively open, and diffuse in their boundaries will be identified with the corruption of values and, later, with Evil. Nevertheless, we must say that every clear definition of the symbol tends to have greater semiotic force than a diffuse one, but it does not necessarily have to be associated with a superior ethical valuation. The sole function of forcing semantic clarity lies in sustaining a particular ideology.

Objections to the word

Psychoanalysis has always told us that the word heals. What he never told us is that the word also sickens. And it's likely that the latter is the rule and the former the exception. The word, in principle, is not an instrument of liberation. The word liberates what it previously oppressed. The word that liberates must be a "specific" awareness of oppression, since the word that oppresses builds its strength in the nature of the unconscious, in that which seems "natural." The word seeks to seduce, conquer, control, dominate, and—ultimately—oppress. The word is the main builder of the physical world, of institutions, of the symbolic world. That is, the word is the main builder of the mute world. Learning is simple; unlearning is almost impossible. Therefore, if knowledge makes us free, it also makes us slaves. There is no sense in understanding knowledge as a unique entity, amoral or—worse—always ethical and virtuous. Knowledge is used to "become aware" as much as to anesthetize, to liberate as much as to oppress.

One of the most ingrained binary oppositions in collective knowledge is the pair ignorance/knowledge. It is assumed that one is the absence of the other, and therefore, to combat ignorance, we must learn certain *knowledge*. To educate is to teach, to learn is to obey. But this process always occurs on a specific axiomatic basis. Learning certain knowledge based on that is simple; but *unlearning* by removing the axioms is an impossible task for a single individual. Mere ignorance is not so much the cause of our "blindness" but the patient construction of it. The absence of knowledge is not in itself the engine of our errors but rather the concepts we have solidified as true or that we cannot perceive as "concepts"; we cannot see them directly as independent entities, but rather we see the world through them. We use them to see, but we cannot see them. Therefore, overcoming ignorance—a metaphysical assumption of a void, a lack of knowledge—is impossible from an epistemological point of view and very simple from a practical one: we "grasp" and confuse that process with a displacement of ignorance. In this sense, learning is entirely possible and immediate. What is difficult is unlearning, freeing ourselves from those concepts that at some point in our lives we have acquired and arbitrarily consolidated. Here lies the center of our blindness; not in what we ignore, but in what we think we know, or—more so—in what we cannot question because it is part of our way of seeing the world. That learning which comes from the culture in which we are born is conservative: it always tends to reproduce its own tradition, its ethical values, and its dominant ideology. However, this situation is not sustainable over time, across generations. Some ways of seeing the world can survive for centuries, others for just a few generations, but eventually they change. The process of unlearning consists of questioning the epistemological axiom. Then, the paradigm collapses due to lack of support, finally and not in all cases, to reconstruct a new system of meanings. However, this new system will have the same epistemological category as the previous one, meaning it will possess an internal symbolic intelligibility and coherence that is more persuasive and convenient.

Ordinary people have been tasked with learning. Philosophers, we entrust with the atrocious task of unlearning.

Social Paradigm

At any given moment, every society has a paradigm or an ethical consensus. The ideological discourse of any group will seek to identify the social paradigm with the actions and the order that directly benefit it, whether morally or materially. If the identification is successful, the groups harmed by those actions or that order will take their sacrifice as something necessary or inevitable to maintain the paradigm, that which is unquestionable.

For example, in the past dictatorships in Latin America the wealthy classes of society were protected and benefited by the armies. These acted by force, imposing physical and moral punishments on thousands of citizens. Even in the use of this primitive methodology, the military and the upper classes needed legitimizing discourse. Among other strategies, one consisted of identifying their action with the discourse of "national security." The country was in danger—in disorder—threatened in its individuality by traitors who had sold their brothers to the external enemy. Of course, they also used other legitimizing ideological words, such as "honor," "liberty," "peace," and "progress."

Charles A. Beard wrote using another example:

> Marines are sent to Nicaragua to subdue the natives. Why? In the national interest. The Navy must be adequate. Adequate to what? Protect the National Interest. [...] If it is in the national interest, nothing more needs be said to stop the mouths and thoughts of inquirers (Iacobelli, 19).

During electoral periods or in regimes without elections, the struggle is—much like in chess—to take control of the center that enjoys consensus. The fight is to align one's own objectives with "justice," "peace," "freedom" and "progress." If society comes to believe that justice, peace, and freedom have been achieved, the primary focus shifts to "progress." It doesn't matter if the discourse comes from the political left, the right, the top, or the bottom.

Thus, we can observe that struggle only arises when interests conflict, and this only happens when interests operate on the same plane. It's the age-old fight over territory. A Buddhist would have no reason to engage in an ideological struggle with a stock market speculator. But a Marxist would. In our Western history, Christ—perhaps its founder—was the first to assert this: his discourse denied all others without directly confronting them. His aim to negate Roman power and the religious authority of his time had to avoid any confrontation. However, the other denied powers placed him within their own ideological frameworks, where he immediately became entangled in conflict. Christ was crucified alongside two thieves under the ironic title "King of the Jews." In other words, he was placed in a position of conflict that his discourse aimed to negate. But, as he himself said, "Let him who has ears hear." His actions were interpreted from a different perspective, resulting in a clash of interests. That might have ears to hear." His actions were interpreted from a different plane, thus creating a conflict of interests.

Today, for example, the paradigm that has been established as unquestionable is "the fight against terrorism." Terrorism is identified with Evil, as it threatens an even more basic and entrenched paradigm: the "struggle for life." However, anyone who manages to align their actions with these earlier paradigms gains the power to act and classify the rest of society—the world—in their own favor.

To ensure that the creative possibilities of thought do not threaten this position, ideology proceeds by simplifying existing options into a pair of opposites. The strategy is to leave no options other than those that place the discourse on the side of Good and those who do not support it on the side of Evil. 1 In his novel "Requiem for a Spanish Peasant," J. Sender describes a Falangist character who is carrying out human cleansing in a village, putting the following words in his mouth: "You're either with us or against us). After the September 11 attacks, President George Bush, before implementing his war plans, was categorical: "You're either with us or against us." On the anniversary of the invasion of Iraq, the same president again defined the options: "There is no neutral ground. There is no neutral place between Good and Evil; there is no neutral place between life and death." Undoubtedly, (1) the identification of one's actions with the social paradigm—life, good—and the subsequent (2) elimination of alternative options achieve a one-dimensional thought that leaves no way out. The power of identifying a person with life and with Good eliminates any possibility of immediate rebuttal. Social—life, good—and the subsequent elimination of alternative options creates a one-dimensional thought that leaves no escape. The strength of identifying a person with life and with Good eliminates any possibility of immediate rebuttal.

Reading

There has always been rereading, and it has had a dual value: first, due to its "liberating" vocation, it has been a way to question past valuations, expose artificial relationships, or ideological constructions that were previously aligned with a paradigm; second, it has also been a way to justify present dominations—that is, rereading has also had its "oppressive" side.

In the Middle Ages, it wasn't questioned. People referred to Aristotle or an authority. That was the truth: it came from the text, not nature. They didn't reread the text and certainly not nature.

After questioning the authority of ancient texts, the Renaissance carried out the exercise of rereading nature. The Enlightenment solidified this reading, positing a possible and ultimately attainable truth. Encyclopedias, dictionaries: the will to fix the meaning of the sign.

Postmodernity questioned the meaningful validity of the sign. There was an "awareness of rereading," but this in itself is not the novelty: history and nature have always been reread.

Unity of the semantic system

In this way, we can say that a language—at least a spontaneous language, not created *ex nihilo*—is not possible through a simple summation of signs that each mean something. On the contrary, the "coexistence" between them is dictated according to their negative fields. It is precisely the negative field of each symbol that allows it to vary and adapt—according to economic, grammatical, etc., reasons—without entering into conflict with the rest of the symbolic universe, becoming meaningful in all its possibilities. It is the negative field of each symbol that part of the symbol capable of dialoguing with the rest of the symbols that make up a linguistic system. It is the negative field of all significant units that structures a language.

A sign with all meanings

One of the major theological problems faced by the Christian religion—and almost all religions—was pantheism. One could think and affirm that "God is everywhere." But to say that "God is everything that exists in the Universe" is a form of negation. God had to be something that we are not —us— but He could also not be something that was the exclusive property of Evil, of the Devil. That is, God and the Devil could not be the same thing.

The problem with something being everything at the same time lies in its weak and almost nonexistent signification: what is everything is nothing. If God is the Universe, God does not exist. *He must be something more or something less.* That is, even God, to be intelligible, must possess a positive field and a negative field. Traditionally, believers consider themselves as part of His negative field: they—we—are not Him. God may be within us, but we can never say that we are the same thing. If we abuse optimism, we can say that we are part of Him, but it will always be necessary to define what-He-is-not: if God were everything—the good and the evil, the good and the bad—there would be no place for ethics.

Another form of "pantheism" is the idea of "Being" for modern philosophers. Heidegger understood that the word *being* was entirely imprecise, since it could not contain something that was everything. Therefore, it had to be written under an erasure. This idea of erasure was taken up by Derrida and extended to the rest of words, in the understanding that every word is an unstable symbol—inadequate yet necessary—with meanings vulnerable to each situation in the text.

Heidegger felt that Being cannot be contained by, is always prior to, indeed transcends, signification. Being is the final signified to which all signifiers refer, the 'transcendental signified.' (Sarup, 35)

This idea of erasure only refers to the impossibility of "defining a symbol," which does not correspond with our idea of semantic fields. We can better understand this by recalling the idea of Gómez-Martínez that the reading of a text is not "undefined" by its variable context but, on the contrary, is defined by the reader at the very moment of reading. Therefore, there is no reason to claim that every symbol always has a relative and necessarily unstable meaning.

Society and individual, or *sociividuality*

When we speak of negative and positive fields, we are not referring to a condition inherent to the sign, but to one inferred by the reader. That is, even in the case of a clear definition of the symbol through a clear definition of semantic boundaries, we cannot say that it must necessarily be shared by two different readers. We can assume a common area, though it always remains conjectural. This is, of course, a phenomenological view. But none of this means that there is no will—and the effect—of a clear and solid definition of the symbol by the reader, without which there would be no language of any kind.

On the other hand, the process of inferring/deducing a meaning to/from a sign is never the product of individual arbitrariness. When I interpret, I am drawing upon memory and the reading codes I've adopted from society, since interpretation is never an isolated act but rather, ultimately, a social one. Even when I exercise my freedom and deconstruct the previous process (meaning), I do so based on prior learning and certain rules that allow me to remain within the realm of potential external intelligibility, within the possibility of communicating my thoughts, my interpretation, the new meanings derived from the process.

The same can be said of a traumatic *experience*: the psychological consequences depend on a *semantic definition* and its corresponding *valuation* of what is "taboo," what is "normal," "moral," or "immoral," etc. These meanings, these valuations, are grounded in a collective reading of the sign. However, a radical act of semantic rebellion could invert or nullify the valuation. For this, a prior social struggle is usually necessary, which consolidates after a certain period of time, during which the inherited sign (an event, a behavior) is resignified and a different consciousness is achieved. This can be the case with the sexual claims of some minorities.

3.5—The Dialectical Adversaries

THE DISPUTE OVER MEANINGS and the explication of a *logos* can, in some cases, be conditioned by moral precepts, judgments, and prejudices, and may even be motivated by sectoral, corporate, social, and political interests that are not necessarily evident, neither to the defender of an ideology nor to the one who suffers from it. Rarely is the struggle for meaning a dialectical dispute based on antiseptic abstract concepts; rather, it is tainted by an innumerable accumulation of ideas and human passions.

To say that Latin Americans have an "underdeveloped mentality" different from those who belong to the successful first world can be an attitude akin to that of the conquerors who justified the miseries of the indigenous people—and their exploitation—by their "superstitious and lazy mentality." It is the same contempt that the Calvinist doctrine derived, contempt for economic failure as a sign of divine condemnation, contempt for the poor rather than for poverty (Fromm, 107).

In his prologue to the *Manual of the Perfect Latin American Idiot*, co-authored by Alberto Montaner, Mario Vargas Llosa summarized the central thesis of this book, which became a best-seller since 1996:

> Without intending to, Mendoza, Montaner and Vargas Llosa seem to have arrived at the same conclusion in their investigations on the intellectual idiocy of Latin America as the American economist Laurence E. Harrison, who, in his controversial essay, asserted years ago that underdevelopment is a "mental illness" (15).

If we view underdevelopment from the perspective of The Open Veins, as part of an international political and economic context where the strongest prevail, this "mental illness" becomes a simple "defeat." This idea can be affirmed using another historical parallel that gives continuity to the narrative of The Open Veins: the indigenous cultures of pre-Columbian America were also defeated, not because of their mental or cultural deficiencies but because they had less military technology. In other words, they had not perfected the art of conquest and domination like the Spanish.

The idea of a "wrong mentality" is not in itself an argument; it is merely a label that one dialectical adversary hurls at the other. The label is not part of an *explanatory logos*, but is rather freely associated with a particular observation that, depending on the case, can be one of development or underdevelopment, success or failure. The same association can be made with a rich man and a poor one. The rich man could be freely associated with the label "intelligent" or "hardworking," while the poor man could be associated with its opposite, "clumsy" or "lazy." However, countless examples show that this could be a rule with more exceptions than confirmations, meaning we cannot articulate any logos through labels.

An important difference between the supporters of the thesis of *Las venas abiertas* and those of *Las raíces torcidas* lies in the fact that the former consider their ideological adversaries—the empires, the great capitals—as endowed with a perverse intelligence. Perverse, but intelligence nevertheless. Unlike these, the supporters of Montaner's thesis sustain a dialectical confrontation based on the "idiocy" of Latin Americans from the first group (Manual del perfecto idiota latinoamericano, 1996). Innocent, but idiocy nonetheless. It could be said that they agree on one thing: the intelligence of the North and the idiocy of the South.

In this sense, even the book *Las venas abiertas* begins with a single quote:

«...*We have kept a silence quite similar to stupidity...*»

(Proclamation of the Junta of Tuitiva in the city of La Paz, July 16, 1809)

Now, this "stupidity" as self-criticism, as a state of unconsciousness, ceases to be a temporary condition to become, in Montaner's thesis, a permanent, historical trait of the Latin American character: the "idiocy"—which, as the only synonym in the Microsoft Word dictionary is "deficiency"

But since Montaner is a supporter of an optimistic ideology—similar to Galeano's, though of a different ideological sign—he does not deny the possibility of recovery from the "mental retardation" of our peoples. The solution consists in starting to think like him and ceasing to be, as Giovanni Papini said, "the stupid continent" (Montaner, 125).

Despite the long list of medical disqualifications used as arguments, the idiocy of the South does not prove the intelligence of the North—rather the opposite—while the intelligence of the North is not enough to conclude the natural idiocy of the peoples of the South. These attitudes simply reveal the initial form of relationship between the dialectical adversaries, which does not differ much from colonial times, when the exploitation —or the backwardness, according to the text— of the Indians was justified by their inability for work and for the Catholic religion —the true faith.

> [In Mexico] the prison, the barracks, and the sacristy were in charge of the fight against the natural defects of the Indians, who, according to a member of a distinguished family of the time, were born "lazy, drunk, and thieves" (Galeano, 194).

The "natural defects" of the Indians —lazy, drunk, and thieves— were also widely used to justify the enslavement of Africans. Even this ethical ideology transitioned into science, taking on a character of objectivity.

Arthur Schopenhauer once wrote that the fact that Black people had fallen predominantly and in large numbers into slavery was evidently a consequence of having less intelligence than the other human races, which, however, did not justify the fact. In the not-too-distant *Dictionary of Psychiatry* by Antoine Porot (1977), a disease is defined as "psychopathology of Black people," referring to the intellectual incapacities of the indigenous people of Africa. After enumerating different syndromes, which could be considered as cultural qualities —oneirism—, "psychosomatic" —such as depression, alcoholism—, and economic —like intestinal parasites and syphilis—, the specialist recommends the repatriation of the sick Black people, not without a large number of escorts, given their dangerousness.

3.6—Two Opposite Vectors of Reading

AS WE SAW AT THE BEGINNING, IN THE dialectical dispute between Sarmiento and Alberdi, the opposition between the supra and infrastructural conceptions was starting to become evident. A bit later, José Martí expressed the same problematic implicitly: "The vain villager believes that the whole world is his village [and] takes the universal order for granted, without knowing that the giants who have seven leagues in their boots and can step on him, nor about the fight of comets in the sky, which move through the sleeping air swallowing worlds. What remains of the village in America must disappear." However, Martí —like many others who maintained this reading— did not renounce the "suprastructural" resource of ideas and consciousness as promoters of change, of criticism as subversion. "Trenches of ideas are worth more than trenches of stone," he wrote, and shortly after confirmed the same idea, always resorting to visual imagery: "No prow can cleave a cloud of ideas" (Martí, America).

Postmodernity, represented in our essay by thinkers like Alberto Montaner, rejects this vision from an extreme standpoint: it is not macropolitics that influence history and the fate of peoples, but their own micropolitics, independent and autonomous thanks to their omnipotent "mentalist" resource, translated into society as a certain cultural expression —of success or failure.

At the other extreme, we find the essays of Eduardo Galeano. For the reading of history that manifests in The Open Veins of Latin America, a change that eliminates the relationship hindering development —and justice— consists of first dismantling the socioeconomic structure upon which society and the unjust order, both domestic and international, are organized. But since every economic and power structure tends naturally to perpetuate itself above individuals and societies, there is no other solution but the rupture, sometimes violent, of the prevailing order. For the same reason —it can be deduced—, and to avoid the rule of Darwinian law, which is the Law of the Jungle, it is necessary to control the freedom of the strongest. Once this stage is reached, the cultural revolution and the psychological change of the inhabitants will gradually transform. Social justice, on the other hand, should be an immediate achievement.

Opposed to this conception of history are thinkers like Alberto Montaner, for whom it is first necessary to change the superstructure —the culture, the psychology of individuals, their motivations— in order to subsequently achieve economic change and, consequently, greater material development. Both also differ in the moral conception of social justice. But this is not so much due to their ascending or descending readings of history as it is to the ideology from which each observes the problem. This would be demonstrated if we see that the political ideology Montaner defends —liberalism, market freedom— is, at its roots, an ascending reading of social dynamics, just as the Marxist reading is. That is, for liberalism or neoliberalism, the unrestricted mobility of individuals and capital results in economic development and, consequently, in moral and cultural development, which should then in turn enhance the freedom of individuals and capital. The metaphor of the invisible hand proposed by Adam Smith is zealously defended by proponents of postmodern liberalism. In it, too, there is an ascending, i.e., materialist, conception of history: once the economic and social conditions for the "invisible hand" are established to operate freely, the economic success of a society is guaranteed. Or at least it will be greatly enhanced.

Let us observe a characteristic of Latin American governments throughout the 20th century: in fact, though not by law, the "prime minister" of governments is the minister of economy. Usually, the appointment of one of these technocrats is awaited with great expectation, and once in office, he is persistently held responsible for economic crises. Ministers of education and culture hardly count. Few care, unless it is a teacher or someone closely linked to traditional culture.

However, and despite the fact that these two opposing conceptions of history are refined in both authors, we can trace some "impurities," that is, certain ideas that each expressed based on an inverse reading to the one they usually make.

Both readings, the ascending —materialist— and the descending —culturalist— are, at their core, "positivist." Both understand history as a process of progress that, though it may go through centuries of catastrophes and injustices, tends naturally toward perfection or, at least, toward overcoming the primitive nature of human beings. For one, this progress consists of greater equality in the opportunities for individual and societal development; for the other, it consists of an increase in the freedom of individuals in their own development, as a precondition for the development of society. For both, the material development and social justice are the objectives of human progress. For both ideological conceptions, the ideal state is anarchism. It was for the early communists until the "transitional authoritarianism," like any great power, always had the aspiration of perpetuation; and it was also for the most optimistic liberals: the near absence of the State. Both survive only as utopias, if not in the writings, in the hermeneutics of them.

Now, distancing ourselves from both authors, we can see that both readings can be partially demonstrated. In other words, we cannot confirm or deny either in relation to the other. On the contrary, we understand that both readings are valid without necessarily being mutually exclusive. Both the economic structures, production, their institutions, and their laws condition the development of individuals and society just as culture, the character of individuals and peoples can do in relation to their economic and social organization.

The scope of history

The scope of history

248

4.1—The historical formation of characters

IN FEBRUARY 2005, AN EVENT occurred that was entirely common for the Mexican people and, by extension, for any people in Latin America: the appearance of the Virgin Mary and the subsequent pilgrimage of thousands of faithful to the place of the miracle. As in many other occasions (these collective sightings happen every week) this image of the Virgin was a kind of elongated oval —vaginal, virginal—, a flat stain rather than a three-dimensional figure. Often these stains or the Virgin Mary appear in very different places, such as a wall, due to a light source, a piece of bread, or a piece of cheese that has been toasted in one way or another. In the case of the Virgin who appeared in the Mexican ravine in February, it was a sewage pipe that, rather unhygienically, freely discharged into that topographic formation. Of course, one could argue that the sewer pipe was only an instrument of the miracle. But it is strange to think that a divine miracle needs some logical mechanism to occur. By definition, a miracle is something improbable, something that contradicts the logical and the necessary. Of course, this warning, about the origin of the stain, was insignificant to the believers, and the image of the "black virgin" —like the Virgin of Guadalupe— continued to be venerated as a new miracle. The message of these apparitions is never clear, and the believers care nothing more than the phenomenon of the image itself. When they do not go to ask the image to solve problems that a more just society could have solved or, at least, avoided.

This is one of the religious and cultural traits of much of Latin America. Despite their similarities, we can also see great differences within the apparently uniform body of this continent. There will be no shortage of those offended by this note, as if being different in some way endangered the "identity" of each of the parts.

These differences can be explained by the very history shared by the Ibero-American peoples, which can be better appreciated in contrast with the other, the North American one. Unlike this, the Spanish conquest was not only a process of land occupation and displacement of indigenous peoples. It was also a process of miscegenation and syncretism of their own blood and customs with the blood and customs of the natives south of the Rio Grande. The large populations the Spanish found in America and the more developed cultures of peoples such as the Aztecs, the Maya, or the Incas caused an encounter and confrontation that did not occur, with the same drama and with the same consequences, in the north.

Perhaps for this very reason, the Spanish colonization in those American lands that were the seat of great indigenous cultures was carried out differently from what took place in other regions of the continent, such as the Southern Cone. This region shares with the rest a Spanish heritage, a history, somewhat similar to the rest: the administrative bureaucracy of the Crown and the cultural and economic dependence on the European metropolis; the perception of the state and the law as a distant and invisible power, at the same time illegitimate and omnipresent. It does not share, however, a history of impositions, of "cultural traumas," as could have been the conquest of the spirit of great civilizations that still survive hidden, beneath the Christian habit, the distrustful gesture.

In the Río de la Pata, the fate of the (relatively) few natives was not very different from that of those encountered by the Anglo-Saxon colonists in North America: exile or death, which doesn't even weigh in the collective memory of its current inhabitants.

The fervent —and sometimes fanatical— veneration of the Virgin Mary is more characteristic of the peoples of Mexico, Central America, and the Andes than it is of Chile, Argentina, and Uruguay. These countries, while they have received the influence of indigenous culture mainly from the rest of the continent, have never been characterized by a massive religious fervor for any Virgin, as is the case in Mexico, for example.

We know that the ancient indigenous deities mixed with the new Spanish deities; that the Virgin Mary —venerated here as nowhere else in the world— not only took the place of ancient mother goddesses but also had to fill the enormous "emptied" space of pre-Columbian spirituality. Coatlicue also conceived the god Huitzilopochtli without sin, through feathers that fell upon her from the sky. This blending of deities is expressed in their own representations and ancient rituals, which, thank God, no longer include human sacrifices, partly due to the new faith and partly due to the inevitable evolution of human customs through history.

However, this salvation (or spiritual colonization) was not achieved simply through dialogue and love. There was no possible dialogue between the Virgin Mary and the barbaric Aztec deities. Simply, the one with the greater military power prevailed, not without long and bloody battles. The new faith, the true one (for being victorious), was imposed by any means necessary, often resorting to physical and spiritual punishment, imposing the forgetting of ancient beliefs that were an inseparable part of a great civilization that included millions of men and women. Today, the ancient Aztec fanaticism has turned into a peaceful fervor for different mestizo variations of the European Virgin (a variation, in turn, of the improbably blonde mother of Jesus). If we cannot call it obsession or fanaticism, it is due to a cultural consolidation that imposes the representation and interpretation of this sensibility as the genuine act of the highest faith, rather than mere iconoclastic fetishism. But the veneration of the maternal icon persists, even above the worship of her own Son. As if the spirit of the ancient Aztec mother goddess had taken over the Christian image, after years of religious indoctrination of a deeply religious people.

4.2—The Millennial Heritage of Ideas

PARADOXICALLY, NEITHER EDUARDO GALEANO nor Alberto Montaner, in their essays on Latin America, will spend much time analyzing the culture of Latin American peoples compared to European culture, in its two variants: the Latin current and its Anglo-Saxon variation. For most of The Twisted Roots, Montaner traces the origins of certain psychological traits of contemporary Latin American society — sexism, racism, xenophobia, slavery — to medieval Spain, ancient Rome, and even older Greece.

> If the premise of this book is that the institutions and behavior of Latin Americans must be traced back to Western tradition, the obligatory starting point is Greece (77).

In Plato and Aristotle, he finds the representatives of statism and free trade, respectively. According to Montaner, "there are ideas centuries old, sometimes millennia old, that become embedded in the intellectual memory of peoples" (100). These ideas, in turn, are responsible for beliefs and superstitions that are transmitted through cultural heritage and define certainties that are unconsciously unquestioned.

> It is highly likely that a Bolivian rural unionist or a Paraguayan small businessman has never read a word of Aristotle, or may even be completely unaware of the existence of Thomas Aquinas, but that ignorance does not spare them the consequences of these and other powerful thinkers in our tradition (Montaner, 100).

The central thesis of the book *The Twisted Roots* is a widely shared principle, though not immune to questioning: the present character of the Ibero-American people is the consequence of their history. A second postulate stands with the first: this cultural character is responsible for its own failure. Under these premises, there is a risk of holding Plato accountable for Latin American underdevelopment.

This choice is questionable if we consider that, as we saw before, the central idea of Latin America's failure is a direct consequence of the comparison with a certain idea of success, specifically with the idea of success in Anglo-Saxon America. That is, the crucial and, therefore, significant moment should not be sought in a history that is common to both groups but in the historical moment when this cultural split, the difference, occurs. A moment that, in any case, is not overlooked by Alberto Montaner, but is delayed by a pile of probably dispensable pages that help distract or diminish the importance of this historical split.

On the other hand, the idea that the identity and current order of a given people are a *cumulative* consequence and are *determined* by a historical chain of events is refutable. Without a doubt, individuals and peoples are full of history. Often, their choices, behaviors, and ways of thinking are indebted to their own history, sometimes in ways unsuspected until a meticulous analysis brings them to light. But it would be hyperbolic to think that each event completely contains the series that precedes it. We can see in history that in each event there are persistences of previous events as well as absences and forgettings, both confirmations and negations. The difference between two simultaneous historical events is explained not mechanically, as an almost infinite relationship of causes and effects of each and all previous events, but by the omission of some and the continuity of others. In this dynamic, not only is the new produced but also the difference, a product of different novelties, different persistences, and different omissions. We can think that everything on earth is a variation of past ideas and that, therefore, absolute originality does not exist. However, with ancient elements, novelties can be obtained, just as white is the composition of the seven colors and is something different from blue, yellow, or red.

This means that, although we can find the Platonic origin of Latin American authoritarianism in Greece, the idea that only the best-prepared individuals are capable of governing a people, we can also recognize its absence in the societies that the same author is pointing out as "different" in this regard: the Anglo-Saxon society. This society, in turn, shares the same Greek heritage. The difference, then, lies in the choices made at each moment by individuals and peoples. And each choice is, at the same time as the affirmation of something, *the denial of something more* or of the rest.

Beyond the already analyzed "failure of Latin America" (3.2), Montaner observes other traits that he recognizes as characteristic of this society. For example, sexism, racism, and xenophobia. However, he does not take the time to prove that these characteristics are unique to Latin America and uncommon elsewhere in the Western world. Montaner presents them as indisputable observations whose origins must be traced as new offshoots of twisted roots. He also finds these origins in Europe one thousand and two thousand years ago. Xenophobia, for example, is not only an ethical distortion but also another cause of economic backwardness. The proof, according to Montaner, lies in the fact that while the countries of Central Europe encouraged the immigration of artisans, Spain expelled the Jews in 1492 and the Moors in 1606, while also prohibiting the presence of foreigners in America (155).

One might think that in a *cultural split*, the Anglo-Saxon and Protestant world freed itself from these original characteristics of Europe, which allowed for greater development. However, it is not proven that the Anglo-Saxon world lacked widespread racist, sexist, and xenophobic practices... quite the opposite.

As a conclusion to this point, we can say that although (1) the hypothesis of cultural heritage as defining a present social trait can be traced through history, (2) its scope is not entirely clear. Moreover, (3) this history, responsible for the character of Latin America is also the same history of Anglo-

Saxon societies, and therefore does not constitute a "distinctive factor" that helps to understand the assumed difference between the two societies.

4.3—The Modern Revolution That Never Arrived

UNDER THE TITLE "THE REVOLUTION THAT CHANGED THE WORLD," Montaner discusses the rejection of scholasticism represented by Erasmus of Rotterdam or Juan Luis Vives (143) and the educational reform of Protestantism (144). At this point, Montaner emphasizes what, in his view, will signify the cultural, social, and economic differences between the Protestant world and the Catholic world of Spain and Portugal. The latter will continue with an intellectual tradition that will not allow for the modern revolution that was taking place in the countries of Central Europe.

> By the end of the 16th century, Jesuit pedagogy was systematized with the *ratio studiorum*. It is a comprehensive method used in all disciplines: preselection, concentration, exercises, repetition (Montaner, 145).

Meanwhile, in England

> what Newton represented in the scientific field had its political equivalent in the work of his friend John Locke, also English, a physician, jurist, and pedagogue who laid the theoretical foundations of the modern liberal state. (150)

For its part, France had a heavyweight anti-Jesuit: Voltaire.

> This vast movement of paradigm shifts reached Spain in a muted form and was almost imperceptible in America. [...] It likely has to do with the attitude of the Habsburgs and, especially, the ironclad control that the most orthodox religious figures had over education and cultural dissemination. (151)

The Counter-Reformation —characteristic of Spain— strengthened scholastic culture as a reaction not only to religious changes but also to the social, political, and ideological shifts coming from beyond the Pyrenees. It was a reactionary movement, as its name suggests, which perpetuated itself both in the peninsula and in the New World.

4.4—The Legacy of Social Orders

The Demographic Component

LATIN AMERICA NOT ONLY INHERITED from Spain its rigid social order, its ancient educational systems, and its top-down conception of power, its laws, and many of itsinstitutions. It also inherited part of the pre-Columbian social structures, especially those from the western strip of the new continent, from the countries that today belong to the mountainous regions with coastlines along the Pacific Ocean. In the books of Galeano Montaner, this inheritance is not read with the same intensity as the cultural heritage of Spain and Portugal.

Furthermore, the encounter—mestizaje and discrimination—between native and colonizing cultures gave rise to a new order, a particular order that shaped the identity of the continent. An order distinct from the peninsular one.

One characteristic of this new order is that it was born conservative. Montaner notes in the early pages of his book what may be his most solid hypothesis: political and social power was born illegitimate in this land and remains so to this day. Another observation about the peculiarities of the new society is debatable: the high indigenous component is the cause of its underdevelopment, as it is why Latin America could not absorb the values and modern mindset of old and revolutionary England.

According to Montaner, there was a demographic imbalance of a different nature between North America and Latin America. When the Spanish and Portuguese conquered the center and south of the continent, they encountered numerous populations and societies organized with strong and ancient traditions. In contrast, in North America, Australia, and Canada, the population was "insignificant": the tribes were small and scarce—compared to the Incas, Mayas, and Aztecs—, while European settlers quickly became an absolute majority. (19). However, it is not specified that in vast regions of South America the demographic condition and even the displacement of the sparse indigenous populations was very similar to that encountered by the Anglo-Saxon settlers in what is today the United States.

The idea that a significant native population was an obstacle to the development of a modern and progressive mindset—the English one—would be proven, according to Montaner, by observing colonization in India, where the

Anglo-Saxon mindset did not imprint its material develop-ment, whereas it did in Canada and Australia, where the in-digenous presence was insignificant or disregarded (19). Along the same ideological lines, Carlos Rangel expressed a similar idea in different words:

> The Anglo-Saxon colonists came in search of land and free-dom, not gold and slaves. The indigenous peoples, having been expelled from the territory or exterminated, did not need to be rejected or integrated socially or psychologi-cally. In contrast, this need has been the central fact and continues to be the cancer of Latin America [...] As a result, we Latin Americans are simultaneously the descendants of the conquerors and the conquered people, of the masters and the slaves, of the abductors and the violated women. (Rangel, 31)

The idea of the search for freedom by the Anglo-Saxon colonists is no less romantic nor less mythological than that of the Noble Savage. The extermination of indigenous peo-ples as the cause of North American progress and mestizaje as the cancer of Latin America is, at the very least, repugnant. But it also represents a thesis widely disseminated among a portion of Latin American "thinkers" and, therefore, we must take it into account.

Eduardo Galeano responded to arguments of this type thirty years earlier. According to his view, many other coun-tries that belonged to the British Empire and that fulfilled the same economic role as Latin American countries—sup-plying raw materials to English industry—fared the same fate as those that were Iberian colonies and provided wealth to the Crown for other purposes. That is, the same fate of exploitation and underdevelopment.

> It was not racial factors, as it appears, that determined the development of some and the underdevelopment of others: the British islands of the Antilles had nothing of Spanish or Portuguese [...] North American industrialization benefited, even before independence, from official incentives and protections. England showed tolerance, while strictly prohibiting its Antillean islands from manufacturing even a pin. (Galeano, 216)

The initial idea of an "illicit" conception of power in Latin America — as a result of the relationship between the Crown and its Spanish subjects and the indigenous peoples dispossessed and enslaved by the Crown's subjects — loses weight with the new "demographic" hypothesis — not to say "racial" — supported by Montaner. In the "demographic hypothesis," there is a risk of concluding that the origin of "success" lies in Anglo-Saxon culture, in its purity. The problem now would be non-Anglo-Saxon cultures, not necessarily pre-Columbian ones — as in the case of India — and not the previously held notion about the "illegitimacy" of the State and power, of conquest and colonization.

Iberian society

For his part, Eduardo Galeano sees no origin of economic backwardness in the indigenous component. Consistent with his conception of the conquest and colonization of the new continent, he attributes a negative legacy from ancient Spanish and Portuguese society.

According to Galeano, the expulsion of Jews and Spanish Arabs deprived Spain of artisans and capital. The same effect had resulted from the expulsion of Protestant Flemish, who were welcomed by England, giving a significant boost to British manufacturing. At the same time, the upper classes had a clear idea about honor and wealth. Spanish aristocrats devoted themselves to luxury and income, without paying taxes or being imprisoned for their debts.

> Anyone who engaged in industrial activity automatically lost their noble status [...] Each year, between eight hundred and one thousand ships unloaded in Spain products manufactured by others. (Galeano, 38)

This same idea will be revisited by Montaner in his critique of the Spanish and later Latin American conception of wealth. He will also share with Galeano a strong critique of the Spanish way of conceiving and organizing public affairs. In Spain, according to Galeano, by the mid-16th century, the import of foreign fabrics was authorized while the export of Castilian products to anywhere other than America was prohibited. A decree from this same period prohibited the import of foreign books and prevented students from studying abroad. Both the looms and the students of Salamanca were dramatically reduced (37).

Due to its bureaucracy, its complexity, and the distances that documents had to travel from America to Spain, lawsuits lasted decades, and there was a sense of the near impossibility of justice. "In Spain, that [jurisdiction] worked poorly. In America, worse" (Montaner, 46).

Despite the gold from America, the Spanish state went bankrupt five times in the 16th and 17th centuries. The Crown conceived its possessions as a source of income to fund itself. (Montaner, 112).

> The capital that remained in America [...], did not generate a process analogous to that of Europe to lay the foundations for industrial development but was diverted to the construction of grand palaces and ostentatious temples. [...] To a large extent, that surplus also remained immobilized in the purchase of new lands or continued to circulate in speculative and commercial activities. (Galeano, 46)

The Iberian conception of wealth through the possession of gold and silver deposits contrasted with the new British thinkers: wealth lies in development, and this is generated, primarily, through work and human capital.

At this point, our two dialectical opponents will agree. However, while Montaner will affirm the thesis of Adam Smith (1723-1790), according to which this mechanism works better with minimal state intervention and maximum freedom for private capital, Galeano will find in "the invisible hand of the market" a different historical meaning: the invisible hand is not the hand of a wise and just god but that of a perverse demiurge: the "invisible hand" does not save and administer justice and progress but steals and enslaves for the benefit of capital accumulation, thus producing greater social injustice and, consequently, preventing "true development."

Fragmentation of an Imagined Union

But, for Galeano, the negative legacy was not only what the Spanish Crown left at the time of colonization. On the contrary, he also considers the existence of another growing empire, a substitute for the Spanish one, which meant not a colonization of lands but an economic colonization: Galeano sees in the intervention of the British Empire one of the reasons for the dismemberment of Latin America.

Another reason, consistent with it, for the fragmentation—frustration—of the new great nation lay in the nature of the new Creole society.

"An archipelago of countries—says Galeano—, disconnected from each other, emerged as a consequence of the frustration of our national unity" (431). At the moment of the birth of the Latin American nations, there was unity of languages but a lack of "economic unity"

The existence of a landowning ruling class and the absence of an entrepreneurial and capitalist bourgeoisie, as in the United States, made the state fulfill the role of industrialization. But the new industrialization was inserted into an immovable social structure—conservative, aristocratic, semifeudal—which also produced great social inequalities. (Galeano, 347).

In this last selection of historical "facts," and in the attribution of their significance—their responsibility for the backwardness of Iberoamerican societies—there is a tacit agreement between our contenders.

The Myth of Latin American Unity

The idea of Latin America as a unit is more a product of the dreamers of independence and the intellectuals of the 19th century than a reality expressed in history. On the contrary, history shows a strong tendency towards fragmentation, a product more of the political and economic interests of the dominant landowning classes, who were never willing to give up some of their privileges for the benefit of a union or integration. This division may have been favored by international interests, according to an interpretation of *The Open Veins of Latin America*, but it materialized above all in a culture predisposed to it. Already in 1830, José María Luis Mora wrote in Mexico:

> Our federation was formed in an inverse manner to that of the United States of North America; the latter went from the circumference to the center; ours from the center to the circumference; there, the states created the federal government; here, the federal government gave political existence to the states; in the North, many independent states were constituted into a single Nation; in Mexico, an indivisible and unique Nation, divided itself into independent states to a certain extent. Assuming these principles, who could doubt that, if in the North the States gave the law to the Federal Government, in Mexico the Federal Government must give it to the States? (Mora, 633)

Thus arose smaller and smaller regions —such as in Central America, as in other unjustified regions further south— each of which responded to chiefs and caudillos who could better monopolize power in the form of *a country* created to their measure, to the measure of their personal influences and not of a province based on a constitution that went beyond the individual and the renowned families. Even today we can see this myth of "Hispanic" unity in the United States that goes no further than the self-interests of each group, of each social class. Even today we can see the terrible difficulties of integration in the continent south of the Rio Grande (as José Martí imagined in Our America, more than a hundred years ago) when cultural elements such as language, history, and customs would seem to indicate that this integration should be more "natural" than what the European countries have actually achieved, despite their great cultural, political, and historical differences.

4.5—The Legacy of Economic Structures

THE ECONOMIC SYSTEM AND SOCIAL STRUCTURE are expressed in culture in many ways. One of them is the organization of its physical space, an incorruptible document though not free from conflicting interpretations. In these human traces on the Latin American territory, Galeano sees other proofs of the lack of communication and, therefore, of the real fragmentation of the imagined unity.

> The result is evident: today, any of the international corporations operates with greater coherence and sense of unity than this set of islands that is Latin America [...] The drama is reproduced on a regional scale. The railroads and roads created to transport production abroad through the most direct routes still constitute undeniable proof of the

> impotence or incapacity of Latin America to bring to life
> the national project of its most lucid heroes. (Galeano,
> 433)

As examples, he mentions the absence in Brazil —in 1970— of connections with Colombia, Peru, and Venezuela. The cities of the Atlantic had no cablegraphic communication with those of the Pacific "so that telegrams between Buenos Aires and Lima or Rio de Janeiro and Bogota inevitably passed through New York" The same was true for telephone lines between the Caribbean and the South. "Latin American countries continue to identify each with its own port, a denial of their roots and real identity" (Galeano, 434).

The struggle between centralism and federalism was resolved in favor of the former. Most Latin American countries have the highest concentrations of population in their capitals. The federalist ideas of José Artigas failed before the central power of Buenos Aires.

> The centralism of the Peninsular government did not encourage responsibility and self-government in the vast territories of the Indies. (Montaner, 46)

This centralism is also a legacy of the Spanish Crown —dating back to the times of the commercial monopolies imposed on the colonies— and will deepen according to the economic model of "exporter countries of raw materials" after independence, which can be read in the road and railway maps of the continent.

The Ownership of Land

In 1836, in *El Araucano* of Chile, Andrés Bello wrote that those who criticized the Hispano-American peoples believed that representative principles could not be applied to our peoples. These principles, "which have been so happily applied in the United States, and which have made English settlements a great nation that daily increases in power, industry, commerce, and population, could not produce the same result in Spanish America" Bello observes an initial different condition in the North and the South. "The situation of these peoples at the time of achieving independence was essentially different: some had properties divided, so to speak, evenly, while others saw property accumulated in a few hands" The same idea will be taken up by Eduardo Galeano one hundred and thirty years later in The Open Veins (121), without the reality of land ownership in 1970 being much different from that in 1836.

> The former were accustomed to the exercise of great political rights while the latter had not enjoyed them, nor even had an idea of their importance. The former were able to give liberal principles the full scope they enjoy today, and the latter, though emancipated from Spain, had within their midst a large and influential class, with whose interests they clashed. These have been the main reasons why the enemies of our independence have affected despair over the consolidation of our Governments (Bello, Republics).

This long quote, written 169 years ago, summarizes not only the thesis of *Las venas abiertas* and *Las raíces torcidas*, but also expresses a problem and an awareness (or *tardocon-science*) that is dramatically experienced today by many Latin American countries, especially Mexico and Venezuela: the problem of land distribution as the key to economic development and a social justice order. The global, economic, and technological context has changed drastically; however, the problem continues to be viewed as it was then.

In 1970 Eduardo Galeano observed that the road networks, which expressed a particular economic and productive conception, also demonstrated a form of land ownership. For Galeano, both the latifundio and "its poor relative", the minifundio —in Colombia, Costa Rica, and Mexico— were responsible for agricultural backwardness and the rest of the economy (203). As we noted earlier, this form of ownership and production was not seen by the land workers as a benefit for themselves but rather in terms of a proprietary class or the holder of the price and final consumption of the goods produced. This idea coincides with Montaner's later note on the illegitimacy of wealth and power. "The region progresses without freeing itself from the structure of its backwardness," Galeano understood (407).

The large capital cities, where political power and the concentration of wealth were established, were increasingly encircled by belts of poverty, characteristic of Latin America, where the dispossessed rural populations were displaced. This physical structure, an expression of illegitimacy and underdevelopment, in turn constitutes an obstacle to development itself. According to the metaphor of Sadosky, cited by Galeano, "It's like a clock that is running slow and is not fixed. Even though its hands keep moving forward, the difference between the time it shows and the actual time will keep growing" (407).

The scope of history

Twisted Roots

5.1—The Illegitimacy of Wealth

Social Disparities

THE COEXISTENCE OF THE WRETCHED with the ostentation of the rich forms, a priori, a representation of underdevelopment, according to modern conceptions of progress and social justice. And it is precisely this reality that is first recognized in Latin American societies as part of their present and historical particularity. Which immediately leads us to the idea of illegitimacy or injustice. This idea of "twisted roots" is noted by Galeano when he cites Alexander von Humboldt:

> Perhaps nowhere is inequality more ghastly. The architecture of public and private buildings, the refinement of women's attire, the air of society—everything declares an extreme of care that stands in stark contrast to the nakedness, ignorance, and rusticity of the common people (Galeano, 56).

Already in the early 1800s, a European observed what many commentators repeat today: "perhaps nowhere is inequality more ghastly."

The Original Sin

In the reading of the two texts under study, we will find repeated mentions of the stripping of minerals first, and of basic consumer products later. The first due to political and military imposition; the second due to international economic reasons. The interpretation of this "exploitation" carries valuations of different signs.

With less insistence, the fate of millions of indigenous people who were enslaved and killed in the name of religion or European interests first, and creole interests later, is noted. Tens of millions of Indians died from disease or were exploited in gold, silver, and, above all, mercury mines. The same applies to the lucrative exploitation of African slaves who died at sea or in production fields. This history, marked by dispossession and genocide, is often set aside but cannot be forgotten. Monuments and museums dedicated to the indigenous and African holocaust are practically nonexistent; instead, bronze monuments to caudillos who ordered or participated in the massacres of indigenous people are not uncommon. The American Indians not only lost their civilizations, but also their lands. They were displaced when not outright killed. Among the ancient indigenous cultures, their bloody rituals are often remembered as a way of justifying their exploitation, just as the Catholics who exploited them to death for not abandoning their beliefs used to do.

The perception of injustice and illegitimacy survived the Iberian conquest. As in other realms, a rigid continuity was established. This is evident in another quote from Humboldt:

> In 1802, another cacique descended from the Incas, Astor-
> pilco, was visited by Humboldt. [...] as he walked, he spoke
> of the fabulous treasures hidden beneath the dust and
> ashes. "Do you not sometimes feel the urge to dig for treas-
> ures to meet your needs?" Humboldt asked. And the
> young man replied: "No such urge comes to us. My father
> says it would be sinful. If we had gold branches with all
> golden fruits, the white neighbors would hate us and harm
> us" (Galeano, 70).

That is to say, Galeano once again rescues the idea that
one's own wealth attracts the greed of others and, consequently, misfortune. This idea leads us to another: wealth is
evil, it is immoral—sinful. Ultimately, it is illicit. The notion
of wealth as the origin of sin is of Christian and later Catholic
origin. Undoubtedly, this religious factor could have perme-
ated the mentality of the colonized, but in this paragraph,
Galeano refers to the inappropriateness of wealth from a geopolitical and commercial standpoint. Wealth has brought
more slavery and death than poverty. Therefore, poverty is
better than wealth in the historical consciousness of the colonized. This idea is, of course, entirely opposed to the Calvinist ethic of economic success, as noted in Chapter 3.

According to Galeano, the dispossession continued with
the enslavement of those indigenous people who were dedicated to agriculture and who were forced to work in mines
or on the lands from which they had been dispossessed. In
this way, he not only continues his historical narrative but
also reinforces the logic he intends to highlight: the enslavement and exploitation of indigenous peoples. The dispossession—according to this author—continued until the 20th
century. As an example, he mentions the moment when

agrarian reform was announced in Peru in the late sixties: "still, newspapers frequently reported that the Indians from the broken communities in the highlands would, from time to time, invade the lands that had been stolen from them or their ancestors, waving flags, and were repelled by gunfire from the army" (70).

Galeano does not preach poverty, but he finds its origins—both psychological and structural—in (1) the dispossession by others and (2) the dispossession by one's self. The former is driven by ambition; the latter by injustice and lack of consciousness. Montaner would agree only with the second point, though not with the interpretation of the terms "injustice" and "awakening of consciousness."

5.2—Education and Intellectual Production

The Persistence of an Anachronistic Model

UNLIKE *TWISTED ROOTS*, in *Open Veins of Latin America* there is not the same insistent reference to formal education, particularly concerning the characteristics of new Latin American universities and their historical origins. However, there is no imminent discrepancy noticed in this aspect; rather, some phrases and ideas seem to confirm a possible agreement had Galeano dedicated a chapter to this issue.

According to Montaner, both Spain and Portugal scorned the scientific and technological knowledge that was fundamental in Anglo-Saxon societies. Citing Miguel de Unamuno, with one of his outbursts, "Let them invent!", the author traces this mentality into the 20th century on the Iberian Peninsula. Conversely, the Iberian conception of art fostered significant development in painting and literature.

> The contribution of our people to the cultural adventure of the West is minimal in the scientific and technical fields, though not in the artistic sphere, where the presence of Spain and Latin America is truly remarkable (Montaner, 126).

This same idea of Montaner was already explicit in Open Veins of Latin America: "Portugal, too, could not rescue any creative force other than the aesthetic revolution" (Galeano, 89). The Spanish Golden Age only manifested itself in the arts, since they did not clash with the traditional conception of society (Montaner, 152). To make matters worse, educational institutions remained tied to scholastic tradition. That is, there was no productive aim in intellectual creation. "Curiously, the first educational institutions established by the Spanish in America were not created for the benefit of whites, but for the Indians. However, there was no altruism in this but a clear intention of social control, coupled with missionary zeal" (Montaner, 130). Education was a tool of indoctrination and intellectual colonization.

> Naturally, children learned little in the "Indian schools": sacred history, letters, numbers, religious hymns —they sang incessantly, which seemed to please both the priests and the Indians, and some trades. Neither originality nor independent formation was expected of them. It was formative-repetitive instruction (Montaner, 131).

The first universities in Latin America were based on the scholastic model, Verba, non res, where experimentation and proof were of little importance compared to the authority of a prestigious author. For the 12th-century Church, "lay" studies meant "idiotic" studies: Laicus comes from lapis, which means "stone" (Montaner, 139). That which was intelligent, wise, then, consisted in following the authors consecrated by the ecclesiastical tradition. These authors might not be the same, but the intellectual attitude remained unaltered: the alumnus —the "nourished one"— was to study and assimilate without question the texts imposed by the education system. This submission had, moreover, a medieval religious motivation (Huizinga): "few things could be more displeasing in the eyes of God than 'intellectual pride.' Not even being a recognized master is enough to have one's own ideas. One of the bitterest complaints of Roger Bacon —a scholar himself— directed against Albertus Magnus, later proclaimed a saint and doctor universalis, was that the German, lecturer at the University of Paris, presented his theses, his opinions, as authentic. It is worth returning to the example: what invalidated the reasoning of Albertus Magnus was not the merits or errors of his approaches, but the lack of auctoritas" (Montaner, 133)

The current academic model, inherited from ancient Greece and based on the *trivium* and the *quadrivium*, was valued and prioritized in different ways according to the European societies of the 16th and 17th centuries. The *trivium* (trivial) referred to grammar, rhetoric, and dialectic (the formal). On the other hand, the *quadrivium* studied arithmetic, music, geometry, and astronomy. "There was the irrefutable reason" —wrote Montaner— in the quadrivium (135).

Meanwhile, the Iberian societies that had scorned the scientific and technological revolution in favor of rhetoric and the formality of discourse had become mired in the past. Montaner even cites the Stoic from Córdoba, Seneca, who centuries earlier had stated that the classic seven pillars of wisdom —the seven classical subjects— did not make men better, as they needed an education of correct values (134).

> What was the essence of Latin education? Without a doubt: form, word, gesture. They sought eloquence above all else, the cultured citation of some classical text, uttering a felicitous phrase in the appropriate tone and with precise gesture (Montaner, 136).

This "Latin" and "Greco-Roman" heritage maintains its continuity until finding a safe place in Latin America, through its Iberian colonizers. "There is a connecting thread that starts from Greece and, in its time, will reach America" (138).

A Reactionary Society

When in 1492 Isabella the Catholic and Ferdinand of Aragon expelled the Moors and Jews, they deprived themselves of their best intellectuals. Montaner makes this observation and corresponding judgment (142), and it aligns with Galeano's view regarding the same historical events: "The defense of the Catholic faith served as a mask for the struggle against history," says Galeano, emphasizing the loss of the artisan class —the technicians of the time— with the expulsion of Moors, Jews, and Flemish, who, in turn, went into exile to

England to contribute to the process of changes then taking place in Northern Europe (38). Neither text mentions the printing revolution as a democratizing factor for the lower classes. Only Montaner notes the trend toward literacy as part of the process of social revolution: "By the end of the 17th century, seventy-five percent of the French are illiterate. In Germany, this proportion is reduced to fifty-five percent" (144).

However, consistent with the reactionary impulse against these changes, the rigidity and social immobility in the Iberian Peninsula were consolidated with the Counter-Reformation. At the Council of Trent (1545-1563), the (1) Counter-Reformation was organized, (2) the Inquisition was revitalized, (3) the Index was established, a kind of thought police that judged heretical books to be destroyed, and (4) the Society of Jesus emerged, a kind of militia for the Pope (Montaner, 145). Ignatius of Loyola founded the Jesuit movement, so influential in the Americas, and shortly thereafter, several educational organizations governed by them emerged.

> By the end of the 16th century, the Jesuit pedagogy was systematized with the Ratio Studiorum. It is a comprehensive method used in all disciplines: preselection, concentration, exercises, repetition (Montaner, 145-146).

The ex-Jesuit René Descartes criticized in his Discourse on the Method the education he received at La Flèche. Descartes was banned by the Church for questioning the idea that truth comes through revelation and authority. Instead, Descartes proposed doubt and analysis. (Montaner, 146). On the other side of the English Channel, Francis Bacon proposed reaching true knowledge through experiment and progress through science, while in the Iberian Peninsula, they insisted on formalist methods.

This tradition, the foundation of formal education in Latin America, had its consequences in the 20th century. As Galeano puts it, "Latin America does not apply the results of scientific research for its own benefit for the simple reason that it has none. [...] the mere transplantation of technology from advanced countries not only implies cultural subordination but also [...] does not solve any of the problems of underdevelopment" (406). He adds that "Latin American universities train, on a small scale, mathematicians, engineers, and programmers who, in any case, cannot find work except in exile" (408).

On the other hand, in the nationalization processes initiated in some countries, such as in Juan Domingo Perón's Argentina, "the state did not realize in time that if it did not give birth to its own technology, its nationalist policy would take off with clipped wings" (349).

Meanings of 'The Twisted Roots'

It is significant that a book like *The Twisted Roots of Latin America*, which proposes to analyze the ideological culture of Latin America, and whose central thesis is the idea of its almost absolute responsibility for its own failure, devotes more than fifty percent of its pages to the analysis of the history of Europe and the United States. Montaner traces "the twisted roots" of Latin America in an intellectual tradition that developed in Europe over twenty-five centuries. To clarify this apparent disproportion, we must understand that what in this extensive period is called "twisted roots" is only so from a contemporary perspective. That is, the flaws noted in Greek, Roman, and later Latin education processes not only belong to the same common trunk from which Anglo-Saxon culture also derives but also do not necessarily need to be considered "flaws" from a Greek, Roman, or medieval point of view. Thus, the meaning of a twisted root stems not so much from its origin but from its continuity. That is, it transforms into a "flaw" or a deficiency—according to Montaner's interpretation—when reacting against the change promoted by countries that would later be recognized as "developed." Quoting Ortega y Gasset, Montaner notes that there was no Renaissance in Spain. Nor was there an Enlightenment (152)

Now, if we seek to evaluate these unquestioned historical facts, we may find conflicts in meaning. In his enthusiastic narration of the new process initiated in Protestant countries, Montaner observes that the ancient bell makers became cannon makers. "The bell, combined with gunpowder, gives the cannon" (Montaner, 154). Later, in a kind of ethical vindication of new technologies, it is pointed out that the cannon gave rise to the internal combustion engine.

The question remains whether progress must be pursued at any cost, whether there is greater progress in an atomic bomb than in the scholastic speculation about the human soul. From the rhetorical perspective that contrasts *success* and *failure*, the answer is not very complex: success is always good for life—without defining *what* life.

5.3—Racism, Sexism, and Xenophobia

Intolerance of Diversity

A PIVOTAL HISTORICAL MOMENT in Spain's history was the expulsion of the Jews—a decree that became effective on the day Columbus departed from Palos[15]—. But this xenophobic attitude corresponded to the ancient struggle of the Christian kingdom against the Moors, which ended not only with their military defeat but also with the subsequent expulsion of Spanish Muslims. The same occurred with the Protestant Flemish. These events are revisited by Galeano and Montaner, though the former emphasizes its economic significance and the latter dwells more on its ethical implications. For both, these expulsions harmed craftsmanship, reduced capital, and slowed Spain's social dynamism.

---

[15] "Your Highnesses, as Christian catholics and princes lovers of the holy Christian faith and promoters of it, and enemies of the sect of Mahomet and of all idolatries and heresies, thought to send me, Christopher Columbus [...]; and so, after having expelled all the Jews from all your kingdoms and dominions, in the same month of January Your Highnesses commanded me to go with a sufficient fleet to the said regions of the Indies." And a few pages later: "And I departed from the said port [...] on the 3rd day of the month of August of that year..." On August 3, 1492, the deadline for Jews to leave Spain had passed. Christopher Columbus. *Diario del Primer Viaje* (1492-1493). *Literatura Hispanoamericana. Una Antología*. David Wiliam Foster. New York and London: Garland Publishing (1994): 44-45.

Xenophobia is another factor of delay. While central European countries encouraged the immigration of artisans, Spain expelled the Jews in 1492 and the Moors in 1606, while simultaneously prohibiting the presence of foreigners in America (Montaner, 155).

We can add that these hostile attitudes against other peoples not only had xenophobic and racist motivations, as Montaner points out, but also reflected a clear religious intolerance—a reaction against societal plurality. This aversion to plurality, which in the 15th and 16th centuries manifested as religious intolerance, in later centuries could only translate into political intolerance—such as that of Franco or the Latin American dictatorships of the 20th century. Within this mindset, we can also understand the attitude of the conquerors in "the savage continent."

But more than an incapacity to tolerate diversity—of belief and thought, of other possible "true faiths"—Montaner sees in the conquerors two qualities more comprehensible in our contemporary ethical context: racism and xenophobia.

It is this xenophobic and racist framework, characteristic of the era, that the Spanish carried in their minds when arriving in the Americas (Montaner, 91).

As Montaner's thesis on the developmental differences between Anglo-Saxon and Latin societies rests on the ethical and intellectual distinctions between them, we must follow the same method and ask: in this regard, was the mentality of the English and Dutch slave traders very different? Was the attitude of the English in North America—despite the sparse indigenous population—and the colonizing attitude of the

Dutch Boers, which resulted in racist regimes like apartheid in South Africa until 1994, truly different?

As noted earlier, Galeano's opinion is that the difference between development and underdevelopment lies in a relationship of commercial and international power, not in racial factors.

> The northern colonies [...] did not offer the metropolis a complementary production. The situation was very different in the Antilles and the Iberian colonies on the mainland. [...] a small Caribbean island was more important to England, from an economic standpoint, than the thirteen original colonies of the United States (Galeano, 216).

For Galeano, racist practices had, at every moment, economic motivations. From this perspective, we can say that the entire book The Open Veins of Latin America offers a Marxist reading of history. That is, unlike Montaner, it is not Spanish and later Latin American racism that produces underdevelopment, but rather underdevelopment itself, the economic motivations, and the exploitation of one social class by another, and later of one country by another, that produce racism:

> [In Mexico] the prison, the barracks, and the sacristy were in charge of combating the natural defects of the Indians, who, according to a member of an illustrious family of the time, were born "lazy, drunk, and thieves" (Galeano, 194).

We can say that, as in other cases, culture is neither solely determined by the economic infrastructure and means of production, nor is the cultural superstructure what determines the orders of material production and development. Rather, both are part of a reciprocal process that feeds back into itself.

Machismo, immaturity, and psychoanalysis

MONTANER extensively examines Greece and Rome in his search for the Latin American roots of machismo. Since the declared thesis of his book is that the present is a reflection of the past and both are the product of a mentality rather than a socioeconomic system, the author is not concerned with historical distance. On the contrary, he seems to suggest that the further back one can trace a custom or cultural trait, the deeper its roots are assumed to be. It is unlikely that our productive organization is due to an inheritance from some economic system of ancient Egypt or feudal Europe. However, it seems more plausible to recognize a psychological and cultural inheritance from even more remote times, as suggested by psychoanalysis and other anthropological doctrines. Of course, these ancient roots are the same roots of those who will be presented as opposite or different in their characteristics, which would indicate a weakness in the argument.

The model of reading and the paths of historical narration, in order to demonstrate the original thesis of *The Twisted Roots*, blend traditions with psychoanalysis and constantly venture judgments that belong to this literary genre but, unlike it, often do not worry too much about evidence or demonstrations, beyond the meticulous pictorial portrait. The theoretical tools of psychoanalysis are exposed when analyzing the "gallant" behavior of medieval European knights, (un)noble ancestors of the *impolite* "Latin American macho." Not only for supporting a priori judgments that pretend to be deductions, not only for sustaining the idea of self-interest—especially sexual egoism—in every human action, but also for resorting to one of the fundamental principles of psychoanalytic philosophy: just as Heraclitus might have said two thousand five hundred years earlier, what appears to be is not; every declaration of intentions necessarily carries a subliminal opposite, due to a trauma—of inferiority—that drives the oppressor to dominate in pursuit of a hidden, illicit objective.

> Is there in this "revalorization" of noble women [...] a reduction of the macho vision upheld by medieval society? [No,] Absolutely not; what is at stake are masculine values [...] To suffer is a way to express love [...] what is this? An immature, almost adolescent way of exhibiting the most primal signs of masculine identity. It is not, as some think, a form of worship of women, but rather another narcissistic way of adoring the attributes of men (Montaner, 89).

Later, Montaner mentions the burning of witches, mostly women. Although he aims to judge Spanish society for its horrible Inquisition—which would explain the inheritance of machismo in Latin America—, the author forgets that the Spanish Inquisition, though horrible, was insignificant compared to that which took place in the Anglo-Saxon peoples, who are supposedly held up as the model of the opposite (Escudero, 18).

5.4—Psychology of Social Classes

EDUARDO GALEANO provides a social diagnosis at the time of the independence of Latin American countries. According to him, Latin America had the same bourgeois constitutions, many of them modeled after the North American constitution, "heavily varnished with liberalism," but it lacked a creative bourgeoisie like that in the northern countries, committed to the development of "a thriving national capitalism."

This observation suggests a social and psychological cause for the subsequent failure of underdevelopment. That is, a "descending" reading of social dynamics. But immediately, he provides an "ascending" explanation of the phenomenon, typical of dialectical materialism:

> The bourgeoisies of these lands had been born as mere instruments of international capitalism, prosperous cogs in the global machinery that bled the colonies and the semi-colonies. (Galeano, 186)

In other words, the particular character of this social class, which was supposed to be the engine of national progress, was the result of a production relationship — capitalism— that distributed functions on an international scale. The final benefit, then, had to be in the hands of the owners of those means of production — of development —: the Anglophone world.

On the other hand, Montaner marks a difference with traditional Spain. In Latin America, there was influence and admiration for the new revolutions — the French and the

North American. This influence on the educated Latin American class was shared by the new Spanish liberals. Both were readers of the French encyclopedists (160). Thus, the upper classes were not part of the problem but rather a kind of minority consciousness, misunderstood by the rest of the people. In contrast, in The Open Veins of Latin America, the creole oligarchy and its prioritization of luxury over production are cited as one of the main ongoing causes, as seen during the era of Venezuelan oil extravagance. Evidently, in this case, the waste was not in the working classes.

> Free trade enriched the ports that lived off exports and elevated the level of waste among the oligarchies, eager to enjoy all the luxury the world offered, to the heavens. (286)

5.5—Colonizations with Different Approaches

ACCORDING TO GALEANO, in "The Open Veins of Latin America": "The profound imbalance of our days [...] was it born from the imperialist expansion of the United States, or does it have older roots? In reality, in the north and the south, even within the colonial matrix, very different societies had already emerged, serving purposes that were not the same" (Galeano, 213).

Galeano continues to emphasize the different social paths that the societies north and south of the Rio Grande took. The property-owning classes and the bourgeoisie were different, and the peasants and proletarians were different as well. In the south, large landowners dominated — a bourgeoisie focused solely on export, with its gaze always fixed on Europe

— and a working class that never felt ownership of the land it worked or the fruits of its labor. In contrast, in the north, European settlers appropriated small parcels of land and developed a confidence that their labor belonged to them, which eventually led to rapid industrial development and the eventual prohibition of slavery. Galeano does not ground the explanation of these observations — which will be shared by Montaner— in the religious, cultural, and intellectual origins of the North American settlers. As noted earlier, he sees this order as a consequence of a previous state of production, such as the absence of minerals in the northeastern lands, the lack of cheap or enslaved labor from the tribes, and the disinterest of the British Empire — the center of the Industrial Revolution. In Brazil, in 1850, "the rise of coffee as the new 'king product' led to the Land Law, tailored to the taste of the politicians and military of the oligarchic regime, to deny land ownership to those who worked, as the vast internal spaces of the country were opened toward the south and west" (212). In contrast, in the United States, "the 1862 Lincoln law, the Homestead Act, ensured each family ownership of 65-hectare lots [...] They were thus free farmers who occupied the new territories of the center and the west" (121). "In contrast, Brazilian rural workers have never been and are not families of free peasants in search of a piece of land of their own [...], but hired hands contracted to serve the landowners who had previously taken possession of vast empty spaces" (213).

Following the triumph of the industrial North, the agricultural frontiers of the United States expanded westward and southward, followed by the expansion of the northern industry seeking cheap labor.

The agricultural frontier moved swiftly westward and southward, at the expense of the Indians and Mexicans, but its passage did not extend large estates; instead, it sowed small landowners in the newly opened spaces (Galeano, 336).

Once again, the idea of the absence of large estates as one of the causes of a form of production and, above all, as the cause of a particular attitude of the "hired hand," who did not see themselves in the economic prosperity of their employers. But we must not forget that the root of this conception is an "ascending" reading and consists in the fact that this latifundista order, in turn, responded to a preestablished economic and productive logic at a global level.

5.6—Natural Wealth Against Development

NOW, WHAT WERE THE INITIAL CONDITIONS that determined a social structure contrary to its own development? Were these conditions purely cultural, that is, "mental"? Were they purely economic, that is, "material"? Or perhaps both intervened? If so, which determined which? Which had greater weight in the final outcomes?

For Galeano, there is no doubt: "The passengers of the Mayflower did not cross the sea to conquer legendary treasures or to exploit the scarce indigenous labor of the North, but to settle with their families and reproduce, in the New World, the system of life and work they practiced in Europe" (213). That is, in Protestant Europe. The thirteen colonies "quickly took advantage of the handicap posed by the poverty of their soil and subsoil and, early on, generated an industrializing consciousness that the metropolis allowed to grow without major problems" (Galeano, 330).

While it is true that to the south of Delaware Bay, a slave system developed, as in Latin America, the "center of gravity" was in the industrialized region of the North, "in the farms and workshops of New England" from where the victorious armies of the Civil War would emerge.

> The colonists of New England, the original core of North American civilization, never acted as agents of European capitalist accumulation; from the beginning, they lived in the service of their own development [...] (Galeano, 214).

Very different in Latin America, over the centuries, "there was always an enormous legion of idle peasants available to be moved to the production centers: The flourishing areas always coexisted with the declining ones [...]" (241). Not as a cultural or psychological particularity, but due to the initial production conditions, "unlike the Puritans of the North, the dominant classes of Latin American colonial society never oriented themselves towards internal economic development. Their profits came from outside" (215).

This situation, in turn, was expressed in the cultural geography of Latin America: roads led to the ports, but they were not connected between internal production centers.

Probably the same ambition for gold that the first Spaniards who conquered America had, and later the stories, real and imagined, about the fabulous treasures of indigenous cultures and the trafficking of precious metals to Europe, were responsible for a certain exaggeration about Latin America's natural resources. On this point, few have mentioned that our continent also had vast inhospitable expanses, such as jungles, deserts, and mountains. Nor did the North American continent lack gold or other riches, such as extensive forests. Only that, probably, these riches were not complementary to those that the British could find in their own land. This last suggestion is also supported by Galeano, which leads him to assume that New England lacked the obstacle of its natural wealth. It did not possess precious minerals like South America, nor abundant indigenous labor. Although Galeano does not mention the rich North American forests, he does mention that the geographical and geological conditions of the colonies were so similar to those of England that their agricultural production did not represent a complement —like the Antilles— but rather a competition. For this reason, "a small island in the Caribbean was more important to England, from an economic point of view, than the thirteen founding colonies of the United States" (216). For Galeano, these initial conditions began to mark a difference in the structure of the capitalist system prevailing in the world in the 18th century, which translated into a social order and, ultimately, an attitude and mentality. Specifically, Galeano quotes Sarmiento in a letter addressed to Mitre: "We are neither industrialists nor navigators —affirmed Sarmiento— and Europe will provide us for long centuries with its artifacts in exchange for our raw materials" (307).

Then, in the midst of the 20th century, the observed reality is understood as a direct consequence of this dialectical process of history: the fragmentation of the imaginary unity is one of them. A fragmentation that was a consequence of an international production system that went against the original ideas of some of its founding fathers (432). "The result is evident: today, any of the international corporations operates with greater coherence and sense of unity than this set of islands that is Latin America [...]" Nevertheless, this historical determinism, according to the ascending dialectic, is not inevitable. A raising of awareness —which can also be seen as a consequence of a historical process and not just as an individual leap, a product of existential freedom— can nullify the continuity of an unfavorable order, after which revolution will follow. It will be a revolution of economic, social, and production orders, according to the ascending dialectic, or it will be a purely internal revolution within the individual, according to a descending dialectic (see diagram 1).

While this "awakening of consciousness" does not have time and place, the unfavorable social and economic order will continue to be expressed in underdevelopment. This ascending conception of history, according to which economic and production conditions determine social organizations and cultural development, shares points of contact with a Darwinian conception of history. Economic resources are scarce, regardless of whether they can be created or not, and therefore there will be competition and a struggle for their control. At this moment, we are one step away from granting the political dimension of power a relevant place in this interpretative logic. For Galeano, the long history of Latin America's minerals demonstrates that they were exploited by Europeans and North Americans at predatory prices, not only in colonial times but also in our own era. In our time, foreign armies will not be the only agents of domination and plunder, but also intelligence agencies like the CIA or North American companies with the effective power to intervene in the internal political affairs of mining or producer countries. In this aspect, "The Open Veins of Latin America" provides a considerable amount of data with its respective strengths, which is missed in "The Twisted Roots of Latin America".

However, we must remember a difference that strongly defined the character of both colonizations. The 101 lost passengers of the Mayflower, diverted by a storm and their own miscalculations to other shores not mentioned in their contracts, decided to sever all preexisting ties with the authority of London. They recognized themselves as abandoned by fate, unsheltered by the Law, and after some internal disputes, they decided to give themselves their own laws and a government to resolve their own conflicts: the government of the majority.

Very differently, the conquest and exploitation of the rest of the New World was carried out. The Spaniards never ceased to acknowledge the overwhelming authority of the kings and the Catholic Church. Each of their enterprises, each of their ventures, was undertaken with the permission of the authority, based in Europe. The kings never set foot on American soil, but they depended on them for administration and every appointment and decision of their subjects. Even the most rebellious of the conquerors needed to justify himself before the authority, and there are a large number of letters, chronicles, and reports that demonstrate an unbreakable dependence on the invisible authority, on the Crown, on the Church. In other words, they were products of the state and religious bureaucracy, a cog in a larger machinery that justified and legitimized them. Nevertheless, the prevailing sentiment among the conquerors was that of injustice in material rewards and recognition. This was understandable: both wealth and honor could only be conferred by others, by authority. Too many claimants and too few beneficiaries accentuated this sense of injustice on the part of the power. The documents preserved today do not reveal rebellion or independence on the part of those who sacrificed themselves for a project, but quite the opposite: complaints, constant complaints, as a form of acceptance and plea to an authority perceived as unjust and, at the same time, unchallengeable.

The latter is, of course, an observation that has little to do with structural or materialist analysis; it refers to the definition of a historical character, a mentality.

Las venas abiertas

6.1—The Bleeding of Raw Materials

FOR SEVERAL PAGES, GALEANO describes how the cities richest in gold and silver mining became the poorest cities and regions. He also describes the unproductive ostentation of their upper class. These descriptions are often synthesized, sometimes explicitly, in the following expression: the natural wealth of a peripheral country is the cause of its poverty.

The first sentence of *Las venas abiertas* states: "The international division of labor consists of some countries specializing in winning and others in losing." This idea, provocative for its paradox and apparent arbitrariness, is developed and explained in detail throughout the book. According to Galeano, there is a division of labor not only within each society but also among regions of the world. Some fulfill the function of providing raw materials and cheap labor; others benefit from this production, as they possess the force of their own development, which, in turn, is amplified by this very relationship. This relationship, of course, prevents the periphery from developing and becoming independent in the same way as the center, the region that wields political, military, and especially financial and economic power.

Not as economic harm but as a moral sin, he pauses for a few pages to recall the journey of the Spanish conquistadors through the new land, from Columbus to Pizarro. But then Galeano notes that later, foreign greed not only produced enslavement and death but also prevented the initiation of an economic development process like that in the northern colonies. The exploitation of silver in Potosí did not translate into investments for its own development but rather into the construction of lavish buildings.

> By the early 17th century, the city already had thirty-six splendidly ornamented churches, as many gambling houses, and fourteen dance schools. (32)

Now, was this attitude part of an underdeveloped mentality inherited from the Spanish aristocracy, as Montaner might suggest? Or was it part of the logic of exploitation, as an ascending reading would assert? In this case, the luxury of the upper classes and the lust of the lower classes could be understood as forms of social "decompression," essential parts of the same productive system carried out through oppression rather than as a social and individual objective. Meanwhile, Spain was the mouth that received these riches but did not digest them. Gold and silver passed through the Iberian peninsula on their way to European creditors.

> [Ernest] Mandel points out that this enormous mass of capital created a favorable environment for investments in Europe, stimulated the "spirit of enterprise," and directly financed the establishment of manufactures that gave a great boost to the Industrial Revolution. (42)

In other words, as he had anticipated earlier, "the metals ripped from the new colonial domains stimulated Europe's new economic development and could even be said to have made it possible" (34). This exploitation was recorded in Seville but, due to the Crown's war expenses, ended up in the banks of the German Függer family and other lenders like the Weslers, the Shetzes, and the Grimaldis. Meanwhile, in Spain, "the Crown opened war fronts everywhere, while the aristocracy devoted itself to waste" (35).

> A French memorial from the late seventeenth century allows us to know that Spain only controlled five percent of the trade in "its" overseas colonial possessions, despite the legal illusion of the monopoly: nearly a third of the total was in Dutch and Flemish hands, a quarter belonged to the French, the Genoese controlled over twenty percent, the English ten, and the Germans slightly less. America was a European business. (Galeano, 36)

But this trade was not free from violence and illegality. According to Galeano, "plunder, both internal and external, was the most important means for the primitive accumulation of capital" (42). The idea that the wealth extracted from the colonies had significance in the history of capitalism and in the development of Anglo-Saxon societies should be confirmed by a calculation by Ernest Mandel, according to which "the value of gold and silver taken from America up to 1660, the plunder extracted from Indonesia, the profits of French capital from the slave trade during the eighteenth century, the profits from slave labor in the British Antilles, and the English plunder of India over half a century result in capital values that surpass all the capital invested by all European industries by 1800" (42). But, at the same time, "the formidable international concentration of wealth in Europe's favor prevented, in the plundered regions, the leap to capital accumulation" (43).

While the indispensable riches were transported to the center of the modern world to stimulate the incipient industry, the new continent fulfilled its role of servitude. Latin America not only produced metals; it also "specialized in providing Europe with the spices and foods it required. In this way, "each region became identified with what it produced" (44). Just like the silver from Potosí, the gold from Minas Gerais was only in transit through Portugal. Portugal even prohibited textile industries in Brazil. "Portugal produced practically nothing, and the wealth from gold was so fictitious that even the black slaves working in the colony's mines were clothed by the English" (87).

6.2—The Oppressed and the Oppressors

THE SUPPORTERS OF *LAS RAÍCES TORCIDAS* will begin by opposing Marxism and then each of the theses of their dialectical adversary until, for example, they deny the existence of the oppressed and the oppressors. In Manual del perfecto idiota Latinoamericano, Alberto Montaner, along with others, will agree that what "progressive theology calls 'conflictual'—a term that prickles the nerves—is nothing more than a Marxist reading of reality, that is, the division of society into oppressors and the oppressed. [...] the term 'liberation' is in itself conflictive: it fervently summons the existence of an enemy that must be fought" (Mendoza, 206).

On the contrary, for liberation theologians—alluded to in the previous quote—this oppressor/oppressed relationship is inherent in Latin American societies. This is also true for Eduardo Galeano, although this author understands that this (unjust) relationship not only stems from a specific social order (the Latin American one) but is also endemic to the capitalist order of any society. It would suffice to note the relative difference that this production order imposes on human groups. "The city makes the poor poorer, because it cruelly displays illusions of wealth to them" (Galeano, 414).

Once again, we will see that for the supporters of *Las venas abiertas* social and symbolic change follows a change (revolution) in the economic structure of exploitation, production, and appropriation. In any case, this awareness of "being poor in the face of the unattainable wealth of others" is perceptive and passive, in the sense that its reading reproduces the same codes of reproduction imposed by the ideology that it aims to critique. Another form of consciousness is one that deconstructs those same codes of interpretation and valuation, often used, also, by the same dominant ideology to preserve the status quo, such as the one that teaches people to be "good poor." Both run the risk of becoming trapped in their own circle. Simón Bolívar observed that "the soul of a serf rarely comes to appreciate true freedom: it rages in tumult or humbles itself in chains" (Bolívar, Letter). Perhaps we have had nothing else in Latin America since then.

6.3—Debtors and Creditors

IF THE CAUSE OF UNDERDEVELOPMENT is a consequence of others' development, it is necessary to conceive the poor continent as a naturally rich one. Galeano will emphasize this historical paradox —partly real, partly imaginary or exaggerated— of a continent that contributed immense wealth to the old continent, usually through illicit means or coercion, and has been characterized not only by its poverty but by its external debts. To alleviate these, loans are requested from creditors —IMF, World Bank, IDB, etc., where the United States has veto power— who will require weak national governments to sign a Letter of Intent as a preliminary condition (366). In this way, the debtor's dependence on the creditor is perpetuated, not only by maintaining a debt that is difficult to pay and delays any possibility of development but also by allowing intervention in the internal affairs of debtor countries. Galeano will note more economic data: "a fifth of exports in 1955 went to paying amortizations, interest, and profits on investments, [while in] 1968, payments represented 37 percent of exports" (391). "To financial and technological blackmail is added the unfair and free competition of the strong against the weak" (367), he adds before describing different situations where the strongest foreign capitals freely practiced dumping.

Regarding savings and credit, the asymmetry would confirm the structural conditions of the world economy on the uneven development of countries: "no foreign bank can operate in the United States as a recipient of deposits from U.S. citizens. On the other hand, U.S. banks freely manage, through numerous subsidiaries, the national savings of Latin America" (371). And since international relations are based on the Darwinian law of *the struggle for the fittest*, there is no philanthropy. "In 1968, President Johnson assured that more than ninety percent of U.S. external aid in 1969 would be used to finance purchases in the United States (377)."

Galeano also cites the historian Robert Schnerb, according to whom the history of Latin American republics "is, in a sense, the history of their economic obligations contracted with the absorbing world of European finance" (320).

6.4—Conservative Revolutions

POSTCOLONIAL SOCIETIES RETAINED the characteristics of their Spanish predecessors. As we have seen before, the social structure, the relationship between public power and economic power with their different social classes remained in a personalist —caudillist— manner while their inhabitants retained the perception of this order and these powers as illegitimate. Carlos Fuentes summarizes it this way:

> We are a continent in desperate search of its modernity. But too often, we have reacted violently against such a search, preferring to preserve the burden of anachronistic, "patrimonialist" societies, as Max Weber would call them, in which the will of the leader, the interests of his clan, and the rewards due to his armies of parasites and thugs, create

an irrational world of political caprice and "impunity for violence" (Fuentes, 12).

Montaner returns to historical roots to discover there the formation of a character that would explain the subsequent destiny of nations, just as a psychoanalyst traces in a child's childhood the origin of their neurotic impulses, their successes and their economic failures, rather than in the economic history of credits and means of production that are part of their context.

Under this analytical principle, he notes that while new financial instruments were being developed in Europe — stock exchange, credit, forms of capital investment— "the accumulation of capital was not the result of industry, trade, or increased productivity, but of war spoils, land distribution, slave labor, and privileges granted by the Crown" (117). The greatest source of capital, as it is today, was the possession and accumulation of land. This tendency to hoard land came from the Castilians, for whom being a landowner was a form of distinction and nobility. An observation with which Eduardo Galeano agreed.

The Church was one of the main landowners, accumulating unproductive lands, especially until the disentailment, which meant the return of the Church's assets to the Spanish state in the 19th century.

> [According to Alexander von Humboldt] No less than half of the real estate and total capital of Mexico, according to his testimony, belonged to the Church, which also controlled a significant portion of the remaining lands through mortgages. Mexican miners invested their surpluses in the purchase of large estates (47).

This idea is picked up by Montaner: the large estate as a sign of nobility. But if in Spain there was a peasant and statist conception—compared to the rest of Europe—in Latin America it was worse: "according to the mercantilist mentality of the time, the role of the colonies was to be a captive market in service of the producers of the metropolis. Latin Americans were not to manufacture what the Mother Country produced" (Montaner, 119).

6.5—Ruling Classes and Dominant Ideologies

THIRTY YEARS EARLIER, EDUARDO GALEANO recognized the same trait inherited from Spain, related to the Spanish capitalists who "became rentiers, through the purchase of Crown debt titles, and did not invest their capital in industrial development" (38). Later, he would observe the same attitude in the dominant classes of Latin America. In contrast to the North American bourgeoisie, he defined the Creole bourgeoisie as the gendarmes who would fulfill the role of administering the bleeding for their own benefit without the creative imagination that would have been necessary for industrial development. At the same time, and consistent with this vision of oppressor-oppressed, he had a passive view of the working classes: "the well-being of our ruling classes—ruling internally, ruled from the outside—is the curse of our multitudes condemned to a life of beasts of burden" (4).

But these attitudes, these psychological and cultural traits, in turn, respond to an infrastructure: the system of production and capital accumulation —both national and international— has been shaping the attitudes and responses of each social class. At the core of this idea lies a certain determinism, since, although we act based on a mentality, this mentality would be defined in its form and functioning by its economic and social context.

Carlos Fuentes, who in Valiente mundo nuevo seems to adopt a psych culturalist —descending— reading of history, appears to agree with Galeano on this point:

> Since independence, our dependence depended on a mirage: the prosperity of "Latin" America was conditioned by the prosperity of the upper classes. Unfortunately, these classes have been very agile in copying Western consumption models but very slow in adapting to European and North American modes of production (Fuentes, 15).

Later, Carlos Fuentes will once again emphasize the psychocultural dimension, which would be transmitted like an epidemic. According to Fuentes, "the foundation of a democratic culture in Ibero-America is cultural continuity, of which both democracy and literature are manifestations." Both are responsible for the creation of a society that remains subjected to the legacy of the "autocratic traditions" of the indigenous empires and the Spanish Empire through "Habsburg paternalism and the centralizing, modernizing activism of the Bourbons"

> The church, the army, and the Spanish Imperial State were our oldest institutions. Civil society is our most recent reality. Independence expelled the Spanish State. The church and the army remained, sometimes stronger than

the incipient national states, though always stronger than the weak civil societies. The result was anarchy and dictatorship, alternating to the point of despair in most of our countries (17).

In this way, on one side, we have the oppressors —the ruling class— and the oppressed —the "beasts of burden." This is the same relationship that Galeano identifies as existing between classes and between nations, determined not so much by an internal, cultural, and psychological factor, but by an external factor, economic in nature, of political and ideological power.

> Unlike the Puritans of the north, the ruling classes of Latin American colonial society never oriented themselves toward internal economic development. Their benefits came from the outside (215).

Therefore, a change—a revolution—that eliminates this relationship that hinders development and is also unjust would first consist of changing *the socioeconomic model* upon which society is organized. Once this stage is reached, the cultural revolution and the psychological change of the inhabitants should gradually occur. Social justice, on the other hand, should be an immediate achievement.

Power and freedom

ttt

7.1—Freedom and the "logos" of history

THE DETERMINISTIC CONCEPTION OF HISTORICAL materialism, represented mainly by Marxist models of interpretation, had one of its earliest and most convincing objectors in Max Weber. In the words of Milton Fisk, Weber understood two factors in certain cultural regions of Europe:

> first, a moral ideal was prevalent that he described as secular asceticism—an attitude that promoted frugality and hard work. He believed this ideal had its roots in the theological conception, common at the time of the Reformation, of a distant and unapproachable God. Proof of being elected by such a God would come, not through communication, but through secular works (Fisk, 164).

A broader and deeper analysis of this issue can be found in *Escape from Freedom*, by Erich Fromm.

Now, besides these objections to the materialist conception of history and its consequent emphasis on a *metaphysical* factor, we must also note that these models of interpretation (descending) also conceive the world as a larger whole composed of parts. Parts with a sufficient degree of freedom in which both an individual and a society or nation are capable of changing their own history without changing the order they are part of. Due to this relative independence of the parts, the individual possesses a significant margin of social and personal movement in proportion to their own mental attitude toward their surroundings and themselves. The same goes for a society: its underdevelopment does not depend as much on the fate of its neighbors or the more distant nations of the planet, nor on a structuring global logic, but rather on its own internal organization. In this conception of history, we perceive a positive belief in existential freedom.

On the other hand, the *ascending* or Darwinian conception of history and social dynamics is, at the same time, integral. If in the *descending* or culturalist reading, the philosophical parallel of the 20th century could be existentialism, in the *ascending* reading, the parallel is not only Marxism but, from an individual perspective, it is psychoanalysis. Both in "Las raíces torcidas" and in "Open Veins of Latin America," the present is explained by the past. However, the very conception of each suggests that the culturalist reading would be in a better ideological position to conceive the present as a consequence of the future.

Conceiving the present as a consequence of the future is the first acknowledgment of human freedom. This conception is not outrightly denied by its opponent, as it also recognizes that the solution to the "problem" posed lies in awareness. Awareness to change the structure, to deconstruct the oppressive order; not to change the individual or society from the inside out. However, this attitude, militantly revolutionary, will continue to base its conception of history and social dynamics on a meta-social logos that will give meaning to the term freedom. The individual will be free within a logos of social justice—generally, during most of the 20th century, this logos referred to Marxism—or they will not be truly free in a logos of social injustice, that is, in a capitalist order.

For a materialist reading of history, every order is a consequence of a pre-established logic driven by economic and productive power, which, as if that weren't enough, is also inherent in human nature: the domination of some as the engine of progress for others.

In the ascending reading, each part is explained by the functional logic of the whole, the set of parts. Each individual belongs to a social class and fulfills their role in the division of labor; each society, each country necessarily responds to the economic and power logic that organizes and structures the world. In this scenario, there are few possibilities for a true *independence* of nations, for a true *freedom* of individuals. Freedom and independence could only be achieved by destroying this order, dismantling the social and global mega-structure that constrains individuals and colonized nations —the countries of dependent capitalism—. Paradoxically, this liberation from the mega-structure had as its ideological alternative the submission —of individuals and nations— to a new and revolutionary economic, social, and productive order: the dictatorship of the proletariat.

It is significant how each dialectical opponent understands consciousness-raising. For the supporters of *Open Veins*, this would be the understanding of the individual or society —before or after the revolution— of the logos of history, of the unjust and oppressive order that not only subjugates bodies and minds to make them produce more for the benefit of others' happiness but also imposes a false —or at least inconvenient— idea of freedom, property, justice, and, ultimately, happiness.

On the other hand, for the supporters of *Twisted Roots*, this same conception of history and power as determining structures —of the social order and its meanings— is responsible for individuals' inability to become conscious: as long as it is understood that the social order depends on an external structure to the individual and not on their own mental attitude, they will not be able to *become aware* of their own prison and their own possibilities.

However, for the culturalists, these possibilities are not referred to a joint, organized action of society in favor of a specific goal, as the dialectical opponents of the structuralist reading would argue, but rather to an individual action that, as an inevitable consequence, must produce a social collective effect.

7.2—The Illegitimacy of Power

IT IS LIKELY THAT POWER has been, for most of its history, arbitrary. The idea of the wise and just king dates back to the times of Solomon, but there were also those who were considered despots, especially if they came from another people, another culture. Generally, and from the ancient Egyptians to modern dictators, passing through the Maya and Inca, power was granted by a divinity (the religious ideology of the highest class). That is, it was a descending power. Well into the 20th century, in Western countries, this legitimizing conception of power could still be seen. The coins in Spain included the icon of General Francisco Franco with the following legend: "Caudillo of Spain by the grace of God."

But this descending relationship of power had historical exceptions and, in Europe, began to reverse in the Modern era with parliaments and later with democratic systems. Spain, the "motherland" (an expression that is not resisted for being a kind of oxymoron but for its hierarchical connotations), resisted this change for a long time. Perhaps, as exceptions, we could name the renewal movements of the 20th century, such as that of the Republicans, although they always represented a very short-lived experience. Both *The Open Veins* and *The Crooked Roots*, focus on Spain, in the early years following the discovery of America. Eduardo Galeano reminds us of the conflictive relationship that Spanish society experienced with power at the beginning of the 16th century, which would ultimately prove dramatically significant for the American colonies:

> Charles V, of the Habsburg dynasty, had spent sixteen years in Spain out of the forty that his reign lasted. He had taken the throne without speaking Castilian, governed surrounded by a Flemish entourage, extending safe-conducts to take mules and horses loaded with silver and gold out of Spain (Galeano, 36).

Charles V (or Charles I for the Spaniards) was not only not representative of the Spanish people, but he also sought to impose a Renaissance culture that they did not feel. (It is also probable that the people identified the new humanist and Renaissance culture with a power that did not represent them, and thus remained tied to the Gothic and Baroque sensibility).

On the other hand, let us recall the great social inequalities of the vast Spanish Empire, illustrated by works such as

El Lazarillo de Tormes. Obviously, the anonymous author of this proto-novel belonged to an economically superior class to the one he portrayed, though this does not mean he was unfamiliar with the lower strata of society. His own class is not depicted in El Lazarillo (paradoxically, since the story is told in the first person), because this is not simply the tale of a rogue but rather, inadvertently, through mockery of an inferior class, an exposition of the survival rules of the hungry poor and, by extension, an indirect account of the social injustice and exploitation of the time. Here, lies, deceit, and the legitimization of illegality abound as common currency. All of these were conditions that the dominant ideology of the "nobles" attributed to the wicked people, to the "villain." Briefly, let us provide an example of this character of the 16th century, the century of conquests in America.

When the blind man asks his guide to listen through the ear of a stone bull, and he obeys, he strikes him against the statue. In this way, the first lesson that Lazarillo de Tormes learns from his first master is to never trust anyone. Later, we find summarized an attitude that will be repeated many other times, when the same blind man offers "his protégé" to eat a bunch of grapes, taking one each time and promising "not to cheat." However, the blind man begins to take two at a time, so Lázaro, accustomed to the greed and deceit of his master, begins to take three at a time. When the bunch is finished, the blind man says:

> "Lázaro, you have deceived me. I swear to God that you ate the grapes three at a time."
> "I did not eat," I said; "but why do you suspect that?"
> The very wise blind man replied:

> "Do you know how I see that you ate them three at a time?"
> "In that I was eating two by two, and you kept quiet" (Ceja-
> dor, 92).

At the same time that the Spanish kings began to be perceived as illegitimate, they were, in turn, historically subor-
dinate to another power—of divine origin—, according to a
relationship of strategic interests: the Pope. This relationship
stemmed from centuries of the same tradition that was not
willing to change, without realizing that the historical center
of Europe was beginning to migrate to the countries of the
north, to the countries of the Holy Roman Empire (Montaner, 36).

This perception of the illegitimacy of power, of the injustice of its administration, was documented in the chronicles
and fictions of the Spaniards who crossed the Atlantic. Even
in the last writings of the first conqueror, Christopher Columbus, we can read his bitterness and complaint about the
injustice of the rewards administered by the King (the highest representative of political power). Montaner notes the
conquerors who followed Columbus and recognizes in this
cultural trait the genesis of the future Latin American social
character.

> Not only the Indians, mestizos, and settlers resented the
> Spanish State; also the conquerors like Pizarro, Cortés and
> Almagro were dissatisfied with the benefits received for
> their enterprises (37).

Albero Montaner traces this state of mind of the Spaniards of the time and formulates a continuity that is hard to
refute: the conflictive relationship that the subjects—later

citizens—would maintain with the power of the kings—later creole governments.

Both the Indians and the creoles had known reasons to resent the Spanish State. But the conquerors did as well. How does Montaner, then, interpret this conflict on the part of the conquerors? According to the Cuban author, and in line with a contemporary reading made from a liberal ideology, the conquest was driven and carried out as a private enterprise. Its goal was the material enrichment of the protagonists and social prestige, not of the conquest itself but that which derived directly from fortune and property. Both the expedition leaders and the soldiers who followed them came from social strata far from a comfortable aristocratic position. As an example of this foundational state of dissatisfaction with authority due to the injustice of the rewards for personal effort—of a not-so-individual enterprise—, Montaner cites the conqueror of Peru, Francisco de Pizarro:

> "At times when I was conquering the land and walked with a backpack on my shoulders, I never received any help, and now that I have it conquered and won, they send me stepfathers." The same frustration, though at different times, was felt by Christopher Columbus, Hernán Cortés, and Diego de Almagro: the Crown did not allow them to exploit the Indians freely, limited their political decision-making, and often denied them social distinctions or haggled over material rewards (41).

Four centuries later, in 1946, Jorge Luis Borges observed that "the Argentine, unlike the North Americans and most Europeans, does not identify with the State [...]; the truth is that the Argentine is an individual, not a citizen." He immediately recalls that "films produced in Hollywood repeatedly present for admiration the case of a man [...] who seeks the friendship of a criminal only to later hand him over to the police; the Argentine, for whom friendship is a passion and the police a mafia, feels that this 'hero' is an incomprehensible scoundrel." He reinforces his reasoning by recalling a significant moment in Argentine literature, "that desperate night when a rural police sergeant shouted that he would not tolerate the crime of killing a brave man and began fighting against his own soldiers alongside the deserter Martín Fierro." With his sharp intelligence, he concludes that "the European and the North American judge that a book must be good if it has received any award, while the Argentine admits the possibility that it might not be bad despite the award" (Borges, Ficcionario, 217).

This conception of power, perceived as illegitimate by the three major groups that formed the early colonial society, would have become embedded in the subconscious of the new creole society, which persists to this day. In this sense, we can understand how a mindset survives social and economic structures and, in turn, becomes responsible for their permanence or conservation. If the process were strictly the opposite—as proposed by the materialist reading—it would be difficult to understand how certain cultural and psychological characteristics survive political and socioeconomic orders that have been toppled, as seen in the examples of the French, Russian, or Cuban revolutions.

Montaner identifies, in the subsequent historical process of Latin America, the preeminence of men (caudillos) over the State. That is, arbitrariness over the Law, over an abstract system, over institutions.

All of this originates from the idea of the illegitimacy of the State. At the same time, another Peninsular heritage survives that will lead to a tragic contradiction. Yes, power, the State, is illegitimate, but power—salvation—comes from above, power is descending.

7.3—Descending Power

OF COURSE, THE ORIGIN of a conception of the nature of "descending power" is not in Spain. As we have noted before, we can find it as an unconscious assumption in the origins of history and as a conscious denunciation in Averroes, in the Middle Ages.

> [For Mohamed Ibn Rushd, Averroes] authority should flow from society as a whole through rational decisions. It was the ascending theory of power, a pillar upon which democracy would later be built. It did not flow by the grace of God—the descending theory of power—but by the consent of the people. Legitimate power, therefore, ascended from the citizens to the summit (Montaner, 29).

Averroes dies in exile in Morocco in 1198, but his thought is translated in Paris, which is seen as a threat to the authority of Pope Gregory IX (29).

The roots of a given ideology can be traced back to the origins of history. But what gives it historical significance is not this possibility—quite the opposite, since it brings it closer to an idea of nature rather than history—but the identification of crucial moments, that is, those moments in which upheavals, revolutions, or continuities occur.

In what we could understand as one of the undeclared theoretical foundations of Montaner, in history, changes and reactions to those changes occur continuously. In the resistance to abandoning what we might riskily call "obsolete mentalities" lies the true origin of the illness, of the malformation—of the twisted roots. In this resistance, religion must have played an important role, since it was, at the time, the ideological source of the era as ideas, beliefs, and feelings were measured and shaped. Religion must have been, then, the physical and spiritual arena where the eternal struggle for power took place. Far from the Reformation and close to the Counter-Reformation—or Restoration—which consolidated an ancient tradition of uncritical subordination to the papacy in Rome, Spain became trapped in this vertical and descending conception of power. Montaner reminds us that "the Pope does not have to obey anyone. He cannot be judged by his subjects. He answers only to God. The organization he presides over is vertical, and power is top-down" (3).

Unlike the individual-system conception, the American Revolution of 1776 arose from the perception that England violated the Law by imposing taxes without consultation. The revolution was not about replacing one power with another but about defending the Law.

The rationalization that Averroes spoke of aimed to replace the Machiavellian control of individuals and transfer it to a system, a set of social norms upon which the new faith of the people would be established (Arocena, 46). It is clear, for Montaner, that in this historic decision "the Americans adopted a bottom-up approach to exercising power" (162).

Of course, many Latin American revolutionary leaders and some of their intellectuals viewed the novel process taking place in the northern United States with favor.

> While in Europe enlightened Spaniards were divided between Francophiles and traditionalists, those in America were almost all Francophiles, admiring the revolution that had ended the monarchy of Louis XVI and also the process that had liberatad the Americans from British control a few years earlier (Montaner, 160).

José Artigas, the great defeated and later elevated to bronze in his country, admired this revolution and conceived of power in the same way, summarized in a phrase likely polished in its grammar: "My authority emanates from you, and it ceases before your sovereign presence."

France, unlike the new United States, remained halfway, according to Montaner's reading, in terms of a revolutionary vision of power. For the French Revolution—Rousseauian— the natural rights of individuals did not exist. The majority had the right to impose their rights over minorities, and leaders had to be, above all, enlightened. But from the blind absolutism of the king, it transitioned to the violence of the revolution and from there to the rise of Napoleon, which was a form of absolutism but military (163).

The idea that kings held power "by the grace of God" was abolished by the Glorious Revolution in England (1688-1689), which stripped the crown of power, leaving it only as a symbol (164). However, the revolutions in Latin America drew more from the French source than the North American one, according to Montaner.

> With inspiration more French than North American, a good dose of Masonic conspiracy, and the persistent encouragement of England, the insurrection against Spain finally took shape across the length and breadth of Latin America (165).

In addition to the previously analyzed "mentality," formed in those times, "the primal instinct of Latin Americans led them to propose local monarchies that suspiciously resembled those they had just overthrown" (165).

7.4—The Contradictory Consciousness

AS WE HAVE SEEN, THE ACCEPTANCE OF A DESCENDING *nature*-power coexists in conflict with the established idea in our societies of its illegitimate *nature*. Montaner summarizes this significant contradiction as follows:

> Inevitably, the underlying idea established that the interests of society would always be better safeguarded by the State than by greedy capitalists, a contradictory conclusion in societies that simultaneously hold that the State is a corrupt, wasteful, and inefficient administrator. (Montaner, 97)

Latin America was populated by this ideology of power. However, as we have seen earlier, while its inhabitants absorbed this idea about the nature of authority, they resented it, recognizing in it the source of their oppression. This contradictory reading of power can currently be seen throughout Latin America, but it is perhaps in countries like Mexico and, above all, Peru where it appears with greater intensity —although we cannot yet affirm whether the coincidence that both countries were the cradles of the greatest indigenous civilizations is significant or not for this analysis.

According to Montaner, a particular psychological fact then occurred that would characterize our continent: the creoles and the colonized adopted the perspective of the conquered. The same did not happen in Anglo-America (18).

The Mexican writer Carlos Fuentes offers a brief portrait of the psychocultural profile of what, in simplified terms, we could call the "Latin American people." Here, we have a descending, psychoculturalist reading, with its religious origins and its contemporary political and ideological translation:

> With Saint Augustine, we find it hard to believe that the grace of God communicates directly with the individual; against John Locke, we find it hard to believe that the purpose of civil government is the protection of private property. We rather believe in the powers of hierarchy and mediation. We believe, with Saint Thomas, that the common good and the unity required to achieve it are superior to individual goals and private interests (Fuentes, 13).

Even military leaders like Simón Bolívar revealed their distrust in full democracy, despite their republicanism: "Elections —he wrote— are the great scourge of republics."

The contradictory feeling about the nature of power is once again expressed with starkness in the expectations regarding the public organization of these countries. Montaner tells us that all postcolonial societies "agreed on the key point: the economic solution for the Latin American peoples lay in strong states that would guide societies towards a superior destiny of collective development and happiness" (175).

According to the psychoculturalist view, this conception is the product of an inheritance, of an education that stems from history and from which a society, at a certain moment, has been unable to liberate itself by using what Averroes called the "discovery of rational laws" capable of harmonizing the needs of society with its own laws and its own organization. For a materialist reading of history, this is nothing more than the result of an order of production and exploitation of wealth, the result of a Darwinian struggle. In *Las venas abiertas* we can read that "within each country, the international system of domination that each country suffers is reproduced" (Galeano, 415).

7.5—The Darwinism of nations

Eduardo Galeano begins *Las venas abiertas de América Latina* in a provocative manner: not only does he point out historical responsibilities but, above all, he takes his materialist reading of history to the extreme with the idea that some countries specialized in winning and others in losing.

> Our corner of the world, which today we call Latin America, was precocious: it specialized in losing from the remote times when the Europeans of the Renaissance leaped

327

across the sea and sank their teeth into its throat (Galeano, 1).

In addition to the high-figuration metaphor —poetic— which gives the book its name and visual force to its thesis, Galeano will, in his own way, provide a more reasonable foundation for his initial outburst. However, this condition of "reasonableness" is framed within a particular reading of history: the ascending, or materialist, reading.

We have already partly analyzed this type of reading. Let us now observe that another of its consequences results in a Darwinian consideration of international relations and history. A logic that is reproduced at different scales, from the international to the domestic.

> To each one has been assigned a role [...] within Latin America the oppression of smaller countries by their larger neighbors, and within the borders of each country, the exploitation that big cities and ports exert over their internal sources of sustenance and labor (Galeano, 3).

The reflective impersonal "has been assigned" suggests the presence of someone or something that has decided this order, which shows that even this Darwinian idea of history is not fully conscious in Galeano at the time of writing. This ambiguity is confirmed shortly thereafter, attributing to others —to potential dialectical adversaries— this same idea that will be reinforced throughout the course of his own book:

> For those who conceive of history as a competition, the backwardness and misery of Latin America are nothing more than the result of its failure. [...] But it so happens

that those who won, won because we lost: the history of underdevelopment of Latin America integrates, as has been said, the history of the development of global capitalism (Galeano, 3).

We can envision a way out of this impasse. It is possible that history has been a struggle of the fittest, of the triumph of the strong over the weak. Its ultimate expression is imperialism, but its internal logic is the capitalist system, since "the strength of the entire imperialist system rests on the necessary inequality of the parts that compose it, and that inequality assumes increasingly dramatic proportions" (4). According to this conception, history is governed by Darwinian laws, but it is not inevitable that it operates according to this principle, that is, according to the capitalist system. Once this savage system is overcome, societies could recognize an ethical code of justice that nullifies Darwinian laws —the *Law of the Jungle*— just as we can observe in any community where the weak are more protected than the strong. For Galeano, this historical parallel would be socialism. But not a simple national socialism but an international one.

7.6—Underdevelopment as a consequence of development

ON JANUARY 24, 1812, BERNARDO DE MONTEAGUDO wrote in the *Gazette* of Buenos Aires some enthusiastic reflections on the future of (Latin) America. The confidence in our own forces had a defiant tone in the face of the world's greatest powers. The political divisions of the continent had not yet been defined, its peoples had not yet gained independence from the Spanish empire, and it was already read that "we have time and resources to arm our hand and make it fearsome to our enemies; the fate of America does not depend on them, no, but on ourselves: its ruin or prosperity will be the result of our energy or indifference" (Monteagudo, *Reflections*). However, although Monteagudo speaks of a "revolution of the globe," he does not directly mention the geopolitical, ideological, and cultural context that included Europe, Africa, and the Americas. A factor that would be considered, by the mid-next century, as decisive and —for the radicals— determinant.

For Galeano's thesis, the fate of the colonies was determined from the outset by their natural conditions, but even more by the needs of the nations that were developing based on the nascent industrialization of their economies. Thus, "the colonial economy, more of a supplier than a consumer, was structured to serve the European market" (Galeano, 44).

> The American colonial economy, although formally displaying some feudal traits, acted in service of capitalism emerging in other regions. After all, even in our time, the existence of the rich centers of capitalism cannot be explained without the existence of poor and subjugated peripheries: both integrate the same system (45).

The thesis of "subdevelopment servitude" could be summarized as follows: "The small islands of the Caribbean had been infinitely more important, for England, than its northern colonies. Barbados, Jamaica, and Montserrat were prohibited from manufacturing a needle or a tool on their own. Quite different was the situation of New England, and that facilitated its economic development as well as its political independence" (129).

After the fate of sugar and coffee, Galeano achieves a new continuity in the historical narrative by describing the fate of rubber in Brazil. Its exploitation did not serve to industrialize its own region but rather for the ostentation of a few. The inventions that made its exploitation possible came from the North. When rubber seeds were taken from Brazil by the English bound for Malaysia, Brazil's production was ruined.

> Thus, the workers, who had been brought from afar to be put at the service of someone else's venture, were left to survive as best they could. Foreign, even, to Brazil itself, which had done nothing but respond to the siren call of global demand for raw materials, without participating in the slightest in the real business of rubber: financing, marketing, industrialization, distribution (Galeano, 143).

The same fate befell Venezuela and Brazil's cocoa: "Like sugar cane, cocoa brought with it monoculture and the burning of forests, the dictatorship of international pricing, and the relentless hardship of the workers" (146). For many pages, Eduardo Galeano pours out data on the relationships of interests between North American companies—especially oil companies—and the dictatorships in Latin America. Unlike Las raíces torcidas, the data, quotes, and references are abundant and meticulous. However, all this data serves a single idea, a single metaphor. Parallelism and continuity function as metaphor, detaching themselves from the thinker to create their own history according to their own signifying nature. After exposing the situation of minerals on the continent, Galeano continues with crops like sugar and concludes that "the more coveted a product is by the world market, the greater the misfortune it brings to the Latin American people who, through their sacrifice, create it" (94).

In summary, "underdevelopment is not a stage of development. It is its consequence" (470).

On these notes, proponents of the culturalist thesis might object that this history was not the direct imposition of industrialized nations but rather the inherent incapacity of the producer countries to take advantage of their natural benefits. To which the supporters of *Open Veins of Latin America* will respond by recalling that the same logic of international oppression is reproduced within each society, especially within oppressed, colonized societies. That is, the social substitutes of economic and financial empires are the ruling classes that, not just out of mental incapacity, indulged in luxury, waste, and the oppression of their subjects, but because such behavior also reflects and is part of the function assigned to them by the logic of capitalist production: the centers of development do not desire competitors; it is better to have a rich and unproductive aristocracy in the colonies that ensures a proletariat with cheap labor and without the capacity for development, which would imply not just future competition but also the loss of cheap resources necessary for the developed centers.

The following quote gives us an idea of the importance of being far from power: "In Chile, one of Spain's most distant possessions, isolation favored the development of an incipient industrial activity from the very dawn of colonial life" (288). The same is referred to in the case of Paraguay: far from the ports, first distant from the Crown and later from the British Empire, this country had reached a level of development non-existent in its neighboring port cities, based on a primitive development 'inward'" (310). "The [five-year war's] victors, ruined by the extremely high cost of the crime, were left in the hands of the English bankers who had financed the venture" (317).

In the twentieth century, the developed nations, especially the United States, promoted a discourse in favor of democracy in Latin America while simultaneously aiding or imposing dictatorships. Referring to a possible coup in Brazil, just days before it occurred in 1964, The Washington Star published 'Here is a situation in which a good and effective old-style coup d'état by conservative military leaders may well serve the best interests of the Americas' (252). Also, the American ambassador Lincoln Gordon welcomed the coup as necessary to halt communism (252).

The dominion of the global centers of development—economic and military—, the logic of the world capitalist order is based on (1) the periphery exporting raw materials and cheap labor for (2) the benefit of central industry and commerce, which, in turn, (3) need to place such production. This, in large part, will be (4) exported to the peripheral, underdeveloped countries, so that the vicious cycle repeats: (5) the peripheral countries do not compete in commercial and industrial development—we are speaking of the mid-twentieth century—while they continue to (1) produce raw materials and underdevelopment. "Also in Brazil, the textile and metallurgical workshops , which had been taking their modest first steps since the 17th century, were devastated by foreign imports" (288).

Analyzing the decline in the prices of raw materials and the increase in imports of manufactured products, and citing

A. Emmanuel, Galeano says that: "the curse of low prices does not weigh on certain products but on certain countries" (396).

"It is low wages that cause low prices" (396), and not the law of supply and demand. Therefore, poor countries export their poverty, benefiting, according to this law, the rich countries that consume or manufacture it with higher wages.

And for this, everything is valid, even the contradiction in discourse. If democracy is preached, dictatorships are imposed—or favored—in peripheral countries; if the free market is preached and protectionism is combated in producer countries, protectionism for their own industries is established in the developed centers. "Certainly, rich countries have used and continue to use customs barriers to protect their high internal wages" (396). This structuralist vision of the world order and, consequently, of the underdevelopment of some as a result of the development of others is questioned at the same time as The Open Veins of Latin America becomes a best-seller and something more: a kind of political and intellectual reference.

In his commentary on the book *Third Worldism*, by Jean-François Ravel, Mario Vargas Llosa notes in 1983 his agreements and disagreements with the Frenchman's theses:

> Rangel shows that this dogma ["the fallacy that the reason for the misery of underdeveloped countries is the wealth of the developed ones (and vice versa)"] does not withstand historical analysis. The economic takeoff of Europe predates the great colonial conquests in the case of England and France. Colonial policy was more of an obstacle to the development of Spain and Portugal. Germany,

Switzerland, Sweden, and other countries achieved high levels without having colonies" (Vargas Llosa, 335).

We already know Galeano's response to this argument: even countries that did not possess colonies like Spain and Portugal benefited more from them than the peninsular colonizers.

Valuation of the capitalist system

The struggle for meaning

8.1—The dominant system

WE HAVE SEEN THAT, FOR *LAS VENAS ABIERTAS de América Latina*, individuals and societies are subject to a logos that transcends all borders and integrates each part into a coherent whole. In a certain way, this system is "meta-human" and escapes the control of individuals. Therefore, it is not only oppressive and unjust, but it is far from being a model of freedom, as claimed by the other side. Freedom lies in the movement of capital, not of human beings. At least not for those who do not possess capital.

> The system is so irrational for everyone else that the more it develops, the more it sharpens its imbalances [...] New factories are established in the privileged poles of development —São Paulo, Buenos Aires, Mexico City— but less labor is needed each time. The system has not foreseen this minor inconvenience: what is in surplus is people (Galeano, 6).

Those in favor of this "system" will argue that those displaced by machines are inevitable in the historical process. That is, the mechanical progress of production, the displaced individuals, and ultimately —it is deduced— the *historical process* are inevitable. This idea, of course, approaches the fatalism of history, but also the Darwinian conception of it: it is inevitable that the weak be displaced, it is inevitable to replace human beings with machines so as not to lose in the international competition of production. After this process —after the progress of society— wealth will eventually protect the weak as well, though initially some generations must be sacrificed.

But for Galeano, not only is the system perverse; so are those who benefit from it. The birth control measures designed in the developed center to be implemented in Latin America is just one example of this human will that goes beyond the needs of the system: "what do the heirs of Malthus propose but to kill all future enemies before they are born?" (7).

8.2—The Invisible Hand of the Market

THE DOCTRINE OF THE "FREE MARKET" or "free trade" is fundamental to the defenders of liberalism from Adam Smith to the so-called "neoliberals" in Latin America, towards the end of the 20th century. This doctrine proposes that the liberation of international trade will benefit nations, as each specializes in producing what it has a "comparative advantage" in, while importing other products more cheaply than if it were to produce them itself. Both nationally and internationally, these prices would be regulated by a natural Law or invisible hand, a metaphor that, while not entirely divorced from an anthropomorphic will, possesses a divine character.

However, and according to the thesis of *The Open Veins*, not even Britain (the cradle of these commercial doctrines and their defender internationally) practiced them without contradictions. Instead, it not only preferred commercial and industrial protectionism within its borders but also, especially in the 20th century, with the practices of John Keynes's economic theory, engaged in systematic state intervention in the regulation of demand for goods and capital.

Galeano will interpret this lack of correspondence between theory, discourse, and practice in his own way: "There has never been a free play of supply and demand in the so-called international markets, but rather the dictatorship of one over the other" (394).

The commercial monopoly with the Spanish metropolis had effectively ceased to exist by the early 19th century. There was illegal, contraband trade, and most products were English. By 1810, trade was liberalized, and taxes on imports and exports were reduced, which meant a triumph for the English. Galeano views this liberalization as something negative for local manufacturing:

> Free trade enriched the ports that lived off exports and sky-rocketed the level of waste of the oligarchies eager to enjoy all the luxury the world had to offer, but it ruined the budding local manufactures and frustrated the expansion of the domestic market (286).

That is to say, supply over demand. He will not only point out the "contradictory" protectionism of free trade countries, but will also introduce the gravitational difference between supply and demand. These are not a balanced game; rather, one can dominate over the other. For some economic doctrines, it is demand that determines supply. For others, for *Open Veins of Latin America*, it is supply that prevails and establishes what and how one can or should consume, considering that in a development process, basic consumer goods are far inferior to consumer goods for development itself.

The idea of trade regulations, of legal and state interventions in the national economy, was not only successfully implemented to overcome the global crisis after 1929 —the government of Franklin Delano Roosevelt in the United States was an example—, but they were also maintained in many European countries during their post-war reconstruction process.

This idea of legal regulation is a basic condition in the vision of *Open Veins of Latin America* for an economic order of social justice and international justice: "yet isn't there an International Coffee Agreement to balance prices in the market?" Later, he adds new evidence to confirm the central thesis of plunder, noting that, according to unquestionable organizations like ECLAC, "as incredible as it may seem, coffee yields more wealth in the state coffers of European countries than the wealth it leaves in the hands of the producing countries" (Galeano, 160).

For the supporters of *Open Veins of Latin America*, the "invisible hand" does not have a divine connotation but quite the opposite: it is invisible due to its character of ethical illegitimacy. The *invisible hand* is the hand of the strong who impose their interests over the rest of society, which cannot compete freely but, in a Darwinian regime, are condemned to disappear from the outset, given their initial conditions of birth or class affiliation. Just as in the jungle's law, the weak only serve to nourish the strong with their flesh. Thus, in 1957, in Colombia, "the bloodbath coincided with a period of economic euphoria for the ruling class: is it legitimate to confuse the prosperity of a class with the well-being of a country?" (164).

8.3—Protectionism and the Free Market

"THE RICH COUNTRIES, PREACHERS OF FREE TRADE, apply the most rigid protectionism against the poor countries," Galeano tells us (161). As we will see later, "the free competition of the markets became a revealed truth for England only from the moment when it was certain that it was the strongest, and after having developed its own textile industry under the shelter of Europe's most severe protectionist legislation." Before that, protectionism was legislated and practiced on the island with surprising patriotic cruelty: someone caught exporting raw wool without processing could be mutilated as punishment for their treason (294).

Meanwhile, some protectionist laws for the Argentine industry in the mid-19th century revitalized its own industry. But this development was not enough to withstand the blockade that Great Britain imposed on these measures.

> In reality, protectionism had been languishing since 1841, rather than intensifying. Rosas uniquely expressed the interests of the salting plant owners of the province of Buenos Aires, and there was no industrial bourgeoisie, nor did one emerge, capable of driving the development of a genuine and thriving national capitalism. (Galeano, 304)

When Galeano refers to Paraguay before the War of the Triple Alliance, as a model of "inward" development, he immediately links it to the discomfort of Great Britain due to the resistance it encountered for its trade in the "protectionist" colonies. The war that would end this Paraguayan model was financed by British bankers in Buenos Aires. Based on these observations, Galeano compares the two simultaneous wars of 1865: the War of the Triple Alliance and the Civil War:

> The war that would seal the colonial fate of Latin America was born at the same time that the war which made possible the consolidation of the United States as a world power concluded. Shortly after becoming president, Grant declared: «For centuries England has relied on protection, carrying it to its extremes and obtaining satisfactory results from it. There is no doubt that it owes its present strength to this system. After two centuries, England has found it convenient to adopt free trade because it believes protection can offer it nothing more. Very well, then, gentlemen, my knowledge of my country leads me to believe that within two hundred years, when America has obtained from protection all that protection can offer, it too will adopt free trade» (329).

In line with this thinking, Massachusetts subsidized hemp production for the ropes and cords of burgeoning shipyards, while "other local governments provided incentives for manufacturing of all kinds. At the same time that laws were enacted requiring families to operate looms, the export of unprocessed hides was prohibited" (331). Summarizing these ideas in a single expression, the practice generated an underdeveloped liberalism and industrial protectionism, under the subliminal law of 'do as I say, not as I do.'

The ruling class of Brazil, unlike that of the United States, was not composed of farmers, entrepreneurial manufacturers, and domestic merchants. The main interpreters of the ideals of the ruling classes in both countries, Alexander Hamilton and the Viscount of Cairu, clearly express the differences between one and the other. Both had been disciples of Adam Smith in England. However, while Hamilton had become a champion of industrialization and promoted the encouragement and protection of the state for national manufacturing, Cairu believed in the invisible hand operating in the magic of liberalism: let it be, let it pass, let it sell (332).

The decisive participation of the American state in the recovery from the pre-war economic crisis was nothing new. For Galeano, the Northern State actively participated in the formation of companies and the development of the economy from its origins. Citing North American sources, he tells us that public funds had expanded the dimensions of the internal market. "The state built roads and railways, bridges and canals. By mid-century, the state of Pennsylvania was involved in the management of more than one hundred and fifty mixed-economy companies in addition to administering the one hundred million dollars invested in public enterprises." To make it even more explicit, he directly notes that "the North had also begun to apply a zealous customs protectionism. The landowners of the South, on the contrary, were free traders."

The free trade policies of the Southern states are also part of the economic structure based on a discourse that contradicts practice, but is consistent with the system of exploitation and development. "The Southern aristocracy was primarily linked to the global market, in the Latin American style. [...] When the North combined the abolition of slavery with industrial protectionism, the contradiction erupted into war" (333). "In 1890, Congress passed the so-called McKinley Tariff, ultra-protectionist, and the Dingley Law raised customs duties again in 1897. Shortly thereafter, the developed countries of Europe were in turn forced to erect customs barriers in the face of the onslaught of North American manufactures" (335).

However, while a weakened England or one without the hegemony of previous years reinstated protectionist measures, the new and vibrant North American industry repeated the ideological recipes of its mother country. "Like England, the United States also exported, starting from the second world war, the doctrine of free trade, free commerce, and free competition, but *for foreign consumption*". Even today, the economic policy of the United States remains "rigorously protectionist and, indeed, listens well to the voices of its own history" (336).

Contemporary protectionism does not impose mutilations as in old England, but it is sustained by irresistible laws and strategies. As an example, Galeano mentions the iron industry. Imports of this product are free, "but if it has been turned into ingots, it pays 16 cents more per ton, and the tariff rises in direct proportion to the degree of processing; the same happens with copper and with a myriad of products: it is enough to dry bananas, cut tobacco, sweeten cocoa, saw wood, or remove the pit from dates for tariffs to drop relentlessly on the products" (398).

The same resource is used by Europe: "the common market imposes import taxes to defend the high internal prices of its agricultural products, and at the same time subsidizes those agricultural products to export them at competitive prices: thus, what it obtains from taxes finances the subsidies. In this way, poor countries pay their rich buyers to compete with them" (399). While "rich countries have used and use customs barriers to protect their high internal wages" (396), the ruling class in Latin America defends the free market and free competition.

A highly figurative metaphor serves Galeano to synthesize his ethical perception of the current economic and, above all, ideological order: "the hens grant the fox equal opportunities." This statement concluded the declarations of the Argentine dictator Juan Carlos Onganía, according to whom "foreign investments in Argentina will be considered on equal footing with investments of internal origin, in accordance with the traditional policy of our country, which has never discriminated against foreign capital" (360).

8.4—Development Inward

FROM A LATE 20TH-CENTURY OR EARLY 21ST-CENTURY PERSPECTIVE, this idea of a closed economy may be judged as retrograde and impracticable. But that judgment is not so obvious if we place ourselves in 1810. The nascent United States as well—Eduardo Galeano tells us—first grew by developing inward before outward.

The incipient industries in the interior of Argentina began to decline with the free import of English products.

> The English consul of the Plata, Woodbine Parish, described in 1837 a sturdy gaucho from the pampas: "Take all the pieces of his clothing, examine everything around him, and except for what is made of leather, what thing will there be that is not English? If his wife has a skirt, there are ten chances to one that it was manufactured in Manchester. The pot or cauldron in which she cooks, the ordinary ceramic cup from which she eats, his knife, his spurs, the bridle, the poncho that covers him—all are goods brought from England." Argentina received even the paving stones for its sidewalks from England (Galeano, 291).

The same situation was described in Brazil by the U.S. ambassador: almost all manufactured goods came from England.

Different was the case of Paraguay. According to Galeano, the government of the dictator Gaspar Rodríguez de Francia (1814-1840) had annihilated the oligarchy and relied on the peasants, achieving the greatest development in South America (310). "The American agent Hopkins reported to his government in 1845 that in Paraguay, 'there is no child who does not know how to read and write...' It was also the only country that did not live with its gaze fixed on the other side of the sea" (311). According to this viewpoint, in that historical moment in Latin America, Paraguay's isolationism benefited it. "When the invaders [the Triple Alliance] appeared on the horizon in 1865, Paraguay had a telegraph line, a railway, and a significant number of factories producing construction materials, textiles, canvases, ponchos, paper and ink, ceramics, and gunpowder" (312).

This process of development *inward* in Paraguay came to an abrupt end with the War of the Triple Alliance, an inevitable product of a 'war of interests' that extends its capitalist logic over the rest of the world (317).

Eduardo Galeano's reading of the War of the Triple Alliance aligns with the historical model we previously identified as "Darwinian." A different perspective, from the liberals of the time, can be found in David Rock's essay on the same conflict. This perspective approaches a reading closer to what might be found in Montaner or in the rhetoric of some Western governments at the beginning of the 21st century. For Rock, the Argentine liberals (from Buenos Aires) saw Paraguay "as the epitome of 'Barbarism,' a potential ally of the Federalists, and therefore a major threat to the Liberals and the province of Buenos Aires, the embodiments of 'civilization'." Especially, the propaganda of the time aimed to represent autocratic Paraguay as the antithesis of liberal Argentina. The goal of this war, according to the newspaper El Nacional, was to increase the liberty of the people, civilization, progress, and commerce and industry. And, finally, "to settle once and for all the eternal dispute between civilization and barbarism." According to Rock, for the liberals of the time, their struggle to impose their ideals in Paraguay had its parallel in the struggle of European countries intervening in other parts of the world. According to the Argentine newspaper El Nacional, cited by Rock, they could impose on Paraguay the same conditions that the Europeans had imposed on China, which was nothing more than "Paraguay on a larger scale, forced to open its doors." Therefore, according to this liberal propaganda, there was a natural right to safeguard the continent from the empire of barbarism (Rock, 45).

8.5—Development that produces social injustice

FOR THE STRUCTURALISTS, THE DOMINANT SYSTEM is not only unjust but also produces injustice; its progress may signify a global increase in wealth, but not greater justice. The progress of the center is followed by greater backwardness in the periphery; the enrichment of the upper classes is followed by the impoverishment of the lower classes: in this order, the productive class will always be the poor class, the one that does not benefit from its own production.

In Latin America, "the region progresses without freeing itself from the structure of its backwardness" (407). Statistics show that "the system is organized upside down, when the economy grows, social injustice grows with it" (464).

> Dependent industrialization exacerbates the concentration of income, both from a regional and a social perspective. *The wealth it generates does not spread across the entire country or the whole society but reinforces existing inequalities and even deepens them* (417).

In Brazil, for example, industrial productivity increased by one hundred and thirty percent, while wages grew by only six percent (217). As we have explained before, nothing is produced in isolation, outside the logic of a global macrosystem of exploitation and production: "the low level of wages in Latin America only translates into low prices in international markets" (418).

An unjust system, which produces injustice and dissatisfaction among the productive classes, will, at the same time, generate not only a dominant ideology that controls the meanings and ethical valuations of society, but must also create the necessary institutions to control and repress the tensions, contradictions, and dissatisfaction generated by the system itself: "the abyss that opens in Latin America between the well-being of the few and the misfortune of the many is infinitely greater than in Europe or the United States." This is how institutions characterizing the region, such as armies and military dictatorships, emerge and are sustained: "the methods to safeguard this great distance are, therefore, much more ferocious" (446).

8.6—The Justice of Profits

FOR THE AUTHOR OF *THE TWISTED ROOTS*, "profits in commercial transactions are legitimate, since merchants take certain risks. Every transaction involves uncertainty: one can lose, *ergo* it is morally justifiable to reward with gains those who are willing to face that danger" (107). This reasoning refers to a medieval context that is currently nonexistent: when Albertus Magnus and Thomas Aquinas rediscovered the "mercantilist" thought of Aristotle in the 13th century. We might think this is merely the warning of a line of economic, religious, and moral thought. But it loses validity when decontextualized and presented as an example of a historical truth, equally applicable to our times, to the times in which the author of *The Twisted Roots*—like all of us—is more interested. Our time, the present, is always the time of combat, and any other time serves only to help us in the enterprise of winning in the dialectical struggle.

When Montaner reasons about the justice of profit in a commercial transaction that could also have generated losses, it appears as a moral justification. And indeed, we should think so if we attend to the stark phrase, the simplified thought here. This entire narrative, supported by historical examples and a certain degree of abstraction, suggests a scenario rarely achieved in the context generated by this very practice: the risks and gains are not the same for a weak citizen as for a manager perched in power—let us say, in the power of their own company, without involving other possibilities such as political power often associated with economic power. Of course, many notable exceptions can be found. But they are usually just that: exceptions that mitigate an inconvenient reality that confirms the rule.

Therefore, if we were to follow the same reasoning pattern outlined above, according to which rewards should be proportional to risks, we would have to conclude that the greatest profits should be obtained by the weakest entrepreneurs, by those with scarce credit and capital. But we all know that this is not how the "just" system being defended operates. This is not a condemnation of that system nor a defense of its opposite. To do so would be to operate a generalization and an analytical leap without foundation. This observation must refer solely to the idea previously expressed as an epistemological critique. However, we also know that "analytical leaps" are necessary and quite common. The briefer the narrative, the more it will enjoy these leaps and simplifications. A more exhaustive, long-winded narrative will be exposed to falling into a greater number of contradictions but will strive to narrow these leaps, eliminating as many "strategic omissions" as possible. It is with them that a continuous, coherent ideological narrative is constructed.

The idea that the reward—no quantity is specified, for a practical reason—is proportional to the risks of the investor necessarily omits other types of rewards, such as, for example, the significance of a work: a scientist who invents a vaccine against a disease and saves the lives of millions of people will not necessarily be better rewarded than a soccer player who entertains a similar number of people on Sundays. Needless to say, they will not be rewarded as well as arms dealers who invest in their speculative commercial ventures, "risking" a tiny fraction of their operating capital.

All of this means that even if the ideological model being defended were superior—economically and morally—to any other, the arguments that initially seem solid are nothing more than fiction strategically placed within an essay-like narrative, like a colored tile is placed to form a coherent, continuous, uniform mosaic.

The arguments put forward might eventually demonstrate the superiority of a speculative or entrepreneurial order in the evolution toward a certain level of economic growth. But they are in no way sufficient to prove the moral superiority that is mentioned.

Moreover, we must note that in any historical criticism, moral change is often supported in opposition to the misguided foundations of the past. For example, endless pages are written against the foundations of machismo and religious traditions—and there are ample reasons for doing so—but, on the other hand, an ethical-economic theory is proudly defended by invoking Aristotle, the same Aristotle that the Catholic Church relied on to censor Galileo and burn other heretics.

8.7—The Political Struggle

DURING THE YEARS WHEN The Open Veins of Latin America was written, the political struggle had reached its peak tension. As is often the case, adversaries were largely divided into two political alternatives: capitalism or socialism. A critique of the practical and ideological nature of one usually led to the proposition of its adversary as the alternative. Not attacking one was defending the other; one was either on one side or the other. Because of this, we can understand why the tendency was toward the radicalization of one of the two positions. Any other alternative was seen as improbable or as part of the enemy's interests: one was either on one side or the other.

After analyzing the economic revolution carried out by Lázaro Cárdenas in Mexico (1934-1940), implementing the agrarian reform previously proposed by Zapata, Galeano exposes his political-ideological position explicitly: "Mexican nationalism did not lead to socialism and, consequently, as has happened in other countries that also did not take the decisive leap, it did not fully achieve its goals of economic independence and social justice" (201).

That is to say, from a particular reading of history —a structuralist reading— one arrives at a definite political-ideological position, not without a *leap* deductive leap, since there is no solid connection between the two that is not an act of faith. This leap also carries psychological and ideological meanings: if the current order consists of a vertical oppressive structure, liberation will come after a break or dismantling of that structure. And if the new order is the opposite of the vertical, that is, the horizontal, it must be better.

8.8—The Ethical Meanings of History

Commercial Doctrines

IN *OPEN VEINS OF LATIN AMERICA* LIES THE FOLLOWING conception of international ethics throughout history: the dominant ideology aligns with an ethical discourse whenever it suits its political and economic interests; international law is established to protect the weak, but it is only upheld to the extent that it does not condition the interests of the powerful. That is, as we have said before, at its base lies a Darwinian logic that orders historical events while law and justice seek to abolish its "natural laws."

Free trade was a basic principle for Britain and it was defended even with wars, such as the war against China motivated by opium.

> But the free competition of markets became a revealed truth for England only from the moment it was certain that it was the strongest, and after having developed its own textile industry under the shelter of the most severe protectionist legislation in Europe. In the difficult beginnings, when British industry was at a disadvantage, the English citizen who was caught exporting raw wool, unprocessed, was sentenced to lose his right hand, and if he reoffended, he was hanged; it was forbidden to bury a corpse without the local parish priest certifying that the shroud came from a national factory. (Galeano, 294)

Meanwhile, on the other side of the Atlantic, history repeated itself in the future empire according to the same laws of ethical discourse tailored to their own convenience:

> In 1890, Congress passed the so-called McKinley Tariff, which was ultra-protectionist, and the Dingley Act further raised customs duties in 1897. Soon after, the developed countries of Europe were in turn forced to erect customs barriers against the influx of American manufactures. (335)

At that time, Galeano tells us, the industrialists of the North had begun to apply customs protectionism. Meanwhile, due to different forms of production, the landowners of the South were advocates of free trade. "The Southern aristocracy was primarily tied to the global market, in the Latin American style" (333).

When evil ceases to be good

Consistent with his interpretative model —culturalist—, in *The Twisted Roots of Latin America*, the Cuban Alberto Montaner traces the origins of slavery in the Iberian Peninsula like a psychoanalyst digs into the childhood memories of a mature man suffering from a failure complex. There, he finds a long history of slavery and tolerance toward it, although in the High Middle Ages, it was not very different from other geographic regions. Spain, of course, was on a cultural frontier, more exposed to coexistence and ethnic and religious conflicts. "The [5th-century] Catholic Church," he writes, "did not oppose slavery but merely asked for more humane treatment of its victims" (55). With the Islamic invasion, the slave trade, a product of commerce and war, continued until the Late Middle Ages and intensified with the new Portuguese navigators of the Renaissance (59). Even the defender of Indigenous people in America, Las Casas, tolerated the slavery of Black people, as "in the Bible, Leviticus authorizes slavery." On the other hand, "for a Sevillian like Las Casas, it was very common to see or own black slaves" (60).

Montaner acknowledges that Luther also tolerated slavery for economic reasons, "as he believed that without the assistance of slave labor, the European economic factory could collapse" (66). However, according to the same text by Montaner, this self-interested attitude, based on an ethics tied to power and economy, should not be applied to England, which abolished slavery in the 19th century and sought to extend it, through various means, to Spain and Portugal. Even though the author states that "there is an incontrovertible fact: it was England, in 1807, the first major power to decide to renounce the slave trade" (66), it remains unclear whether this historical, incontrovertible fact was motivated by ethical or economic reasons.

Be that as it may, the effect is the same, and today we can evaluate it positively from an ethical standpoint. But Montaner starts from this present evaluation and deduces past motivations as causes, without the slightest documentary evidence. On the contrary, he seems to start from the reading of Open Veins of Latin America by Eduardo Galeano (where the same "ethical" fact is interpreted from a materialist perspective, i.e., by new economic conditions) to refute it in a simple declaration: "Did England act for economic reasons, as the most cynical claim —the industrial revolution had already begun, and they didn't want to compete with slave labor—, or was the primary motivation moral in nature? It seems that the latter was what most influenced English policy" (67).

The response Montaner gives "to the most cynical" —"it seems that the latter was what most influenced"— is based on perceptions that could be classified as subjective: "for decades, the abolitionist clamor grew until it managed to win the hearts of some important politicians, like Lord Palmerston" (67).

In this way, the reason for great policy is not economic, strategic, or related to power; it is a *raison du coeur*. On the other hand, it takes no small effort not to think of a certain type of cynicism in this kind of lossless benevolence. After all, "it was not the first time that a shift in sensibility had occurred in the West" (Montaner, 67).Which is undeniably true, but it is difficult for the proponents of the opposing thesis to take it seriously.

The latter, on the contrary, explain the struggle between enslavers and abolitionists not simply on humanitarian grounds but, above all, because of political and commercial interests. After all, the humanists (many of them Catholic) who opposed slavery had been fighting in vain for centuries until the Industrial Revolution came along. It seems that people become good when evil ceases to be profitable. Referring to the Civil War in the United States, Eduardo Galeano observed that "when the North added the abolition of slavery to industrial protectionism, the contradiction erupted into war. The North and the South faced two truly opposed worlds, two different historical times [...] The 20th century won this war against the 19th century" (333).

This idea of abolition is repeated in relation to the English abolitionists: it was economic and commercial interests that promoted the abolition of slavery, not a singular ethical principle. Although morality and justice are unavoidable components of the dynamics of history, it is not these factors that drive history but rather interest and power.

The discourse of ethics and justice is constructed by the resistant culture—not by the dominant culture, where interests prevail—and is later used, once the conquests have taken place, by the discourse of the dominant culture as a way to explain a process that was motivated by other reasons.

After detailing the intense slave trade by the hands of Holland and England, Galeano finds an explanation for the change in attitude of the latter: "At the beginning of the 19th century, Britain became the main driver of the anti-slavery campaign. English industry now needed international markets with greater purchasing power, which forced the spread of the wage system" (128).

However—and contrary to Montaner's thesis— for Galeano, this attitude is not specific to a race or culture. It is inherent to a system of exploitation. This can be deduced by considering another observation regarding any Latin American social sector. "The century was already dying when the coffee plantation owners, who had become the new social elite of Brazil, sharpened their pencils and calculated: subsistence wages were cheaper than the purchase and maintenance of the scarce slaves. Slavery was abolished in 1888, leaving combined forms of feudal servitude and wage labor that persist to this day" (155).

It is likely that the universal and age-old impulses of justice and power are the two basic components of history, as oxygen and hydrogen are for water—perhaps in the same disproportion.

Conclusions

SO FAR, WE HAVE PRESENTED—partially, as always—two paradigmatic and opposing visions of Latin America. These visions, which initially claim to share with an objective observation the preexistence of the object to be observed, are, at the same time, the constructors of the observed object. Therefore, we note that vision is simultaneously interpretation, a metaphorical borrowing of language that purports to serve as a description of a solar eclipse and a metaphysical intuition, as if both belonged to the same ontological space. And hence the struggle for interpretation as if it were a struggle for truth. As we understood and stated at the beginning, these operate through the dynamic—ideological or unconscious—definition of two semantic fields, one positive and the other negative.

We also proceeded in reverse, noting other considerations that are traditionally assumed to be different when, on the contrary, we can consider the supposed difference as a mutual identification. As was the case with text and context, the relative and the universal, etc. After these exercises, I think we can easily understand *Latin America* not as an object or independent phenomenon to define—which appears to be assumed in the texts of Galeano and Montaner—but as a text to interpret.

Now, the dispute over a text (T_1) is a struggle of interpretations that can be contemporary or separated considerably in time. In the latter case, discrepancies are the norm, and the latest interpretation always takes advantage of positioning itself over the supposed errors of the previous one.

When the validity of an interpretation (I_1) of an ancient text (T_1) is refuted, arguments are employed and reasoning is structured to provide us with the "revelation" codes, thus obtaining a new interpretation (I_2). This difference concerning the same text —and by extension, the same context, the same reality— is often dramatic, even though it may not initially appear as the product of a fixed ideological standpoint, but rather as "objective." However, it is equally possible to think that the difference between I_1 and I_2 —represented by different "interpretive" texts— does not consider that the existence of *the same difference* between T_1 and T_2 could well be understood —both being assumed as the same physical text, as a historical document. In other words, the difference between the two conflicting interpretations is not the result of reading the same text but rather of reading two different texts. These texts are conflated into one by the tradition that disguises or nullifies the metamorphosis of the *text* due to the apparent permanence of its material support —whether it be writing or a continent. That is, by confusing the paper and the ink drawings with what constitutes a *text*, a partial synthesis of meanings linked to a larger text we call context. The problem is accentuated when the text is not writing on paper but rather a complex and infinite set of social events and products at a specific historical moment, such as what we call Latin America.

This issue can be illustrated with the following example. In *the Introduction by P. García* to the translation of *The Song of Songs*, made by Fray Luis de León, the prologuist says:

> [Fray Luis de León was] precisely moved by the desire to better understand the [biblical] authentic text and delve into its depth through the letter [...] And how could he be labeled a dangerous innovator, when precisely what he advocates is the revision of the Latin translation, not because it contained substantial errors, but due to certain verbal inaccuracies, and demands, at the same time, that the translation be as faithful and correspond to the original, not only in terms of thoughts and the materiality of the words, but also in their order and arrangement, in their turns and metaphors, and even in their archaic form and peculiar syntax? (57)

Let us pay attention to these words: "better understand the authentic text", "dangerous innovator", "revision of the tradition", "certain verbal inaccuracies". Let us attend, above all, to the idea that the interpreter "demands, at the same time, that the translation be as faithful and correspond to the original."

A fruitful and similar exercise was carried out by Erasmus of Rotterdam in 1516, with Novum Instrumentum, when he corrected the traditional Latin version of the New Testament based on comparisons with an older Greek text. But there is a problem: the "original text" does not exist, only a new version of it, supported by the historical authority of what we might call the "vanished text". Only a new version of the text can exist, which, like the sole descendant of a king, inherits the throne and, often, the right to arbitrariness. The revision is legitimate and necessary, but also—and not without contradiction—essentialist.

Nevertheless, this warning about the "nonexistence" of the original text, we can understand that this disputed text, despite the inevitable transformations, possesses something in common "with itself", just as an adult has something in common with the child they once were. Are we the same as we were ten years ago? No. However, it is difficult to deny that these "two different people" do not share something in common that, ambiguously, we call "person" or "identity."

How can we notice the dimension of those changes that the *text* has undergone, not by its own doing but by the generations that are no longer close nor contemporaneous to the material medium—the ink and paper, the celluloid, etc.—that conserves it as a set of signs? The previous observations are not nihilistic or skeptical, but quite the opposite. I believe that, paradoxically, a measuring instrument is those interpretations that were made at each moment in history about the text in question and that, in turn, have become new texts altered or adapted to historical development. That is, those interpretations (I1s) —which the new interpretation (I2) seeks to refute as inaccurate or erroneous with respect to a supposed non-existent text— tell us about the changes in the text. They probably tell us more about the "anthropic" reality —as Gómez-Martínez defined it— than about their supposed "interpretative errors."

The Hebrew text, which was once translated into Latin, is not the same as it was in the time of Fray de León when he attempted to translate it with "greater precision." Why deny precision to those who performed the same interpretative exercise centuries earlier? Is this not a way of ignoring the understanding and particular sensitivity of the time and the individual who then carried out the same interpretative exercise? Does interpretation not mean *transferring* an emotion or an idea from a supposed sensitivity to our own? When we translate, we are not only putting the "original text" into play but also our own sensibility. The difference is that one (the foreign text) is easier to objectify than the other (our own text, supposedly equivalent to the former); one is the origin and the other is the destination. And it is precisely the textual "origin" that is remembered, while simultaneously forgetting the objective of translation: the intelligible and sensitive codes particular to each moment (of the translator and interpreter).

There, "precision" —with pretensions of *truth*— refers to a generational "adjustment." The correspondence between the Hebrew text and its translation into Latin was probably much closer (precise) in its origins than it became later with the passage of time. The degree of "imprecision" reveals to us (1) a change in the interpretative *cosmology* of the translator-reader or, what amounts to the same thing, (2) a change in the *text* itself, which is supposedly arbitrarily fixed, immutable. To deny one of the points is to deny the other.

If we understand that interpretations change and the texts that are the objects of study and dispute do not, it is because interpretations are attributed to the *subjects* who interpret while the disputed text is deceptively identified with an *object*, a physical and stable entity, independent of the former. In this way, we fail to notice that a text is an interpretative construction of the same degree as the interpretation that generates a new text, a new set, physically *different* signs that aim to signify the same as the disputed text. That is, what changes is considered immutable while what remains is considered changeable (the interpretation always adjusts to the metamorphosed text and not the other way around).

But if the search for the textual origin by the reformer does not perceive that the text referred to by ancient interpretations does not exist, nor do those who insist on preserving the ancient interpretation perceive it as if it had not, in turn, undergone the same process of disappearance. Thus, the paradox arises that the conservative pretension of orthodoxy necessarily becomes the involuntary defense of metamorphosis, by negating "correction," by denying change. Therefore, all orthodoxy becomes a permanent transgression. Félix García wrote that "one of the most serious accusations against Fr. Luis made before the Inquisition Court was having translated the *Song of Songs* and turning against the authority of the *Vulgate*" (59). That is, the weight of authority —established by Latin tradition— placed the subjects of the 16th century under the obligation to accept an interpretation that was more foreign to them than it could have been to their translator of centuries earlier. The ancient translation is no more faithful to the new text than to the disappeared text, that is, to the subjects who lived then and can no longer communicate with the contemporary subjects of Fray Luis de León.

Every interpretation is a testimony. By understanding it as such, we (re)value its relationship with the interpreted text; we reveal our own interpretation and the dynamic nature of the text itself. Both texts analyzed in this essay, *The Open Veins of Latin America* and The Twisted Roots of Latin America, are two testimonies. Two testimonies of their times, shaped by specific ideologies with specific purposes. Which of the two is the correct interpretation? Which one comes closer to the truth?

To these types of questions, we have attempted to respond as follows: an interpretation, even one that claims to be objective, is not only the confirmation of an idea but also—and perhaps above all—the negation of the vast complexity that threatens to dissolve it in absolute relativity—or mysticism. As we have noted earlier, this epistemological attitude belongs to the Western tradition of (1) truth beyond appearances—Greek—and (2) the truth of The Book—Judeo-Christian—which demanded a single interpretation beyond any subjectivity: the Law.

In this essay, we aimed to present the idea that an *interpretation* is the result of a *struggle for meaning*; not for truth. Nevertheless, truth remains its ultimate goal and justification, though it is unattainable as it is the primary metaphysical concept of human history, sometimes personified as God.

An interpretation is the construction of a truth and, therefore, cannot share the same semantic space as any other that negates it. As a construction, it requires a minimum of coherence, inclusion and exclusion, affirmation and negation. Because of this, every interpretation shares some common rules with other interpretations, much like two chess players develop different techniques and strategies on the same board, respecting certain rules of the game. A player could not win the struggle if they did not rigorously exercise those rules that make their complex and sometimes strange moves intelligible. As we have suggested earlier, there could be neither agreement nor disagreement if there were no common language shared by both, for if both lacked this common language, there would not even be a (semantic) conflict but, simply, ignorance and indifference. And nothing is further from the struggle and semantic conflict—difference—than indifference. The difference between the game of chess and the vast complexity of human societies throughout history lies in the fact that the rules of the game in the latter change progressively and almost always imperceptibly. Often, these changes go unnoticed, but they are assumed at each moment as the (immutable) basis of new struggles for meaning..

Surely the epistemological challenge that humanity has faced throughout the ages is discovering those rules that transcend changes. Perhaps these rules or principles do not exist in an absolute form, but they have never ceased to be a human obsession. Even when they have been denied, for this denial of skepticism is also an affirmation. As we have said, for meaning to exist, there must be a tension of two semantic fields: one positive and one negative. There is no affirmation without negation, nor vice versa; there is no sign or interpretation without exclusive affirmations and integrative negations. This is the dynamic, according to this essay, of every interpretation; that is, of knowledge, of supposed truths.

Diagrams

(Diagram 1)
Interpretative Diagram

Interpretative Diagram					
context	causes	consequences	preservation	revolution	changes
"Ascending" reading of history. (*The Open Veins of Latin America*)					
Initial conditions (Natural and historical)	Social organization Production and development system	Culture mentality	Perpetuation of the social order	Change in infrastructure (consciousness raising)	Change in the social order Change in mentality
"Descending" reading of history. Culturalism. (*The Twisted Roots of Latin America*)					
Initial conditions (Natural and historical)	Culture mentality	Social organization Production and development system	Perpetuation of the social order	Change in mentality (awakening of consciousness)	Change in infrastructure Change in social order

(Diagram 2)
Scheme of the struggle for meaning

Dialectical semiotic scheme
Dynamics of meanings and their valuations

Adversary I	Adversary II
Symbol I = liberation	
Definition 1 = C1(+).C1(-)	Definition 2 = C2(+).C2(-)
In this case, we can have a result of discordant meanings about the same symbol. A struggle for meaning is established.	
D1 ≠ D2	
Despite this, the valuation of the original symbol is the same by both dialectical adversaries.	
V1 = (+)	V2 = (+)
We can have a different case where the definitions coincide, but the valuations oppose each other.	
Symbol II = disobedience	
Definition 1 = C'1(+).C'1(-)	Definition 2 = C'2(+).C'2(-)
D1 = D2	
Valuation (-)	Valuation (+)
This discrepancy is due to the transfer each dialectical position makes about the same symbol *disobedience*. This symbol is identified or related to other symbols with different valuations. For example:	
C'1(+) = *chaos* + *anarchy* + ...	C'2(+) = *freedom* + responsibility + ...

Bibliography

Alberdi, Juan Bautista. *Bases y puntos de partida para orga-nización política de la república argentina.* Buenos Aires: Ediciones Estrada, 1943.

_____ "Ideas para presidir a la confección del curso de filosofía contemporánea" *Proyecto Ensayo Hispánico.* 1992. November 10, 2004. http://www.ensayistas.org/antologia/XIXA/alberdi

_____ *La barbarie histórica de Sarmiento.* Buenos Aires: Ediciones Pampa y Cielo, 1964.

Arocena, Felipe; Eduardo de León. *El complejo de Próspero.* Montevideo: Vintén Editor, 1993.

Atkins, Douglas. Reading Deconstruction. Lexington: University Press of Kentucky, 1983.

Barreiro, José P. *Domingo Faustino Sarmiento.* Cartas y discursos políticos. Tomo III. Buenos Aires: Ediciones Culturales Argentinas, 1963.

Barthes, Roland. *Elements of Semiology.* London: Jonathan Cape, 1967, p 14

Bello, Andrés. "Las repúblicas hispanoamericanas: Autonomía cultural" Proyecto Ensayo Hispánico. 1992. November 10, 2004. http://www.ensayistas.org/antologia/XIXA/bello/

Berdiales, Germán. *Antología total de Sarmiento.* Buenos Aires: Ediciones Culturales Argentinas, 1962.

Bolívar, Simón. "Carta de Jamaica". Proyecto Ensayo Hispánico. 1992. November 7, 2004. http://www.ensayistas.org/antologia/XIXA/bolivar/

Borges, Jorge Luis. Atlas. Buenos Aires: Editorial Sudamericana, 1984.

____*Ficcionario. Una antología de sus textos.* Edición de Emir Rodríguez Monegal. México: Fondo de la Cultura Económica, 1981.

____*Obra poética 1923/1985.* Buenos Aires, Emecé Editores, 1989.

Braidier, Christopher. Barroque self-Invention and Historical Truth. Burlington, Vermont: Ashgate Publishing Limited, 2004.

Cejador y Frauca, Julio (edición). *La vida de Lazarillo de Tormes.* Madrid: Espalsa Calpe, 1972.

Chalupa, Jirí. "El caudillismo rioplatense del siglo XIX". Universita Palackého: *Philologica 74* (1990).

Chanady, Amarill. Latin American Identity and Constructions of Difference. Minneapolis: University of Minessota Press, 1994.

Colón, Cristóbal. "Diario del primer Viaje (1492-1493)" *Literatura Hispanoamericana. Una Antología.* David Wiliam Foster. New York and London: Garland Publishing (1994): 44-45

De Munter, Koen. "Five Centuries of Compelling Interculturality: The Indian in Latin-American Consciousness". Rik Pinxten, Ghislain Verstraete & Chia Longman, *Culture and Politics.* New York: Berham Books (2004): 89-114.

Escudero, José Antonio. "La Inquisición española". *Cuadernos de historia 16.* Madrid: Universidad Complutense de Madrid (1985).

Fisk, Milton. "Free Action and Historical Materialism". Indiana: Nous, 20.2. Blackwell Publishing (1986).

Freire, Paulo. Pedagogía del oprimido. Buenos Aires: Siglo XXI Editores, 2002.

Fromm, Erich. El miedo a la libertad. Buenos Aires: Editorial Piados, 1984.

Fuentes, Carlos. Valiente mundo nuevo. Barcelona: Edición Narrativa Mondadori, 1990.

Galeano, Eduardo. Las venas abiertas de América Latina. Montevideo: Ediciones del Chanchito, 1999.

Gómez-Martínez, José Luis. Más allá de la pos-modrnidad. Madrid: Mileto Ediciones, 1999.

Goytisolo, Juan. Makbara. Barcelona: Editorial Seix Barral: 1980.

Iacobelli, Michael. "The Semantic Discipline". Athens, Va: *The Modern Languages Journal*. 33.1 (1949): 16-22.

León, Luis de. *Obras Completas de fray Luis de León*. Prólogos y notas del pare Félix García. Madrid: Biblioteca de Autores Cristianos, 1967.

Lèvi-Strauss, Claude. The Elementary Structure of Kinship. Boston: Beacon Press, 1969.

López-Estrada, Francisco. *El abencerraje*. Madrid: Ediciones Cátedra, 1980.

Majfud, Jorge. *Crítica de la pasión pura*. Buenos Aires: Editorial Argenta Sarlep, 2000.

Malinowski, Bronislaw. *Magic, Science and Religion, and Other Essays*. Boston, Beacon Press, 1948.

Martí, José. "Nuestra América" (1891). Proyecto Ensayo Hispánico. 1992. 5 de noviembre de 2004. http://www.ensayistas.org/antologia/XIXA/marti/index.htm

Memorias del subdesarrollo. Dir. Tomas Gutiérrez Alea, Cuba, 1968.

Mendoza, Plinio Apuleyo; Carlos Alberto Montaner, Álvaro Vargas Llosa. Manual del perfecto Idiota latinoamericano. Barcelona: Plaza & Janés Editores, 2001

Mill, David van. "Hobbes's Theories of Freedom". Boulder: The Journal of Politics, 57.2 (1995)

Montaner, Carlos Alberto. Las raíces torcidas de América Latina. Barcelona: Plaza & Janés Editores, 2001.

Monteagudo, Bernardo de. "Reflexiones políticos" (1812) *Proyecto Ensayo Hispánico*. 1992. 15 de noviembre de 2004. http://www.ensayistas.org/antologia/XIXA/monteagudo

Mora, José María Luis. Obras Sueltas. Second Edition. Mexico: Editorial Porrúa, 1963.

Nöth, Winfried, Handbook of Semiotics. Bloomington, Indiana: Indiana University Press, 1995.

Pérez, Alberto Julián. "El país de Facundo". Texas Tech University. March 2004. http://www.sarmiento.org.ar/conf_JPerez.htm

Porot, Antoine, Diccionary of Clinical Psychiatry and Therapeutics. Barcelona: Labor, 1977

Rangel, Carlos. Del Buen Revolucionario al Buen Salvaje. *Mitos y Realidades de América Latina*. Caracas: Monte Ávila Editores, 1976.

Ratzinger, Joseph. Instrucciones sobre la libertad cristiana y liberación. Santiago de Chile: Ediciones Paulistas, 1986.

____ "Instrucción sobre algunos aspectos de la Teología de la Liberación" Proyecto Ensayo Hispánico. Marzo, 2004. http://www.ensayistas.org/critica/liberacion/TL/documentos/ratzinger.htm

Rock, David. "Argentina under Mitre: Porteno Liberalism in the 1860s". Santa Barbara, California: *The Americas*, 56.1 (1999).

Runciman, Steven. *A History of the Crusades. The Kingdom of Acre and the Later Crusades*. Cambridge: Cambridge University Press, 1987

Sábato, Ernesto. Abaddón, el exterminador. Barcelona: Seix Barral, 1984.

_____ *Hombres y engranajes*. Buenos Aires: Emecé Editores, 1951.

_____*Sobre héroes y tumbas*. Barcelona: Seix Barral, 1986.

Sarmiento, Domingo Faustino. Civilización y barbarie. Barcelona: Editorial Argos Vergara, 1979.

_____*Conflicto y armonías de las razas de América*. En Carlos Ripio, ed. *Conciencia intelectual de América. Antología del ensayo hispanoamericano*. New York: Eliseo Torres & Sons, 1974.

Sartre, Alfonso. *Escuadra hacia la muerte*. New Jersey: Prentice-Hall Inc., 1967.

Sarup, Madan. An introductory Guide to Post Structuralism and Postmodernism. Athens: University of Georgia Press, 1989.

Storey, John. *Cultural Theory and Popular Culture*. Athens: University of Georgia Press, 1998.

Tarnas, Richard. The Passion of the Western Mind. London: Pimlico, 1996.

Unamuno, Miguel de. Ensayos. Madrid: M. Aguilar, 1951.

Vargas Llosa, Mario. Contra Viento y Marea. Seix Barral, Barcelona, 1983.

Zavarzadeh, Mas'ud. Seeing Films Politically. New York: State University of New York Press, 1991.

Graphic representation

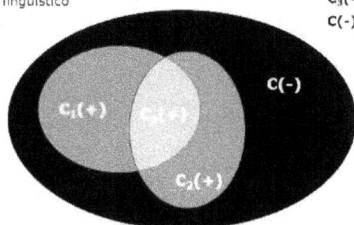

Definición de un nuevo C(s) por exclusiones

Sistema lingüístico (idioma)

$C_3(+) = C_1(+) \cap C_2(+)$
$C(-) = \Sigma C(+) - C_i(+)$

$C_1(+)$ $C(+)$ $C(-)$
$C_2(+)$

Definición del los Campos Semánticos (Signo / Concepto)
Lucha por el significado

Chicano / Paraguayo guaraní / Vasco francés / conciencia revolucionaria
X pero Y, etc

Definición de los campos semánticos de un término-signo-concepto: libertad, justicia, etc.

Sistema lingüístico

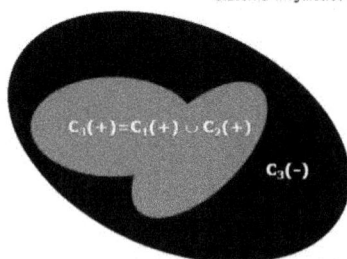

$C_3(+) = C_1(+) \cup C_2(+)$

$C_3(-)$

La actividad intensa, en la doctrina de Calvino, poseía además otro significado psicológico. El hecho de no fatigarse en tan incesante esfuerzo y el de tener éxito, tanto en las obras morales como seculares, constituía un signo más o menos distintivo de ser uno de los elegidos (103). Erich Fromm.

Definición de los campos semánticos de un término-signo-concepto: libertad, justicia, etc.

$$C_4(+)=C_1(+) \cup C_2(+) \cap C_3(+)$$

Sistema lingüístico

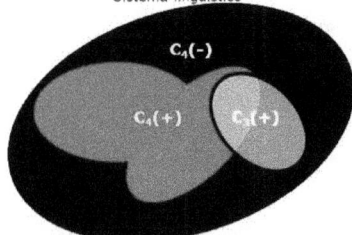

Definición del los Campos Semánticos (Signo / Concepto)
Lucha por el significado

Definición de un nuevo C(s) / Lucha por administrar los significados y valoraciones del signo ("opción por los pobres")

Esta llamada de atención *de ninguna manera debe interpretarse como* [definición del C(-)] una desautorización a todos aquellos que quieren responder generosamente y *con auténtico espíritu evangélico* [Confirmación del C(+) tradicional] a la *'opción preferencial por los pobres'* [nuevo signo —ahora irrebatible— del adversario] De ninguna manera podrá servir de pretexto para quienes se atrincheran en una actitud neutral y de indiferencia [nuevo signo irrebatible del adversario a través de una nueva definición del C(-)] ante los trágicos y urgentes problemas de la miseria y de la injusticia. Al contrario, obedece a la certeza de que las *graves desviaciones ideológicas* [alteración del C(+) del signo y juicio de valor del mismo] que señala conducen inevitablemente a *traicionar la causa de los pobres* [resignificación: el C(+) del adversario es, finalmente, desplazado a un nuevo C(-) que presiona sobre su propio C(+) en búsqueda de una definición con fronteras nítidas]" (Ratzinger. *Teología*).

Lucha Dialéctica por la administración de los signos
Definición de lás Fronteras Semánticas C(+) y C(-)

Sarmianto Educar es disciplinar	Gobernar / Educar Barbarie / poder	Alberdi Gobernar es poblar
Teólogos de la liberación Liberación del pecado (Social)	Liberación / Violencia	Ratzinger Liberación del pecado (individual)
Galeano	Dinámica histórica y definición ética de: Justicia/Desarrollo/Poder	Montaner
Todos	Conciencia (lectura correcta de la realidad)	Todos

Problema: Integración Racial,

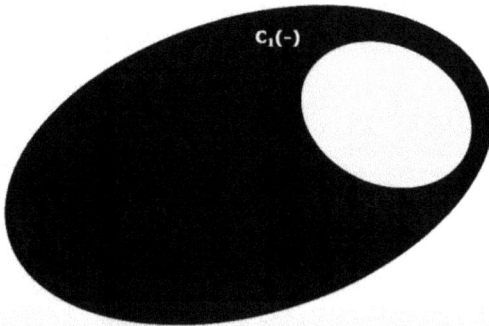

$C_1(-)$

Proceso implicativo

"Race mixing   communism"

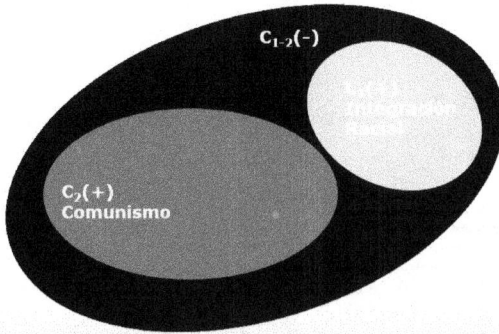

$C_{1\text{-}2}(-)$

$C_1(+)$
Integración
Racial

$C_2(+)$
Comunismo

Proceso implicativo

"Race mixing is communism"

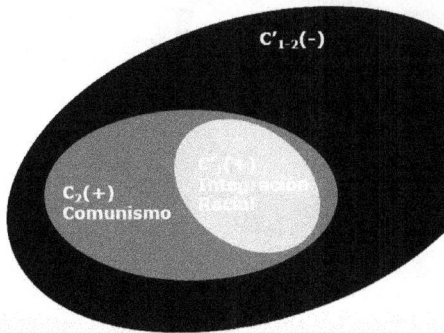

$C'_{1\text{-}2}(-)$

$C_2(+)$
Comunismo

$C'_1(+)$
Integración
Racial

$C'_1(+)$: Campo
semántico a
Definir: Término
de alta
conflictividad

$C_2(+)$: Campo
Semántico
Definido:
Término de baja
conflictividad
(Valoración
negativa)

Implicación de
C'_1 con C_2

Definición de los C(s) por implicaciones

La **lucha semántica** tiene sentido porque se asume o presume una "**lectura colectiva**".

- El *cuerpo* **es** la *cárcel* del alma
- La *religión* **es** el *opio* de los pueblos (marxistas)
- "la *levadura evangélica*, **ha contribuido** al despertar de la *conciencia* de los oprimidos" (Ratzinger).
- El hombre **es** un animal bípedo e implume (gallo sin plumas)

"La *idolatría* **es** una forma extrema del *desorden* engendrado por el *pecado*. [...] Al sustituir la adoración del Dios vivo por el culto de la criatura, **falsea [no es]** las relaciones entre los hombres y conlleva diversas formas de *opresión* (V, 39. p 22)" Ratzinger.

24

Cs de Justicia/beneficio/plusvalía en Galeano

$$C_4(+)=C_1(+) \cup C_2(+) \cap C_3(+)$$

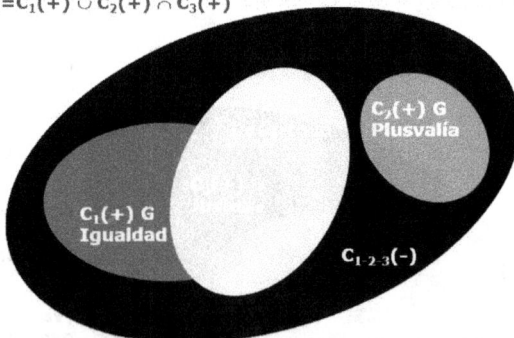

$C_2(+)$ G Plusvalía

$C_1(+)$ G Igualdad

$C_{1\text{-}2\text{-}3}(-)$

Definición del los Campos Semánticos (Signo / Concepto)
Lucha por el significado

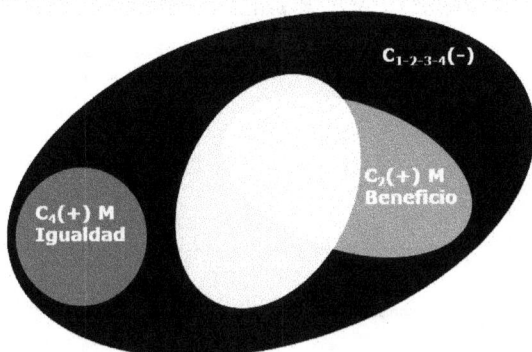

Cs de Justicia/beneficio/plusvalía en Montaner

25

$C_{1\text{-}2\text{-}3\text{-}4}(-)$

$C_2(+)$ M
Beneficio

$C_4(+)$ M
Igualdad

Definición del los Campos Semánticos (Signo / Concepto)
Lucha por el significado

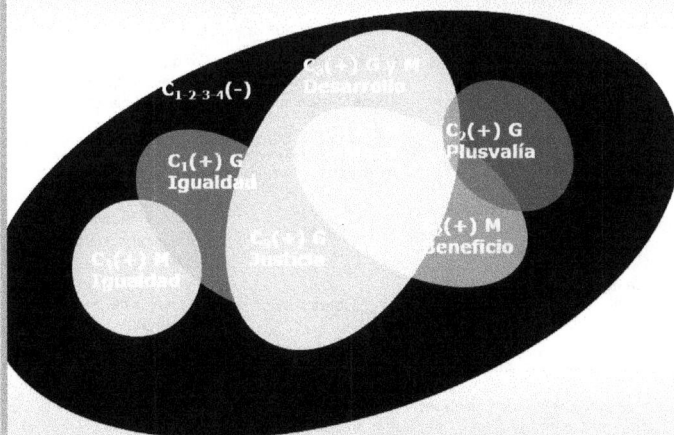

Cs de Justicia en la **Lucha Dialéctica** por el significado

26

$C_{1\text{-}2\text{-}3\text{-}4}(-)$

$C_4(+)$ G y M
Desarrollo

$C_2(+)$ G
Plusvalía

$C_1(+)$ G
Igualdad

$C_3(+)$ G
Justicia

$C_3(+)$ M
Igualdad

$C_3(+)$ M
Beneficio

Eduardo Galeano *Las venas abiertas de América Latina* (1971)	Narración histórica	Alberto Montaner *Las raíces torcidas de América Latina* (2001)
1. Venas abiertas 2. Desangrado, acción externa o autoflagelación; contexto hostil, opresión.		1. Raíces torcidas 2. Defecto de nacimiento / congénito. 3. Incapacidad mental (*Manuel del perfecto idiota latinoamericano*)
Conquista y genocidio. Expropiación de minerales (XVI), cultivos complementarios, mano de obra (esclava, asalariada), capitalismo dependiente (XX)		Grecia, Roma, España, Caudillismo (Racismo, sexismo, autoritarismo)
Población indígena esclavizada y deformada en su carácter.		Población indígena como problema para la modernización
Crítica de la cultura anglosajona e Ibérica. Elogio de la colonización Norteamericana.		Elogio de la cultura anglosajona Crítica de las culturas indígenas.
Estudio filosófico sobre Europa. Historia de las culturas indígenas sólo con respecto a su relación con la explotación extranjera.		Más del 50% del texto es sobre Historia y filosofía europea (raíces "torcidas": Contrarreforma, escolástica, etc)

Eduardo Galeano *Las venas abiertas de América Latina* (1971)	Fracaso de A. L.	Alberto Montaner *Las raíces torcidas de América Latina* (2001)
Estructura / Cultura	Conciencia Cautiva	Cultura / Estructura
Robo y genocidio (La riqueza como origen de la pobreza) (XV-XX)	Ilegitimidad del Poder / Riqueza (Poder Descendente)	1. Conquistadores 2. Pueblos conquistados Caudillismo / beneficios
Grandes poblaciones indígenas como fuente de explotación	El oro de A. L. no posibilitó el desarrollo de España y Portugal	Grandes poblaciones indígenas como obstáculo para la mentalidad moderna
El orden social en función de los intereses del industrialismo (Desunión estructural: puertos)	Fracaso	La educación formal como origen de una mentalidad (Desunión: sist. Colonial, caudillos)
La ética como consecuencia del cambio socio-económico (Esclavismo)	Liberación	El cambio socioeconómico como consecuencia de la ética (Esclavismo)
1. Dictadura del libre mercado 2. El contexto Internacional reproduce la división de clases	Cambio (Revolución) Estructural o Mental	Dictadura de una "mentalidad" Independencia del contexto internacional

Eduardo Galeano *Las venas abiertas de América Latina* (1971)	Fracaso de A. L.	Alberto Montaner *Las raíces torcidas de América Latina* (2001)
Estructura / Cultura	Búsqueda de un *logos* a través de la continuidad narrativa	Cultura / Estructura
El "fracaso" de A. L. Es producto de 1. una "ideología dominante" (proteccionismo, mercado libre) y 2. una "estructura de producción"	Conciencia Cautiva	El "fracaso" de A. L. Es producto de: 1. Una "ideología resistente" y 2. Una mentalidad propia
Estructura$_2$ / Cultura$_2$	Conciencia Liberada	Cultura$_2$ / Estructura$_2$

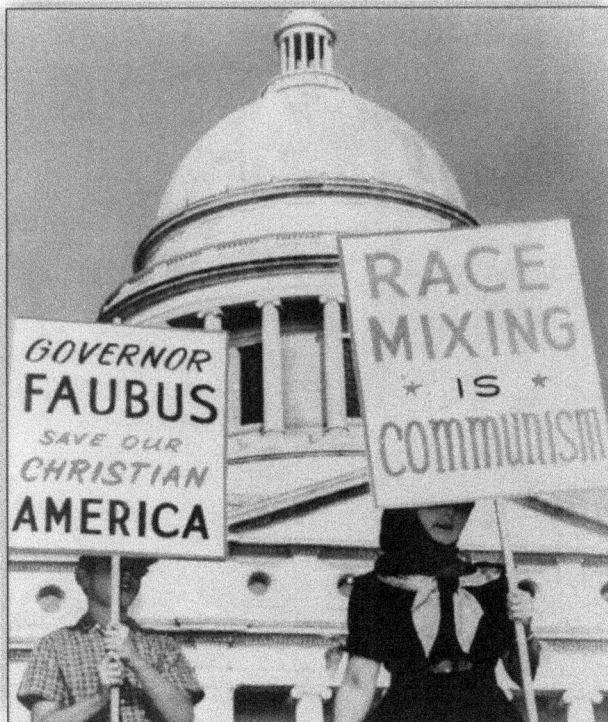

Thematic Index